Defining Russian Federalism

Defining Russian Federalism

ELIZABETH PASCAL

 PRAEGER

Westport, Connecticut
London

Library of Congress Cataloging-in-Publication Data

Pascal, Elizabeth, 1968–
    Defining Russian federalism / Elizabeth Pascal.
      p. cm.
    Includes bibliographic references and index.
    ISBN 0-275-97938-5 (alk. paper)
    1. Federal government—Russia (Federation)   2. Central-local government relations—
Russia (Federation)   3. Intergovernmental fiscal relations—Russia (Federation)   I. Title
    JN6693.5.S8P37   2003
    320.447'049—dc21   2003042925

British Library Cataloguing-in-Publication Data is available.

Library of Congress Catalog Card Number: 2003042925
ISBN: 0-275-97938-5

First published in 2003

Praeger Publishers, 88 Post Road West, Westport, CT 06881
An imprint of Greenwood Publishing Group, Inc.
www.praeger.com

Printed in the United States of America

The paper used in this book complies with the
Permanent Paper Standard issued by the National
Information Standards Organization (Z39.48-1984).

10 9 8 7 6 5 4 3 2 1

To my parents, who instilled in me a love of knowledge and foreign places. To my husband, Robert, who inspires me with his enthusiasm and humor. And to my daughters, Ally and Lara, who give me their wholehearted joy and love.

Contents

Acknowledgments

Many people provided enormous help in the process of researching and writing this book. Participants at the Social Science Research Council Workshop in Kiev, Ukraine, during the summer of 1996 offered me feedback and advice at the earliest stages of this project. Philip Roeder of University of San Diego and Valerie Bunce from Cornell University were particularly helpful with designing the study. I am especially grateful to members of my dissertation committee at the University of Michigan who supported me during the first incarnation of this project. Pradeep Chhibber helped me to better define my thesis, and pushed me to broaden its scope. Valerie Kivelson went above and beyond the job of an outside committee member, editing every chapter and providing a much-needed "non-political science" point of view. Zvi Gitelman offered excellent advice and encouragement throughout the process. A Fulbright Hayes Fellowship and grants from the Social Science Research Council and the Rakham School of Graduate Studies generously funded me during various stages of the dissertation process.

I owe a substantial debt to the many people in Russia who assisted me with my fieldwork. In particular, researchers at the Moscow Carnegie Institute, Vadim Stupin at the Gaidar Institute, and Alexei Novikov at the Urban Institute provided my crucial first interviews and contacts in the regions. I owe many people in Vologda thanks; the region proved to be one of the most friendly and hospitable places that I've ever visited. Ludmila Valokhova, in addition to making sure I was well taken care of in Vologda, devoted countless hours to transcribing many of my interviews. The American USAID consultants at Chemonics International gave me a much-needed break from Russian and welcomed me to their Thanksgiving dinner, replete with a turkey, mashed potatoes, and, of course, beets. In Samara, Andrei Dolgikh, Tatyana Voskoboinikova, and Vyacheslav Aronin were all of great help. In Bryansk, journalists Petr Polinitski and Valentina Maksimyak and lawyers from the *Tsentr Zashita Glasnosti* (Center for the Defense of Free Speech) welcomed me into their offices and their homes.

Various individuals guided and supported me as this project made its way from dissertation to book. Steve Solnick and Kathryn Stoner-Weiss offered valuable feedback on various chapters. Chapter 4 benefited from comments by Jenna Bednar and Steve Solnick at an APSA conference in 2000. I thank colleagues at Wesleyan University, particularly Marc Eisner and Peter Rutland, for giving me the opportunity to teach a course on Comparative Federalism, which helped to deepen my understanding of federalism. I also thank David Patton and Bill Rose at Connecticut College for their support. Mike Gauger edited several chapters of the manuscript and in so doing, made its publication possible.

I am very grateful to my editor at Praeger, Michael Hermann. He gave me great encouragement with his immediate enthusiasm for the manuscript. He immediately put me at ease with his straightforward, professional manner along with a much-appreciated dose of humor. I also thank the reader for the manuscript, Alan Tarr. His thoughtful comments and constructive criticism helped me to make this a much better book.

Finally, I owe my greatest gratitude to my husband, Robert Knopf, who read countless drafts and rewrites of chapters until he could read no more. He helped and, yes, nudged me when I thought the book would never come about, and reminded me that a good laugh can solve just about anything.

CHAPTER 1

The Federal Bargain

Since the collapse of the Soviet Union, both scholars and observers have tracked the development of federalism in the Russian Federation, looking for signs of state collapse or a return to Soviet-style centralization. Despite warnings that one of these is imminent, Russia has undergone no such drastic transformation. Instead, we see an uneasy reorganization of the Russian Federation, in which the long history of centralized government clashes with the center's attempts to satisfy regional demands for authority and with its need to devolve responsibility. Following a decade of Boris Yeltsin's leadership, Russia remained a "political construction site,"[1] with a fragile network of democratic institutions set within the shattered architecture of state socialism. These institutions are the arena for political elites to bargain over the delineation of authority and jurisdiction. A complex process of defining federalism lies at the heart of the struggle among elites at the center and in the regions, in which current choices and compromises affect the opportunities for change in the future.

Post-Soviet Russia presents a unique opportunity to examine the process by which the center and the regions negotiate the rules of federalism in a transitional society. Political participants and outside observers heatedly contest the design of Russian federalism and how it should be best implemented to secure the promise of a stable democracy. Regional actors claim that the center has exerted too much authority over local affairs to allow subnational governments to protect the citizens from the encroachment of the central state, thus continuing the Soviet legacy of "federalist in form, unitary in content."[2] Central leaders under both President Yeltsin and President Putin deride the devolution of power to subnational governments and assert that regional leaders exploit their newfound powers to the detriment of Russian citizens and the nation. A similar debate simmers in the literature on Russian federalism. Russian observers often note the enduring hold of the federal government on power, which leaves the regions beholden to the center for revenue, economic development, and legal reform (Borodulina 1997; Podporina 1997; Igudin 1996). Yet Western scholars, perhaps more fearful of Russian disintegration, focus on the regions' significant powers and autonomy and the resultant economic inefficiencies and legal inconsistencies (Stoner-Weiss 1999; Solnick 1998; Kirkow 1996).

On both sides of the issue, all agree that political and economic asymmetries increasingly came to define federalism in Russia during the Yeltsin administration. The legacy of Soviet federalism accounts for some of the differences among regions. The unequal territorial division among twenty-one republics, eleven autonomous areas, forty-nine *oblasts,* and six *krais,* with the ethnically based republics receiving more control over their affairs, endured after the Soviet collapse, despite attempts to reconfigure the number and size of the eighty-nine regions. Formal documents, including the 1992 Federation Treaty and the 1993 Constitution, reinforced these inequalities, even though they attempted to mitigate some of the grounds for interregional and intergovernmental conflict. Since the passage of these documents, however, asymmetries among the *oblasts* and *krais,* which the constitution purports to be equal in political and economic rights and responsibilities, emerged and intensified under Yeltsin (Ivanov 1998). Extraordinary regional rights ranged from the negotiation of international economic treaties to the retention of tax revenues, from the transfer of federal property into regional hands to individual changes in electoral rules.

Whereas the institutional legacies of the Soviet system produced inequalities between the ethnic republics and other provinces, the asymmetries among the fifty-five *oblasts* and *krais* in Russia did not emerge spontaneously from the uncertainty of the Russian transition, but from central leaders' policy choices. Responding to urgent problems in the intergovernmental relationship and Russian fiscal health, President Yeltsin and his administration chose to employ bilateralism—direct negotiations and treaties between the executive branch of the central government and the executive branch of each individual region—as an alternative to the arduous process of passing multilateral legislation. The choice of bilateralism as an intergovernmental reform strategy altered the development of federalism by increasing the role of regional elites in intergovernmental reform. The 1993 Constitution gave the federal government the power to establish the boundaries of decentralization, but bilateralism gave individual regions the power to set the agenda for federal reform, privileging their own strategies and resources to negotiate these goals. In the complex and uncertain bargaining arena, economically and politically stable regions benefited from the bilateral process, negotiating greater subnational control over local policy and resources, but poorer and fragmented regions continued to depend on a volatile center. Despite the short-term benefits of bilateralism to the center in stability and political support, the resulting asymmetrical rulebook has emerged as a defining feature of Russian federalism. Even as Yeltsin's successor, Vladimir Putin, seeks to redress some of the inequalities within the federation, he faces the uneven resources and powers of the regions. The ongoing competition among regions and between the center and the subnational governments over the demarcation of authority keeps the structure of federalism in flux. Consequently, the question of "Can the center hold?" remains unanswered.

DEFINING FEDERALISM

The study of federalism in transitional societies such as Russia offers insights into the roles of national and subnational actors in structuring and maintaining the federal bargain. This compact lies at the heart of the state-building project, with center-periphery relations either contributing to or hindering the transition to liberal democracy. As Woodrow Wilson asserted in his description of American federalism, "The question of the relation of the States to the federal government is the cardinal question of our constitutional system. At every turn of our national development we have been brought face to face with it and no definition either of statesmen or judges has ever quieted or decided it" (1885; quoted in Ordeshook and Shvetsova 1997, 30). With its economic, ethnic, and territorial asymmetries, Russia illustrates the increasingly prevalent use of federalism throughout the world as a means to address interregional differences. Although federalism has long been associated with stable democracies such as the United States, Canada, and Australia, it also has emerged in the twentieth century as a popular "solution" to a variety of state-building problems associated with ethnic, religious, and/or economic asymmetries, particularly in the post-colonial world.[3] Nevertheless, as numerous authors have rightly noted, federalism has not necessarily resolved these problems or made them less conflictual, and many such federal experiments, as in Pakistan and the West Indies, have failed (Lemco 1991; Tarlton 1965; Smith 1995). There is no established blueprint for creating a stable federation, its myriad of institutions, and the proper balance of power between center and periphery. Leaders of new federal states have imported models from the United States, Germany, and other Western democracies, yet defining federalism primarily relies upon pre-existing institutions, policy-makers' choices, and the intersection of national and subnational interests.

For many scholars, however, the success of American federalism in its constitutional compromise between the states and the national government and the design of its institutions offers a blueprint for nations undergoing political transition or reconfiguration. In one of the classic texts on federalism, Riker (1964) contends that the origins of the federal bargain in the United Sates as a marriage of autonomous units in the interest of territorial expansion and security explain the survival of American federalism. This suggests that federalism emerged as a solution to distinct historical conditions: the tyranny of British imperialism and the ungovernability of the confederation of the founding colonies (Walker 1981). The federal system therefore served the dual purpose of protecting its citizens against the tyranny of the central government and creating a national government strong enough to fulfill its functions, particularly as the provider of military security (Friedrich 1968; Tarlton 1965). The fact that federalism offered a solution to specific state-building problems implies that the American federal project cannot offer a definitive prescription to every nation that seeks to construct a federal system. Many of these countries understand federalism as a means to resolve ethnic tensions or other cleavages that threaten to fracture the state. Alfred Stepan (1999) refers to such systems as "holding together" federations, correctly emphasizing the state-building goals of federalism in such cases. As a newly independent and democratizing state, Russia fits the pattern of a "holding together" federation, but it also seeks the democratic protections that federalism can provide. Russia did not endure a history of confederalism or colonialism;[4] its leaders must address a long history of authoritarianism and a preexisting form of federalism that blended federal rhetoric with centralized bureaucracies and decision making. Simultaneously, Russian federalism seeks to address the problem of unifying an asymmetrical territorial system that defines the relationship between center and periphery—a common state-building problem, but one less central to American federal history. Regional differences certainly played a role in constructing American federalism, particularly during the intergovernmental conflicts over state sovereignty in the 1830s and leading to the Civil War (Whittington 1996; Ellis 1987). But unlike Russian federalism, American federalism was founded upon states' equal relationships with the central government; no state retained powers unavailable to other states.

These historical conditions shape the choice and design of institutions that affect the sustainability of federalism. The need for separate spheres of authority within a unified nation would suggest particular institutions to preserve *de facto* and *de jure* federalism: a bicameral system (Wheare 1953; Duchacek 1970); constitutionally entrenched spheres of territorial autonomy (Watts 1999; King 1982); some type of constitutional court system (Bednar, Eskridge and Ferejohn 1997; Elazar 1995). Yet these institutions are neither necessary nor sufficient to guarantee the survival of federalism. Riker, for example, argues that the American two-party system with its decentralized party organization, rather than the institutions most strongly associated with federations, maintains the federal balance between shared rule and self-rule. Studies of the German and Swiss federations point to cooperative institutional structures, such as concurrent legislative powers in German or the collegial executive in Switzerland, as the keys to federal stability (Watts 1999; Jeffrey 1999). These institutions, however, share a common function: the resolution of conflict between the center and regions. Federal systems require continual readjustment and negotiation to balance national and subnational demands and to sustain the federal bargain. Institutions provide one means of fulfilling this need, by defining the opportunities for subnational input into national policy and constitutional change or by raising or lowering the cost of exit. Multilateral institutions, such as the American Senate, the German Bundesrat, or even the more informal Canadian First Ministers' Conference, traditionally act as the principal forums for center-regional conflict resolution. Yet, not all federal systems emphasize or use multilateral structures to resolve intergovernmental problems. The Russian Federation, Spain, India, and at times, Canada rely upon bilateral relations—direct and dyadic negotiations between center and region—as a means for the federal government to respond to subnational demands. In many of these cases, bilateralism is carried out in frequent but informal meetings. In rarer instances, more formal arrangements support bilateralism. Daniel Elazar refers to these bilateral arrangements—agreements between specific constituent units and the national government that provide the foundation for the federal contract—as *foralistic* arrangements (Elazar 1995, 193). In Spain, for example, the 1978 Constitution provides for bilateral agreements to address the country's ethnic asymmetries, particularly the demands of the Basques and Catalans (Elazar 1994; Diaz 1981). Treaty relations have become the hallmark of an emerging federative-type system in the European Union (Hueglin 2000). The Russian Federation has employed similar agreements in its relations with its ethnically based territories and to address its significant economic and territorial asymmetries. Despite the numerous examples of bilateralism in federal societies, as well as its potential use in other multi-ethnic or asymmetrical states, few scholars have explored this type of federal arrangement, its effect on intergovernmental relations, and its ability to resolve the tensions between the federal government and subnational units that frequently serve as the impetus for building federalism.

Whereas bilateralism might affect federal relations differently from multilateral frameworks, these structures do not exist independently of the ongoing process of intergovernmental relations. As variables affecting the outcome of federalism, structure and process interact, gradually or sometimes radically altering the nature of federalism.[5] As Whittington notes in his discussion of American federal development, "The critical determinants of the nature of federalism are political, not legal" (Whittington 1996, 24). The federal government and its constituent units resolve the inherent tensions and ambiguities of federalism through a principally political process, bounded but not determined by constitutional structures. Particularly in transitional societies, in which central and subnational elites bargain over the rules of the game, leaders' choices and negotiating strategies can alter the boundaries of bilateral arrangements and the division of decision-making power. The institutions noted earlier that traditionally mediate federal conflict are often weak and still accessible for elites to mold their shape and significance. Peterson (1981) rightly notes that national and subnational preferences on the rules of federalism and the implementation of federal policy often do not agree. But the relationships between each constituent unit and the center frequently diverge, resulting in a "federal system [that] may be more or less federal throughout its parts" (Tarlton 1965, 867). Subnational goals and strategies for federal development can also differ, producing an uneven and competitive process. In his influential study on the development of Italian governmental institutions, Robert Putnam describes the way in which these dynamics emerge in the transition from a centralized to a federal-type society:

Devolution is inevitably a bargaining process, not simply a juridical act. The legal and constitutional framework, the administrative framework (controls, delegated powers, personnel patterns, and so on), and finances are both key resources in today's game and outcomes of earlier games. As seen by regional leaders, the central authorities' main bargaining chips were control of funds and control over the delegation of formal authority—the pocketbook and the rulebook. Leaders of the richer, more ambitious regions of the North were more concerned about the rulebook, while the South was more conscious of the pocketbook. (Putnam 1993, 23)

Although Putnam's focus turns to a comparison of political institutional designs in northern and southern Italy, he alludes to an intriguing question: why are some subnational governments, whether in Italy, India, or the Russian Federation, more interested in the rulebook—the legal separation of authority and decision-making—than in extracting more money out of the central coffers? Does the answer simply rely on the distinction between rich and poor regions, or does it go beyond such divisions? Do regions differ in the type of relationships they seek with the central government, or does the variance depend on the regions' degrees of success in devolving decision-making?

This study argues that defining federalism—delineating areas of jurisdiction and authority among institutions at the national, regional, and local levels—encompasses a complex bargaining process among elites over the rulebook as well as the pocketbook. As Riker (1964) asserts, federalism at its very foundation is essentially a bargain among the central government and its constituent units, with each side ceding some authority to the other in exchange for autonomy in other spheres. The bargaining process, however, extends well beyond the initial federal compact. The maintenance of federalism rests on the ability of national and subnational elites to renegotiate the rules of the game and the division of authority within the federation. Although the central government might establish the boundaries and guidelines of the process, it cannot impose its vision of the distribution of authority within the federation. Instead, actors must continually negotiate the federal bargain through cooperation and conflict, with institutional outcomes representing an amalgam of some interests and the exclusion of others. Demarcating power between the center and the subnational governments requires regions to develop and negotiate agendas for intergovernmental reform, using a variety of competitive or cooperative strategies. Yet subnational governments enter into the bargaining process with unequal resources, leaving some regions less equipped to structure the rules of federalism to their benefit. If some regional leaders are more willing and able to attain control over the rulebook as it applies to their concerns, how will the expansion and institutionalization of asymmetries affect the shape and sustainability of federalism?

FISCAL FEDERALISM

To examine the emerging rules of federalism, this study focuses on a key issue for both developing and industrialized nations: fiscal federalism. Intergovernmental finance spans a broad range of economic relations, including revenue sharing, tax sharing, tax privileges, and intergovernmental budgetary mechanisms, as well as federal loans, subsidies, and investments. For a number of reasons, fiscal federalism offers a circumscribed but pivotal realm in which to analyze the bargaining relationship between center and regions. First, decisions over public revenues and expenditures occupy a central role in the intergovernmental relationship. As Hamilton notes in *Federalist Paper No. 30*, "Money is, with propriety, considered as the vital principle of the body politic as that which sustains its life" (Rossiter 1999, 156). Jurisdictional conflicts often originate from struggles over resources, particularly when property rights are uncertain (Eggertsson 1990, 343–44). In a federal system, resources can either enable or constrain governments in the exercise of constitutionally assigned responsibilities (Watts 1999). Second, fiscal federalism provides a context in which to disaggregate the structure of federalism as well as examine how fiscal institutions structure the choices of central and regional actions and condition the resources that they bring to bear on these institutional arrangements. Third, intergovernmental fiscal relations expose the foundations of the federal system by providing a "power map" to the division of authority between center and periphery.[6] The "contractual sharing of public responsibilities by all governments in the system"—most notably the joint control of revenue and expenditure responsibilities—represents a defining feature of federalism (Elazar 1987, 185). By revealing the compromises, conflicts, and coordination in managing and allocating valuable resources, the study of intergovernmental finance lets us explore the development of federalism through the analysis of a single issue.

The study of fiscal federalism has traditionally focused on the effects of federal arrangements—distributional outcomes, efficiency concerns, and public service provision—rather than the process of their design, perhaps an indication of the interest in stable federations such as the United States (Wildasin 1997, 30). Despite the increasing attention to the impact of federal design on economic development and financial stability in developing countries, the focus continues to remain on economic outcomes rather than political consequences (Fisher 1997; Wildasin 1997).[7] Fiscal federalism in Russia has become a particularly intense subject of discussion in the Western and Russian literatures, as scholars debate the balance of economic power between center and periphery (Treisman 1996, 1998a, 1999; McAuley 1997; Lavrov 1995, 1998; Le Houerou and Rutkowski 1996; Tabata 1998; Wallich 1994; McLure 1995). Like the literature on finance in the United States and Europe, the expanding literature on Russia has typically emphasized economic growth and questions of revenue production: What is the most efficient transfer system? To what extent should redistribution level regional incomes? How can Russia best balance subnational revenues and expenditures? Some more recent studies have eschewed efficiency models in favor of analyses of their distributional results. One of the most prolific scholars of Russian intergovernmental budgetary relations, Daniel Treisman, examines the politics of the transfer system, using regression techniques to determine the explanatory variables and consequences of the system's asymmetries. McAuley (1997) and Tabata (1998) employ similar approaches, though McAuley, in particular, disputes Treisman's findings.[8] Although they explore some of the same issues as I do—asymmetrical federalism and the balance between central and subnational interests—they cite distributional differences, particularly in budgetary transfers, as the source of conflict, an argument I challenge in this study. The principal data for their studies, transfers from the Fund for Regional Support, represented less than thirty percent of the total federal financial assistance to the regions in the mid-1990s and only fifteen percent of subnational revenue by 1999 (Lavrov, Litwack and Sutherland 2001). "Mutual settlements," including expenditure adjustments and repayments of federal debt, which rely on bilateral negotiations, still constitute an equally large share of regional financing (Lavrov 1998). Furthermore, the central government perpetually delays or reduces transfers and other federal payments to the regions, giving regional elites incentives to seek financial gains in the form of credits, federal programs, and "experimental" revenue-sharing arrangements and longer-term gains through bilateral treaties and agreements (Lavrov 1998; Litvack 1994). These more informal financial flows are difficult to trace and impossible to quantify, limiting the scope of more traditional quantitative analyses of fiscal federalism. But if we seek to compare the patterns of interaction and their meaning for the development of federalism, comprehensive cross-regional data on financial transfers hold less importance than the institutional context of the transfers and the negotiations of their receipt.

DEFINING CENTER AND PERIPHERY

In the context of fiscal federalism, negotiations over economic resources and their allocation occurred primarily and directly between central and regional governments rather than through proxies such as political party leaders or Duma representatives. By regional or periphery leadership, I mean the executive branch (administration) at the *oblast* (regional) level. I focus primarily on the governor, sometimes known as the head of administration, and his immediate circle of advisers overseeing financial issues, usually the vice governor in charge of the economy and the head of the finance department.[9] Although the regional Duma (legislative council) also controls local financial matters such as the budget, the executive branch has primary responsibility for negotiating with the center. In most cases, I ascribe the goals of a region directly to the governor, as only he is authorized to sign agreements with the central government. Further, he must sign all regional financial proposals, economic plans, and official correspondence with the central ministries. Under Yeltsin, the governor usually had the most contact with high-level central officials through negotiations and his seat in the Russian senate, the Federation Council.[10] One exception is the head of the regional Duma, who also holds a seat on the Federation Council; I will note when this position plays a role in the relationship between a region and the center.

Defining the center presents considerably more problems. It is difficult to conceptualize a single center when the Russian government underwent frequent turnover of vice premiers and ministers under President Yeltsin and witnessed incessant conflicts among bureaucracies and branches of government. Therefore, I focus principally on the president and the prime minister, because one or both of these rulers must sign every major agreement between the federal government and a region, particularly those that affect the delineation of decision making. In addition, Yeltsin's administration held responsibility for regional matters through the presidential representatives to the regions. Article 77.2 of the 1993 Constitution establishes a "single system of executive authority," formally linking the presidential and regional administrations.[11] Moreover, until 1995, the president retained the power to appoint or remove the governors, strengthening the tie between central and regional administrations.

Although the president and his administration led regional negotiations, the fragmentation at the center had a wider impact on the intergovernmental relationship. The picture that emerged from my interviews, supported by the accounts of numerous journalists and other observers, depicted the center as a many-armed creature, and quite often, like Dr. Strangelove in the Stanley Kubrick film of the same name, one arm did not know what the other was doing. This was particularly true in the midst of Boris Yeltsin's illness during and after the 1996 presidential campaign, when the locus of presidential authority was unclear. The frequent leadership turnover in 1995 to 1996, from Yeltsin's pre-election administration to the influx of more conservative supporters during the campaign and a return to the more liberal group led by Anatoli Chubais, only multiplied the confusion at the center. Moreover, Yeltsin's penchant for pitting governmental factions against one another—during the first round of the 1996 presidential elections, for example, when Yeltsin appointed General Aleksandr Lebed to the government in direct opposition to Prime Minister Viktor Chernomyrdin—exacerbated the fragmentation again.[12] The Ministry of Finance, which plays a principal role in intergovernmental fiscal relations, has been a frequent target of accusations that its bureaucracy functions completely separate from and at odds with the rest of the government. The factionalism at the center dramatically increases the negotiating costs for the regional side and for central rulers. Regional elites must negotiate with a variety of officials and ministries, often receiving conflicting answers from the sources. At the same time, the presidential administration might have difficulty coordinating a coherent regional fiscal policy, as it must compile and reconcile information from the Ministry of Finance, the State Tax Service, and the Ministry of the Economy, as well as its own bureaucratic sources. Because of the significance of these conflicts and coordination problems for the institutionalization of intergovernmental rules, the fragmentation of the center becomes the object of study, particularly in chapters 3 and 4.

ORGANIZATION OF THE STUDY

This book focuses on the development of federalism in Russia under President Yeltsin (1990–1999). I give particular emphasis to the period following the passage of the constitution in 1993 until 1998, the height of bilateral negotiations over the shape of the federation. Many studies of Russian federalism examine the First Republic (1991–1993), during which the drama of elite conflict and potential collapse reached its climax. Yet after the October crisis and December constitutional referendum in 1993, the less sensational but no less significant phase of deciding constitutional meaning and allocating authority and resources in specific domains began. It is in this period that the process of defining federalism primarily takes place. The first part of the study examines the center's strategy of bilateral negotiations with the regions to respond to the Russian fiscal crisis and address the issue of federal stability. Two factors influenced the development of the bilateral approach: the persistence of particular historical legacies and the short time horizon of the central administration. Chapter 2 defines the concept of historical legacies—norms and rules that survive beyond the context in which they were created—which draws on the idea of path dependency. According to Margaret Levi, the theory of path dependency goes beyond the idea that "history matters." "Path dependence has to mean, if it is to mean anything, that once a country or region has started down a track, the costs of reversal are very high. There will be other choice points, but the entrenchments of certain institutional arrangements obstruct an easy reversal of the initial choice" (Levi 1997, 28). Policy choices thus constrain the opportunities for future choices by creating or reinforcing particular institutions. Yet the question of how actors can alter existing institutions still remains.

The collapse of the Soviet Union provided the "big bang" for institutional change[13] by destroying powerful institutions, such as the Communist Party's monopoly on political power and the central planning apparatus. It also legitimized new ones, including legislatures and subnational governments. The Soviet demise, however, did not eradicate the entire institutional landscape and create a tabula rasa for democratic federalism. Instead, the exogenous shocks realigned resources, giving new groups such as regional actors and international agencies the power to influence the direction of change and creating incentives for them to alter some institutional arrangements (Moe 1985; Knight 1992). The transition to Russian independence emphasized certain historical legacies from the Soviet period, namely the significance of local resources to the balance of power in the intergovernmental relationship and the importance of the executive leadership to the negotiating process. It did this by constraining actors' abilities or preferences to change these arrangements. Also, the complexities of the fiscal system persisted during this uncertain transition, producing costly interactions between levels of government. Both the center and regions had to expend considerable resources to ensure they received what the other side promised—a potentially costly operation for little reward—or to negotiate an agreement giving them more authority while reducing the constant need for renegotiation as fiscal circumstances change. Although this path offered greater potential for long-term fiscal and political benefits, the cost of negotiation was insurmountable for some leaders.

Chapter 3 looks at the center's options in addressing intergovernmental fiscal reform in the context of these institutional legacies. The mounting fiscal crisis in Russia added a constraint to federal decision making. As the budget deficit rose to more than fifteen percent of expenditures in 1995 and over twenty-two percent in 1996 (Goskomstat 1995, 1996) while measures to improve tax collection failed, the center needed a short-term solution to the financial problems. It could pursue multilateral legislation, particularly the tax code and the budgetary code, to reform intergovernmental fiscal mechanisms and improve fiscal responsibility at the subnational level, or attempt to negotiate bilateral agreements with regions. I argue that bilateralism best served the center's needs in the short term, particularly as multilateral legislation lingered in the State Duma committees. Not only did bilateral agreements offer the center an opportunity to prevent further unilateral action (particularly by the republics), such as single-channel tax systems,[14] they presented potential political benefits as well. Bilateral treaties could strengthen the federal compact, providing a formal and visible means for the subnational governments to pledge their loyalty to the unity of the federation.

At the same time, however, the Russian transition gave the subnational governments incentives to decentralize power and alter the federal structure. Yet if all regions have the incentives to change the rules of the game under the constraints of the same historical legacies and are responding to the center's offer of bilateral talks, why do only some regions seek these changes whereas others do not? To reform intergovernmental rules to their benefit, regional leaders must mobilize resources, ranging from the most quantifiable commodities such as monetary wealth to the fuzzier variables of political leadership.[15] Although the issue of resources enters into many studies of institutional development, political scientists frequently shy away from unquantifiable political variables such as leadership, information, and political legitimacy. Yet it was precisely these more complex resources that differentiated regions more forcefully and successfully negotiating changes to the intergovernmental fiscal rules from those focusing on the implementation of current institutional arrangements. Noting the important role of resource capabilities in explaining institutional change, Hay and Wincott contend, "Access to strategic resources, and indeed to knowledge of the institutional environment, is unevenly distributed. This in turn affects the ability of actors to transform the contexts (institutional and otherwise) in which they find themselves" (Hay and Wincott 1998, 956).

Chapter 4 returns to the historical legacies of the Soviet period to examine how they emphasized particular local resources in intergovernmental bargaining over the rulebook and the pocketbook. All regions were responding to the same institutional factors, but this did not equalize their positions relative to the center. On the contrary, legacies such as the predominant power of the executive in decision making and the bureaucratic complexity of the intergovernmental bargaining environment emphasized economic and political resources that are unevenly distributed at the subnational level. With eighty-nine regions competing for access and consideration at the center, regional elites must determine how to consolidate and target economic and political resources, including local revenues, inter-elite associations, and representatives in Moscow, to construct and bargain their agendas for intergovernmental reform.

Chapters 5 and 6 examine how local economic and political resources affected the development of specific regional agendas for intergovernmental reform and the abilities of subnational leaders to negotiate changes to the rules of fiscal federalism. The study focuses on the *oblasts* in European Russia for several reasons. First, the small number of cases indicates that I should limit the number of independent variables; excluding the republics and eastern regions offers the most simple strategy.[16] Second, numerous scholars have explored the unique relationship between the ethnic republics and the center (Balzer and Vinokurova 1996; Gorenburg 1999; Clark and Graham 1995; Szporluk 1994; Smith 1995; Goble 1994; Lapidus and Walker 1995; Treisman 1997; Kempton 1996; Kahn 2002). The *oblasts* are both more numerous and on average more populous than the republics, suggesting that they deserve more attention. I compare three regions—Samara, Bryansk, and Vologda—that embody many of the predominant characteristics of European Russia, including industrial concentration, densely clustered populations, and substantial economic and social demands caused by the Soviet collapse. All three regions are *oblasts* rather than republics, which maintain a privileged status in the federation, ostensibly because of the ethnic minority populations in their territories. Yet their different political environments, local economies, and levels of economic crisis create quite divergent resource bases, offering different constraints and opportunities to alter the fiscal ties to the center. Chapter 5 examines the specific agendas for intergovernmental reform of Samara, Bryansk, and Vologda. Although the center agreed to negotiate with all three regions, they came to the center with a variety of goals and emerged from the process with very different bilateral relationships. The transitional environment accentuated the differences in objectives between the wealthy and poor regions and the severe economic crisis in some regions shortened their leaders' time horizons. As a result these regions had to pursue central financing to ease their woes while other regions sought more fiscal control. Samara, for instance, sought significant control over the fiscal rulebook, despite the predominance of large and outdated industries in its territory—a possible sign of a strong dependence on the center for reconstruction and conversion aid. One of the most populous provinces in European Russia, Samara emerged in the mid-1990s as a key economic player in the Russian Federation by remaining one of the handful of "donor regions"—those that do not receive transfers from the center's Fund for Regional Support. With this financial independence, Samara's leaders possessed the freedom to seek more control over their fiscal affairs and long-term improvements to the intergovernmental rules of the game.

Vologda, a beautiful area of white birch forests and wooden houses 250 miles north of Moscow, also sought significant changes to the balance of power in its fiscal relationship with the federal government based on the economic potential of its metallurgy industry and agricultural production. But the economic crisis that loomed in the region in 1995 and 1996 limited the degree of fiscal autonomy that Vologda's leaders could seek. With minimal foreign investment, a poorly developed infrastructure, and an underfinanced budget, Vologda needed to maintain the role of the center in supporting the economic future of the region, creating the foundation for a more dependent bilateral relationship with the center than that of Samara. Bryansk, however, had little opportunity to pursue anything beyond an improvement in the implementation of the current fiscal relationship. In the heavily industrialized Central Economic Zone, Bryansk employed fully one-third of its industrial workers in the ailing military-industrial complex, including the production of chemical weapons.[17] In addition to the economic burden of failing industries, the accident at the Chernobyl nuclear power plant in 1986 brought the region's economy close to collapse. Bryansk is on the border of Belarus and Ukraine, making it strategically important for trade and political relations among Russia and the former Soviet states, but also placing it barely two hundred miles from Chernobyl. The province only belatedly grasped the long-term impact of the disaster: the evacuation of agricultural areas to the south; the devastation of its potato farming; and the public health costs. With few places to turn for economic assistance, Bryansk's leaders focused on the federal pocketbook and the immediate fulfillment of the center's fiduciary promises, leaving them few opportunities to consider changes to the development of intergovernmental institutions.

Whereas economic factors helped to determine the goals of regional leaders—whether they focus on the federal rulebook or pocketbook—a wider range of resources affected the strategies and abilities of these actors to negotiate their agendas. The central role of the executive in Russia, for example, privileged regions such as Samara, whose leaders have managed to consolidate local political and economic authority. Samara is one of the few provinces in Russia that has not suffered from frequent political turnover; Yeltsin appointed the governor, Konstantin Titov, in 1991, and he remained in that post for the length of Yeltsin's presidency. Despite significant support in the region for communist candidates in national elections, the widespread popularity of Titov's pro-market reforms and policies with his constituents and local elites gave the governor the resources at home and the credibility at the center to negotiate the decentralization of fiscal decision making and responsibility. But whereas cohesive and stable leadership allowed Titov to translate Samara's substantial economic resources into aggressive and costly intergovernmental reform strategies, the governments of Bryansk and Vologda faced greater limitations. In Vologda, political turmoil limited the possibilities of developing strategies and effectively targeting resources toward the administration's goal of increasing regional autonomy based on local economic potential. Although Yeltsin appointed and supported Vologda's first governor, Nikolai Podgornov, the federal government eventually dismissed and indicted Podgornov on charges of embezzlement and abuse of office. The scandal and political infighting paralyzed governance for more than a year and exacerbated the fiscal crisis in the province, until Yeltsin appointed a popular mayor, Vyacheslav Pozgalev, to the governorship in mid-1996. Corruption and pillage of the treasury by the previous administration hindered Pozgalev's efforts at a radical reform of Vologda's fiscal relationship with the center, yet new leadership also produced incentives to pursue alternative strategies to balance the need for federal financial aid with the desire for more authority over financial decision making.

Bryansk also had its share of political battles and elite fragmentation, which intensified the sense of crisis in the region. Between 1991 and 1999, the governorship changed hands six times, alternating among four politicians. The Communist Party of the Russian Federation and the local nationalist-leftist coalition, *Patrioticheskaya Bryanshchina*,[18] dominate the province, both in the leadership and in the political leanings of the constituents. Three pro-reform politicians have occupied the governorship, but constant conflict with the communist-controlled legislature, corruption, and political stagnation marked their terms, and they were soon removed from office. With little time or support to harness resources toward reform of intergovernmental ties, Bryansk's leaders focused on short-term crisis measures or enriching themselves, even making the federal pocketbook a dubious goal.

Based on these three examples of very different intergovernmental relationships and evidence of further variance throughout the federation, Chapter 7 addresses the consequences of bilateralism for the long-term maintenance of federalism. How do asymmetrical relationships within the federation complicate the delicate balance between responding to subnational demands and national unity? If some regions control key aspects of the intergovernmental rulebook while others remain dependent on the largesse of the center, how will the growing imbalance affect the survival of the federal bargain and the ability of the central government to remedy the inequities? To address these larger theoretical questions, I compare the Russian case with two countries that have employed bilateralism to manage federal instability and to define the rules of federalism: Canada during the last several decades of federal reform and Spain after the passage of

the 1978 Constitution. Like Russia, Canada and Spain face potentially de-
stabilizing tensions as a result of regional asymmetries. Different institutional arrangements, however, have produced contrasting subnational
responses and repercussions for federal reform. In Canada, limited bilateralism and a more recent focus on multilateral intergovernmental institutions have constrained efforts to reform the federal system and reduce
the high level of regional conflict. Spain has also tried to limit the scope
of bilateral bargaining to specific issues and provinces. Yet by institutionalizing bilateralism through the constitution and other multilateral agreements, the government has had only minimal success in trying to control
the process of devolution and eliminate some of the inequities among the
provinces. Like in Spain, bilateralism in Russia provided central leaders
with the opportunity for rapid and extensive reform to the structure of
federalism, but it also contained the seeds for continuing challenges to
federal arrangements and intergovernmental conflict. As the new president, Vladimir Putin attempts to re-imagine the structure of federalism
and the balance of power between center and periphery, existing bilateral
arrangements and intergovernmental bargaining institutions hamper his
ability to recentralize authority and construct a symmetrical federation.
Based on the potential for such subnational challenges to federal authority,
I return to the question posed at the beginning of this study: will the center
hold? The narrative of federation building contains only one part of the
answer for Russia, but it nevertheless draws us away from the old confines
of Sovietology to a new vision for investigating issues of institutional
change and development.

NOTES

1. I have taken this phrase from the title of the book by Pål Kolsto (2000).
2. I am fashioning this phrase on the famous Soviet maxim, "National in form,
socialist in content."
3. Cynthia Enloe (1977) refers to federalism as a type of "conflict management
system."
4. One could argue that Russia was indeed a colony within the Soviet empire,
but given the influence of the Russian Republic within the USSR, it shows few
similarities to the American colonial experience.
5. Cox and Frankland (1995) use such an argument to explain how the interaction between asymmetrical federalism and elite conflict resulted in the dissolution of federalism in Czechoslovakia.
6. The concept of a "power map" comes from Duchacek (1973).
7. Although studies of established federations, such as the United States and
Canada, continue to dominate the literature, there are now extensive readings on
fiscal federalism in India (Thimmiah 1985; George 1988; Sury 1998) and intergovernmental fiscal relations in China (Huang 1996; Oksenberg and Tong 1991; Ma

1997; Donnithorne 1981). Jae Ho Chung (1995) and Linda Chelan Li (1998) provide excellent overviews of the literature on center-periphery relations in China.

8. Alastair McAuley's assertion that the center allocates transfers from the Fund for Regional Support primarily according to distributional concerns rather than a political logic, as Treisman argues, produced a particularly heated response from Treisman. He states, "McAuley's argument has the same structure as that of a medical researcher who sets out to demonstrate that malaria is in fact spread not by mosquitoes but by tropical breezes, identified a correlation between malaria rates and warm, humid winds, and simply asserted that it was not necessary to check whether this correlation remained significant controlling for the local prevalence of mosquitoes" (1998, 894).

9. In referring to the Russian governors, prime minister, and president, I use *he* and *his*, because as of 1998, no woman has served in any of these positions. I try to employ more gender-neutral language when referring to other officials.

10. The rules governing the composition of the Federation Council changed under President Putin. After 2000, governors and heads of regional legislatures had to relinquish their seats and appoint a representative to the new Federation Council. I discuss these and other changes under President Putin in Chapter 7.

11. All translations are the author's own, unless otherwise stated.

12. See, for example, Cottrell (1996).

13. Cortell and Peterson (1999) discuss the various triggers for institutional change more generally than the development of federalism, including the "critical junctures" of war, social unrest, and dramatic technological change, and less dramatic shifts, such as elections, which trigger incremental change in institutions. See also Ikenberry (1988) and Krasner (1984) for discussions of crisis-induced change, or punctuated equilibrium, and North (1995) and Thelen and Steinmo (1992) for attention to more incremental change.

14. Single-channel tax systems allow subnational governments to determine unilaterally the amount of tax revenue they will cede to the federal government. Such systems were particularly prevalent before the passage of the constitution in December 1993, and before the center devoted considerable resources to recentralizing the treasury system.

15. Kathryn Sikkink aptly states in her work on economic policy and implementation in Latin America, "Essential in the study of state capacity is the dynamic interaction between institutions, rules, and procedures of the state and society, and the people, groups, and ideas in political life. . . . Mobilization of resources is the game of politics at its richest and involves ideas, inspiration, leadership, and the unquantifiable qualities that motivate people to believe and act" (1991, 25).

16. See King, Keohane, and Verba (1994), Collier (1991), Geddes (1990), Dion (1998) and the numerous contributions in the *American Political Science Review* (1995) symposium for a discussion of the small-n problem in qualitative research design.

17. According to one estimate, Bryansk produced up to one-third of all the chemical weapons in Russia (Aleksandr Levinskii, interview, 22 February 1997).

18. Throughout the text, I use the U.S. Board on Geographic Names system of transliteration from the Cyrillic.

CHAPTER 2

The Roots of Fiscal Authority Relations: The Soviet Period and the First Russian Republic

At the center of the transition from Soviet centralism to a new federalism was the tug-of-war over resources and the laws that would govern their control. As Wallich (1996) notes, public finance in transition countries permeates all key goals of reform. This is particularly true in transitions from communism in which the role of the state in resource allocation and economic transactions presents a central concern. Furthermore, in a federation, elites disagree over whether the state should retain control over particular resources as well as the *level* of government at which this authority should be located. In addition, the demands of state building, particularly in such a large and diverse territory as Russia, give more potency to the questions of fiscal relations. Although the process of unifying the Russian state involved other equally urgent questions—Russian and ethnic minority nationalism; border disputes; enhancing the power of civilian and military enforcement—unresolved issues of fiscal relations often stood at the crux of them or reflected similar problems. The 1993 Constitution, new tax and budget laws, privatization, and myriad other reforms sought to create an environment that would propel Russia into a capitalist future with the economic prosperity that communism had failed to deliver. Yet the reforms to fiscal federalism—and to the center-regional relationship more broadly—lagged behind other changes.[1] In the vacuum of uncertainty that existed between the scattered new fiscal laws and institutions that the government managed to adopt in the initial years of independence stood the vast tide of Soviet norms and mechanisms of interaction that continued to operate. It is the push and pull between these two forces—legacies of the Soviet "federal" system and the new post-communist institutions—that created the basis for the center-periphery relationship and is the focus of this chapter.

The collapse of the Soviet Union in 1991 not only severed the federal and imperial bonds among the fifteen republics, but signaled the dismantling of a complex system of bureaucratic and administrative hierarchies. Yet there was no violent revolution or civil war to eradicate entrenched Soviet institutions.[2] Instead, many bureaucratic and political elites maintained their former positions, sometimes in different guises, and continued to carry on business as usual (Kryshtanovskaya and White 1996; Higley, Kollberg, and Pakulski 1996; Wollman 1993). Although one could argue that national institutions in Russia underwent significant turnover and change, these changes reached the provinces more slowly. In the economic sphere, the so-called "red managers" maintained their positions in Russia's enterprises, looking for ways to hold onto the privileges of running state enterprises while gaining from the movement towards privatization. In public administration, the provinces had neither the resources nor the political will to remove any but the most stalwart and hard-line communists.[3] The mechanisms of center-periphery interaction reflected the continuity of personnel in the provinces and the center, relying on Soviet institutional norms to function in the face of rapid legal and economic change.[4] Although center-periphery relations underwent unmistakable change in post-Soviet Russia, this relationship maintained its roots from the Soviet system. Soviet institutions were not wiped out in 1991 but continued a process of transformation—albeit one that was greatly accelerated and extended—that began in the late 1950s under Khrushchev.

This chapter explores the roots of fiscal federalism in Russia and the foundations for bilateral bargaining within this framework between central and subnational leaders. I argue that the Soviet system bequeathed to its Russian heir a set of institutional legacies—norms of interaction that remained resistant to change—which structured the range of options for fiscal reform in the Russian federation. The system of fiscal relations that Soviet leaders devised in the 1930s created the basic parameters of center-periphery relations and of the behavior of regional elites. As the Soviet economy developed, the budgetary system became an immense bureaucracy, with overlapping and competing jurisdictions, and with the center increasingly unable to monitor activities at the local level.[5] Even under Stalin's totalitarian regime, the center had difficulty balancing the desire for strong centralization and the need for some decentralization in the economic realm to address local problems and projects. Numerous attempts at reform by Khrushchev and Brezhnev re-negotiated the balance of power among the party, the ministries, and their local organs, yet they proved incapable of eliminating the substantial uncertainty and complexity from the hierarchical system and often further obscured the locus of decision-making authority (Breslauer 1982, 79–80, 107–14; Hahn 1991). As a result, the provinces had more opportunity to question policies relevant to the periphery but more obstacles to circumvent. Subnational leaders were left to cope with a morass of bureaucratic officials, party edicts, and budgetary rules, particularly as central financing became less dependable. With no clear rules of reform or negotiation, republic and local leaders relied on informal networks and connections to lobby for increased central financing or to manage outside the purview of the center. Consequently, local leaders had to depend on their own abilities to gather and utilize information, lobby the central government, and construct agendas, rather than await the consideration of central elites. For regional elites that survived the transition from state socialism, these well-honed skills would prove invaluable.

The fiscal demands on the provinces served to highlight their differences in terms of economic resources. The uneven distribution of natural resources and industry clearly distinguished the importance of particular regions to the national economy (Bahry 1987; Gaddy 1996), but local economic structure also affected the fiscal relationship with the center. The division between "regulated" and "own" revenues under the Soviet fiscal system depended heavily on the industrial composition of the province and determined whether a locality had even a modicum of fiscal autonomy from the center.

The lack of clarity in authority relations, informal norms of negotiation, and the significance of local resource asymmetries continued to influence the reform process even after the collapse of the Soviet Union. Russian leaders, facing a seemingly endless array of economic and political problems, were cursed by the dysfunctional remains of the Soviet system of public finance but could do little to quickly or effectively repair them. As Gorbachev and then Yeltsin sought to address the contradictory needs for central revenue control and the devolution of expenditure responsibility, they continually confronted, and often relied upon, pre-existing institutional arrangements. Each attempt at reform only exacerbated one or more of these structural problems while providing subnational elites with the fodder to argue for even more authority over local issues. In the aftermath of Russian independence, the government focused on urgent fiscal reforms, such as monetary stabilization and price reform, leaving many of the Soviet bureaucratic structures in place. As central leaders, faced with increasing regional demands, turned to issues of federalization, they confronted many of the same structural problems as their predecessors, compounded by the new pressures of a rapid but chaotic transition to capitalism, fiscal deficits, and expectations for true democratic federalism.

THE SOVIET FISCAL SYSTEM AND THE FIRST ATTEMPTS AT REFORM

In the 1930s, Stalin's economic elite designed a fiscal system intended to ensure the dominance of the communist party and the central government. The basic organizational and management hierarchy remained in place for the next 60 years, shaping the roles and relationships of elites that worked within it. A complex, two-year process to formulate the state budget evolved gradually from Stalin's basic plan, but the primary economic navigator was the five-year plan that plainly reflected the party's political and economic goals. The state did not construct extensive financial planning for pricing, long-term investment, or developmental goals (Hutchings 1983). Instead, *Gosplan* (the state planning committee), along with the Ministry of Finance, established annual and five-year production and fiscal targets for each level of government to correspond with the five-year plan. As this information "trickled down" to the localities, the local soviets and finance departments would draft budgets detailing local revenue sources and local financial needs to pass up to the center (Bahry 1987). Local budgets depended heavily on state financing; although localities held some responsibility for expenditures, particularly in the social and cultural fields, the union budget controlled the majority of revenues, transferring two-thirds of all local budgetary revenues flowing from the center (Ross 1987). Republic-level budgets were similarly dependent on the center, unable to meet even half of their expenditures from their own revenues (Hutchings 1983).

Both the tax system and the fiscal bureaucratic system mirrored the vertically dependent budgetary structure. The tax system emphasized two indirect taxes: the enterprise profit tax and the turnover tax—a "handling" tax primarily on consumer goods that was calculated by the difference between the wholesale and final prices (Nove 1986)—which made up two-thirds of total revenue. The turnover tax was wholly assigned to the union budget and was used, in turn, to balance the republic budgets, accounting for approximately forty percent of their total budgets (Bahry 1987). The assignment of the profit tax depended on the subordination of the individual enterprise to a particular level of government (see below). On average, revenue from enterprise profits made up less than thirty percent of republican budgets, with less than ten percent ending up in oblast-level budgets (Ross 1987, 85). Two central agencies, the Ministry of Finance and the State Bank (*Gosbank*), along with their subordinate republic-level and local agencies, held primary responsibility for fiscal management. The Ministry of Finance functioned as the fiscal executive director, responsible for preparing the state budgets, approving financial plans and financing of enterprises and state agencies, and overseeing tax and other revenue collection (Gallik, Jesina, and Rapawy 1968). The center (all-union) and republics held joint jurisdiction over the Ministry of Finance; similarly, local finance departments were subordinate to both the Ministry of Finance and the local governments (soviets). In practice, however, the fiscal bureaucracy operated according to a strict hierarchy. The Ministry of Finance answered only to the Council of Ministers and the Politburo and the Ministry of Finance in Moscow controlled the fiscal bureaucracy at the union and local levels. *Gosbank* was similarly organized into hierarchical agencies and managed the implementation of the decrees and plans of the Finance Ministry. Without private banking in the Soviet system and with cash limited to the consumer sector and wage payments (Hutchings 1983), *Gosbank* played a key role in the Soviet financial system. It handled all transactions among enterprises and between enterprises and state agencies. These included settling accounts for payments and sales between one enterprise and another whereby payment could take place from an enterprise's account without the consent, or even knowledge, of the payer (Gallik, Jesina, and Rapawy 1968, 272). The concentration of fiscal control and management into two primary state agencies centralized not only decision making but also access to information. Local soviets and enterprises lacked the information on tax rates, inter-enterprise accounting, and revenue flows that is vital to the functioning of an economic system. Consequently, enterprise managers acted more as opportunistic contractors than responsible partners with the Party in economic growth.[6]

The economic system as a whole did not mirror the territorially organized structure of the fiscal system. Industry, while also hierarchical, was organized by sector rather than territory. The contradictions between these two systems of organization—the territorial-based fiscal system and the sectoral ministries—and the power struggles among political and bureaucratic officials that resulted from overlapping jurisdictions became key targets of Nikita Khrushchev's numerous attempts at reforms. Although many of these reforms were reversed after his fall from power in 1964, they had an impact on the Soviet system that outlasted the career of their architect. One of Khrushchev's prime goals was to break the power of the central bureaucracy by reinvigorating the power of local party and state officials, including their power over the economy (Breslauer 1982, 42–46). This initial attempt at decentralizing the system after years of Stalin's centralizing policies met with strong opposition from Soviet bureaucrats who propelled the policy's demise. Yet the overall design of the reforms was equally fatal. Instead of authorizing the local soviets to take control over local industries based upon their greater knowledge of provincial conditions and needs, Khrushchev dismantled the majority of the central economic ministries and transferred their functions to regional *sovnarkhozy*, or state economic councils. Beginning in 1957, the center transferred the control over many industries to the 105 *sovnarkhozy*, which were responsible for plan fulfillment by the enterprises in their region. With the creation of a new "master," enterprise managers were often caught between the contradictory directives of the regional *sovnarkhoz* and those of the central planning agency, one of the few remaining ministries, which sought to seize the power previously held by the economic ministries (Nove 1986, 63). In addition to complicating the bureaucratic structure,

the reforms drew criticism from above and below: from central bureaucratic elites, who accused the new councils of localism or concern for their
individual regions over the good of the entire Soviet Union, and from
local enterprise managers, who complained of conflicting information and
a lack of coordination with enterprises in other regions. The *sovnarkhozy*,
created in part to eliminate the coordination problems among the various
branch ministries, now oversaw the same problems of communication
between the regions. The consequent territorial insularity led to the dismantling of the *sovnarkhoz* experiment. As the conflict between the central
planners and the *sovnarkhozy* increased, more decision-making power was
transferred back to the center, making the regional councils even less able
to fulfill their functions.

The reversal of Khrushchev's reforms in 1965 resulted in a more centralized economic system than had existed under Stalin. With the elimination of the *sovnarkhozy* and the reinstatement of the central ministries,
the center once again took responsibility for overseeing local industry, a
process that was well under way by 1962 (Bahry 1987, 48). Enterprises
that had been subordinate to the local soviets before Khrushchev's reforms
were transferred to the central ministries (Ross 1987). Although some of
these enterprises were transferred back to republics and oblasts in the
1970s, the center maintained total control over key sectors of the economy,
such as machine building (Bahry 1987). The finance system also remained
centralized, with control over revenue staying primarily in the center's
hands. Nevertheless, the growing complexities of the bureaucratic system,
as well as the increasing problems and shortages in the Soviet economy,
strained the vertical hierarchy, giving the central leadership reasons to
seek new arrangements with the subnational territories.

THE PERIOD OF *ZASTOI* AND
RECENTRALIZATION

The Brezhnev period, later known as the era of *zastoi*, or stagnation,
brought a level of stability to the bureaucratic system through the abrogation of personnel reshuffling and systemic reform. At the subnational
level, this stability solidified the arrangement of regional elites and the
bargaining relationship with the center. But the reintroduction of the ministerial system also renewed the conflict between the industrial sectors
and the territorial fiscal system. As Cameron Ross (1987) argues, the contradictions inherent in the two competing systems increased the significance of a locality's economic resources and industrial structure to its
relationship with the central government. Brezhnev's policy of the stability of cadres, which aimed to counteract Khrushchev's attempts at reorganization, created a closer bond between regional elites and their
localities. As a result, the political success of these elites became tied to

the economic success of their regions (Moses 1985). Yet local leaders did not necessarily control the enterprises located within their jurisdictions. Heavily industrialized regions, particularly those with important military factories, such as in Kiubyshev (Samara) or in Vladivostok, had little input into the investment and planning decisions for these enterprises. First secretaries of the Soviet republics, however, had more discretion in overseeing the disbursement of funds. Beginning in the 1960s, funds channeled to the regions through the ministries surpassed those dispersed through the budget (Lewis 1977). The reforms of Brezhnev and Kosygin granted republican leaders the right to control and consolidate subsidies to enterprises for capital construction and social welfare. The 1971 legislation also gave this right to local soviets, but their control over these funds was often limited by oblast and republican leaders (Ross 1987, 62–71). With the increase in their responsibility under Brezhnev, the leaders of the republics also faced growing pressure from local leaders to respond to their financial needs and demands. Despite the stability of the political system, there was now an even more complex bureaucratic maze to negotiate, making lobbying for the economic success of one's territory an intricate process. Therefore, subnational leaders had to choose their battles with the center carefully based on their opportunities for access and likelihood for success.

Republic and local leaders retained a number of pathways to improving the economic and financial health of their territories. Subnational leaders had significant, albeit not always successful, opportunities to lobby or complain to central leaders for increases in state outlays to their regions (Bahry 1987). As investment resources became scarcer in the 1980s, subnational elites also directed more attention to expanding their degree of decision-making power over resources. Regional lobbying usually focused on either areas of joint jurisdiction between the center and the republic or enterprises subordinated to local authorities. Regional elites could appeal to a variety of central bureaucracies, but they were forced to navigate an enormously complex system, since no single ministry held complete decision-making responsibility for regional budget outlays. For example, in an article in *Pravda* (2 March 1986), Sverdlovsk's Iu. V. Petrov observed that the controlling bureaucracies were so numerous within the construction industry that even the Ministry of Finance—technically the chief controller—did not know all of their identities (Bahry 1987, 163). Both Gosplan and the Ministry of Finance had formal review procedures for requests and complaints, but neither bureaucracy had the ability or desire to handle most of them. If these agencies failed to answer these requests, regional leaders could turn to Party elites, the Supreme Soviet, or the Council of Ministers. But the Forestry Ministry, for example, might not carry out a decision by the Ministry of Finance to allocate more investment funds to a local timber processing plant. Regional leaders would then once again need to lobby for the implementation of the decision. Similarly, the Council of Ministers might authorize more funds for a local project when there were no budgetary funds available. In the short-term, the Council could show concern for local problems and perhaps even gain some assistance with an issue under local or joint jurisdiction in return. When no funds were allocated, the sympathetic bureaucrats could simply claim that the authority to provide the funds belonged to another bureaucracy and was outside their purview.

Whereas the sheer size of the central bureaucracy would seem to offer regional elites numerous opportunities to press their claims—surely one could find a personal or regional connection to a central bureaucrat—their widespread availability gave no clear advantage to any particular region (Gustafson 1981). Opportunities, however, differed according to the sector of the economy of a particular enterprise (Bahry 1987; Ross 1987). Certain industries, such as machine building, defense production, and other spheres of "national importance," were subordinated directly to the all-union government. Managers of these enterprises might sit on central ministerial committees, giving them occasions to lobby directly for their interests. Yet if enterprise managers in centralized sectors did not have committee appointments, they remained at the center's mercy since they lacked the protection of regional elites who might advance the interests of the enterprise. Regional leaders tended instead to act as intermediaries for locally subordinated enterprises since subnational elites shouldered more responsibility for them. Consequently, they had greater incentive to lobby the center for increased financial allocations to enterprises under regional control (Bahry 1987).

The industrial structure of a region—i.e., the distribution of enterprises in a region between union, republican, and local subordination—affected not only the lobbying relationships among elites, but the amount of local revenue available to a region. By the late 1970s, central elites were looking for incentives to increase enterprise production rates and profits and to decrease the amount of direct industrial and regional subsidies. In place of subsidies, the Soviet government began to develop revenue-sharing arrangements, whereby the controlling government body would receive a percentage of the enterprise's profit tax. State revenue was divided into regulated income—money that went directly into the state budget and could be allocated to regions through transfers or grants—and secured income—tax revenue, primarily from the profit tax, that was divided among levels of government or came from local revenue sources.[7] Thus, local governments would receive a percentage of the profit tax from locally subordinated enterprises whereas enterprises under the direct control of the central government paid the entirety of the tax to Moscow. With this arrangement, some regions gained an advantage in secured income according to the local economic structure rather than their political ties.

In 1974, for example, while Kuibyshev (Samara) oblast managed well with a 35.1 percent secured-income base in its budget compared to the average of 29.8 percent, a smaller oblast such as Bryansk had only 21.9 percent secured income. The discrepancies were even wider between the non-industrialized regions such as Murmansk (9.1 percent) and the cities with special status, Leningrad (53.8 percent) and Moscow (67.5 percent) (Ross 1987, 79). As a result, regional elites now sought to lobby for a broader tax base by subordinating more enterprises to subnational governments, rather than simply begging the central government for more direct transfers (Bahry 1987, 60).

If these methods of lobbying the central government failed, regional elites had one more source of bargaining power: information. Central elites depended on the information passed up to them on policy implementation including plan fulfillment, capital investment projects, and social welfare issues. Local leaders had incentives to conceal failures to fulfill plan targets, but they also sought to exaggerate their problems and the need for financial assistance. Despite attempts at oversight, central authorities did not have the resources to monitor every local investment project. Instead, they depended on the same bureaucrats who were in charge of implementing central policies to provide evaluative information as well. Local bureaucrats had numerous incentives to distort information, including opposition to policy change, poor wages, and staff shortages (Ross 1987, ch. 6). Although regional and local party elites also oversaw the implementation of central policies, they spent more time lobbying for increased investment than managing the projects already in place. In addition, their concern for local economic success motivated them to collude with other local bureaucrats to subvert national policy. With investment decisions and targets often decided by political elites who had little understanding of economic development and little knowledge of the policy's implementation, local leaders worked with economic managers to reformulate national policy to suit local needs (Smith 1980).

Informal control over information and implementation notwithstanding, regional leaders remained at the mercy of Moscow's agenda. As the economic crisis deepened in the 1980s, the center grew less able to fund new investment projects or complete older ones. Regional demands for funding did not abate in this environment of domestic fiscal austerity. In order to stave off potential insurrections from the periphery, central ministries often promised funding without actually allocating the money (Bahry 1987). The death of Leonid Brezhnev and the political turmoil brought on by the rapid succession of aged leaders briefly overshadowed the growing economic conflicts between Moscow and the republics. Yet they would soon reemerge with new vigor following the advent of perestroika and systemic renewal.

GORBACHEV'S REFORMS AND THE COLLAPSE OF THE SOVIET UNION

Mikhail Gorbachev once again brought the issue of decentralization into a reform agenda and offered new hope to regional elites to increase their control over local fiscal issues. During his short-lived tenure as General Secretary, the regions only saw the beginnings of these reforms, with any newly won authority overshadowed by the confusion and uncertainty caused by increasing conflict.

Gorbachev renewed Khrushchev's battle against the tight grip of the economic bureaucracy with similar goals but a different approach and magnitude to the reforms. Like Khrushchev, he aimed to break the power of the central ministries, which he saw as hostile to *perestroika*, and build the necessary political framework within the Party and the bureaucracy for his reforms (Hough 1997; Urban 1990). Gorbachev outlined his plans for decentralization in 1987 with the "Basic Provisions for the Radical Restructuring of Economic Management." This document, along with a decree on the rights of regional authority, sought to address the conflict between the sectoral and territorial bureaucratic structures by emphasizing the authority of the republics and decreasing the concentrated power of the individual ministries. Gorbachev eliminated many of the subdivisions in the ministerial bureaucracy and transferred control to the localities. Simultaneously, he sought to give more responsibility for policy implementation to the localities by concentrating the administration of enterprises serving local markets in local bodies, giving more coordination functions to territorial (republican) governments, and ensuring that funds for the social development of a region depended on its economic performance. In addition, he decentralized some fiscal authority by channeling more funds into local budgets through a union-republic tax-sharing arrangement with the profit tax[8] and increased autonomy for formulating local budgets (Schroeder 1991a, 210).

The increased economic authority and autonomy given to the republics combined with the growing nationalist movements to produce a dramatic effect as the political situation in the Soviet Union became more precarious. In 1988, the Baltic republics introduced their demands for economic sovereignty, including full control over property and resources on their territory and a separate currency. As a compromise, Moscow offered to transfer to republican control all economic enterprises other than those crucial to the Union government such as energy and defense industries. In addition, they agreed to raise tax-sharing rates, and increase expenditure responsibilities under self-financing (*samo-finansirovanie*) arrangements (Remington 1989). In 1990, in an effort to halt the complete disintegration of the country, Gorbachev put forth a draft of a new Union Treaty. In this document, the Soviet Union was renamed the "Union of

Sovereign Soviet Republics" and Article 1 stated that, "Membership of a republic to the union is voluntary" (Henderson 1991). The debate over Soviet federalism and the relationship between the Union republics and the center became the "most disruptive element to the economy" in the early 1990s (Hewett and Winston 1991, 332). Although 69 percent of all industrial production was still controlled by all-union ministries in 1989 (Schroeder 1991b), by the following year the republics, led by the Baltics and Russia, began exerting authority over the enterprises and resources on their territories. In the Russian republic, for example, the Supreme Soviet led by Boris Yeltsin proclaimed the republic's sovereignty—raising the ire of Mikhail Gorbachev and other central officials—and attempted to take over Gosbank as well as the ministries under joint union-republican control (Hewett and Winston 1991).

The dangerous combination of a rising "tide of nationalism,"[9] state collapse, and unclear property rights also arose within the RFSFR. Both Gorbachev and Yeltsin attempted to harness the nascent ethnic nationalist movements within Russia to consolidate political power. Yeltsin bid for the loyalty of Russia's autonomous republics, such as Tatarstan and Yakutia, by promising them control over resources and property in exchange for their declarations of allegiance to Russia over the Soviet Union (Filippov and Shvetsova 1999). As economic disintegration of the Union seemed imminent, republican parliaments and central banks sought the loyalty of large state enterprises, particularly within the military-industrial complex, by offering them generous credits and low interest rates (Lipton and Sachs 1992, 226–7). By 1991, many of the republics had halted payments into the federal budget, asserting the independence of their own budgets.

The dissolution of the Soviet Union later that year seemingly put an end to the crisis in the federal relationship. Yet in the Soviet system, bureaucratic and administrative hierarchies *within* the republics simply mirrored those between the Soviet center and the 15 republics. Russia, with its 89 regions and concentration of economic resources, inherited both the wealth and the problems of the Soviet system. The division of authority between the center and the regions over Russia's resources was hardly clearer than it had been during the final years of the Soviet Union. With the future of the Russian Federation still in doubt, the resolution of federal relations and, along with it, fiscal federalism, became a matter of survival. Swiftness of action and short-term crises were the primary focus. There was little time or political will to invent new solutions to or engage new actors in what appeared in many ways to be the same problems of uncertainty and resource asymmetries that plagued the old system. Soviet norms of center-periphery relations thus continued to function even after the edifice around them collapsed.

DEFINING FEDERAL RELATIONS IN THE FIRST
RUSSIAN REPUBLIC

Despite the rapid succession of transformational reforms—the end of communist party rule, the abrogation of a command economy—Russia's leaders quickly realized that it was easier to dismantle Soviet institutions than to build their replacements. When Boris Yeltsin assumed the leadership of the chaotic Russian Federation, he focused on short-term measures to prevent a total collapse of the economy. Yeltsin and his team made some crucial economic decisions at the outset regarding currency convertibility, price liberalization, and anti-inflationary measures, leaving more comprehensive structural reforms, especially in the fiscal sphere, for the future. In part, the center lacked the resources to engage in a complete overhaul of the economic system. Moreover, the country could tolerate only so much change without inciting political and social unrest. Just as Soviet attempts at reform under Khrushchev and Gorbachev had generated more confusion, Russia's reform plans also increased the level of chaos and uncertainty in the system. With the borders of the Russian Federation still somewhat in question and political or civil unrest very much a possibility, stability became a principle goal for Yeltsin and his administration. In the context of an often uneven and ad hoc reform process, Soviet bureaucratic norms of behavior continued to function, filling the gap between institutional breakdown and institutional creation (Easter 1996). These often took the form of informal mechanisms, such as clientelism, barter, and more nefarious types of behaviors.[10]

Local leaders sought to reinforce their spheres of control as the Soviet economic system collapsed around them. Gorbachev's moderate attempts at decentralization, and the subsequent jurisdictional confusion as the republics assumed administrative control over their territories, produced strong centrifugal tendencies. At the same time, the ethnic nationalist movements within Russia—Tatars, Bashkirs, Chechens, and Ingush, among others—that had been growing since Gorbachev initiated his policy of *glasnost'* underscored the potential for dissolution along the lines of the Soviet Union.[11] Ethnic leaders in Russia's republics could now demand increased autonomy not only on the basis of democratic federalism or economic necessity but on the grounds that they deserved some type of cultural, political, and therefore economic autonomy. In order to reassert central control over the federation, Yeltsin replaced the hierarchical party apparatus with a "presidential vertical" system of decision making by concentrating power within the executive branch (Shevtsova 1996, 36). The "presidential vertical" sought to revive a system in which subnational leaders remained accountable to the central government for their positions and the resources to govern their territories. Yeltsin also used more formal means to reintegrate the federation with the 1992 Federation Treaty. He strove simultaneously to extend the hierarchical structure of executive power to the rest of the federation while responding to regional demands by decentralizing some decision-making powers.

Like previous attempts at decentralization, however, the process gave regional leaders an appetite for more authority and power. The center, still struggling to maintain its control over the federation, had difficulties in establishing clear boundaries to the decentralization process—a problem never faced by Soviet leaders who preserved a tighter reign over reforms through Communist Party control. With the expectations of regional elites as to the intent of federal reform differing from those at the center, the Federation Treaty failed to fulfill its purpose as the foundation for cooperative relations between the federal and regional executive branches. Rather than institutionalizing a system of power sharing between center and periphery, the Treaty forged a stalemate among the players. It established a wide array of shared powers, such as the establishment of general principles of territorial division, organization of self-government, and taxation, without determining how these powers would be negotiated. Moreover, it did not create an implementation mechanism—perhaps relying on the Soviet system of informal norms of implementation—an omission that drew increasing criticism from the regions.

The Federation Treaty[12] modeled the federation's basic organization on the structure of the old Soviet Union so that Russia's ethnic republics received substantially more rights and authority than the other regions. It not only preserved the complexities of the Soviet system, with a combination of republics, oblasts, krais, federal cities, and autonomous areas, but it upheld republican sovereignty, which had arisen in Gorbachev's 1990 draft of the Union Treaty. Yet the term "sovereign republic" in the 1992 Treaty became even more contentious in post-Soviet Russia since it pertained to only 21 of Russia's 89 territories rather than all 15 union republics as part of the Soviet Union. The Federation Treaty accorded to Russia's republics control over all of the resources on their territories whereas it required the provinces to share this control with the central government. The bestowal of sovereignty without any clear demarcation of its limits was an issue ripe for conflict.[13] Some republics insisted that "sovereignty" meant that they could institute their own regulations, such as a single-channel tax system that allowed the republics to decide the percentage of revenue to be transferred to the center. Although the center disputed such economic rights, the republics had a strong foundation for their claims—a last-minute addendum to the Federation Treaty granted these privileges to the republic of Bashkortostan in exchange for its signature on the document (Sharlet 1994).

Although the Federation Treaty was intended as a short-term political solution to the federal crisis in lieu of a new constitution, the pact disintegrated almost immediately. With more than one hundred legislative laws needed to enact the Treaty (Sharlet 1993), the central government had little incentive and few resources to fully implement the terms of the document, particularly since both Tatarstan and Chechnya had refused to sign despite continual pressure and the promise of economic concessions. In the months before the signing the Treaty, Tatarstan withheld all taxes from the center and declared its full sovereignty, even as its president, Mintimir Shaimiyev, carefully explained that the republic was not seeking to secede. Tatarstan's official position was that it would not sign without a prior agreement between the Tatarstan and Russian governments. In essence, Shaimiyev saw the Russian Federation as a set of pacts between separate states rather than a set of multiple governmental ties within a cohesive whole, or a confederation rather than a federation (*Rossiiskaya gazeta*, 15 February 1993). Chechnya's position was less equivocal, particularly following the vote for full independence by the republic's parliament in November 1991.

The issues of federal relations left unresolved by the Federation Treaty highlighted the pressing need for a new constitution. As the constitutional conference approached in the summer of 1993, the provinces presented their own agenda, demanding fiscal and economic equality for all regions, with the center. A parade of provinces, including Vologda, Irkutsk, Chita, Sverdlovsk, Chelyabinsk, and six other provinces in the Volga region, declared their intentions to acquire the status of republics. Whereas Vologda administered a referendum on the question in April, most of the provinces used the constitutional conference as the forum to announce their plans. The declarations and referenda emphasized the desire for economic equality in relations with the center and uniform decentralization of control over local resources. In Sverdlovsk's proclamation as the new Urals Republic governor, Eduard Rossel', asserted that the province was not aiming to separate from the Russian Federation or to give "ultimatums like the republics have done," but only trying to respond to those republics that "suck out" from the Federation budget more than they need (*Rossiiskaya gazeta*, 3 July 1993).

At the constitutional conference in July, forty provincial representatives presented a joint statement detailing their conditions for signing the draft constitution based on the demand that the constitution must affirm the basic equality of all members of the Federation, particularly in the demarcation of budgetary and fiscal rights. In addition, the provinces took advantage of the republics' position on maintaining their status vis-à-vis the center so as to seek more radical decentralization. Although their statement eliminated the right to secede from the Russian Federation, the forty provinces demanded to equalize the legal and economic standing of the subjects of the federation by using the current status of the republics as the baseline for delimiting power between the center and periphery, thereby achieving two goals simultaneously (*Rossiiskaya gazeta*, 7 July

1993). Meanwhile, the Council of the Heads of Republics, a body established by the Federation Treaty and comprised of each republic's president, continued its demands for full implementation of the Federation
Treaty independent of any future constitution. In trying to balance republican and provincial interests, Yeltsin offered the preservation of "special
republic status" to the Council in exchange for equality in financial and
tax policies across the Federation. As the conflict grew, both between the
center and periphery and within the center,[14] the republics offered to mediate in exchange for a constitutional provision stipulating that the republics would retain full power over their territories with the exception
of those powers voluntarily given to the center (*Segodnya*, 11 June 1993).
In essence, they sought to redefine the Russian federation as a bifurcated
system in which the republics would maintain a confederal relationship
with the center and the other regions would retain a more centralized
federal relationship. Given the level of discord within the country, such a
system or even a confederation with all 89 regions did not seem outside
the realm of possibility.

In the Fall of 1993, while the war of words intensified and Yeltsin became increasingly preoccupied with fending off a hostile legislature, many
regions unilaterally appropriated decision-making power. In August and
September, a number of provinces and republics (many of which had
adopted this strategy much earlier) began withholding part or all of their
contributions to the federal budget. In addition, many regions declared
the establishment of single-channel tax systems, a strategy employed by
Russia toward the Soviet government in 1991 (Filippov and Shvetsova
1999). These actions met with little response from the Ministry of Finance
or elsewhere in the embattled central government.

The situation changed drastically after Yeltsin disbanded the parliament
in October. During the crisis, fewer than half of the provinces supported
the President. Most of the republics chose not to get involved, an outcome
that did not meet Yeltsin's expectations of loyalty in exchange for his
promises to implement the Federation Treaty. In the Republic of Bashkortostan, leaders continued to work on a new constitution that declared
Bashkortostan a sovereign state with the right to secede from the Federation (*RFE/RL News Briefs*, 8–12 November 1993). Facing a combination of
lukewarm support and outright defiance that threatened to break apart
the Russian Federation, Yeltsin initiated a series of decrees aimed at crush-
ing the power of regional leaders. He decreed that representatives to the
new Federation Council would be popularly elected rather than appointed as the regional representatives had wanted. Next, Yeltsin took aim
at the regional legislative branches, calling for the "voluntary" dissolution
of the soviets, but dissolving the Sverdlovsk soviet by decree as a warning
to those who failed to take the recommended action. As a bulwark against
future consolidation of power within the pro-communist regional legis-

latures, Yeltsin reproduced his actions at the center by transferring some decision-making powers, particularly in the budgetary sphere, to the executive branch of the regional governments. He revoked the power of the soviets to pass a budget without executive approval and gave the local head of administration the power to disband the local legislature if it could not produce a quorum (Teague 1993, 10–11). While enhancing the authority of regional executives, Yeltsin's show of power demonstrated that the political hierarchy remained in place. His use of decrees to construct the "presidential vertical" implied that any new authority granted to regional administrations could just as easily be revoked. Focusing on the republics, he decreed new sanctions against the nonpayment of taxes to the center and announced that the concept of republican sovereignty would not be included in the new constitution. Finally, Yeltsin cleverly eluded any further shows of disloyalty from legislative or regional elites by appealing to "the people" to pass his version of the constitution, a strategy that served him well throughout his presidency.

The 1993 Constitution of the Russian Federation,[15] approved by popular referendum in December, responded to the threat of disintegration by affirming the power of the central government. It eliminated the idea of a confederal system or even a weakly federal one. Rather than underscoring Russia's diversity and, by implication, the need for some measure of regional autonomy, the constitution emphasizes the identity of Russia as a single entity. Article 5.3 emphasizes "the unity of the system of state power," replacing the endorsement of "decentralization of government" in earlier drafts of the document (Sharlet 1994, 123). The federal government retains the sole power to change the organization and borders of the Russian Federation (Art. 71.b). It also addresses the unilateral actions of the provinces by expressly stating that changes in status must be approved by the Russian Federation (Art. 66.5). Although the constitution incorporates the Federation Treaty as one of the treaties governing the division of state authority, the constitution prevails over any other regional or federal document. Consequently, the contradictions between the terms of the Federation Treaty, including the economic privileges accorded to the republics, and the constitution's affirmation of equality of all subjects of the federation render the earlier document meaningless.

While reasserting the authority of the central government, the constitution holds the potential for future decentralization, as well as for continued conflicts between center and periphery. Article 71 establishes the areas of sole competency of the federal government. In addition to symbolic and territorial rights as well as the protection of individual rights, the document accords the federal government a number of important economic rights. The federal government is solely responsible for the federal budget, federal taxes, and funds for regional development (Art. 71.h), the management of federal state property (71.d), and external economic relations of the Russian Federation (71.l). Article 72 establishes the areas of joint authority between federal government and the regions. The federal government retains authority over the disposal of many resources according to Article 71, whereas the subjects share in the establishment of "general principles" to govern many of these resources. These include the demarcation of state property (72.g), general principles of taxation and levies (72.i), general principles for the organization of state authority (72.n), and legislation on administration, labor, family, housing, land, water, and forestry (72.k). Authority over external economic relations is accorded to the central government, but coordination functions for the external economic relations of the federation subjects are shared (72.o). In addition, questions relating to the use and disposal of natural resources fall under joint competency. The constitution does not accord specific competencies to the regional governments, leaving all residual powers not covered by Articles 71 and 72 to the member states.

Like the Federation Treaty, the constitution does not establish a clear procedure to determine the exact jurisdictional boundaries in these areas of joint competency. Article 11.3 contains the clearest language describing the formal documents that will govern the center-periphery relationship. It states that "the demarcation of spheres of power and authority between organs of state power of the Russian Federation and the organs of state power of the subjects of the Russian Federation are realized in the current constitution, federative and other treaties on the demarcation of spheres of power and authority." Article 78, which calls for the organization of executive bodies to implement federal laws in the territories, also permits the federal or regional executive authorities to "transfer a portion of their authority" through bilateral or multilateral treaties and agreements. Within this institutional context, there is no clear hierarchy among multilateral agreements, legislation, bilateral treaties, and inter-regional agreements; only the constitution clearly stands above them.

With hundreds of laws necessary to implement and clarify its statutes, the 1993 Constitution provides only the broad outlines of federal relations. Although this is not unusual for a federal constitution—the U.S. Constitution is one of the briefest documents of its kind—it is more problematic in a federation with far-reaching areas of joint jurisdiction. The German Basic Law, the Swiss Constitution, and the Belgian Constitution, for example, establish numerous institutional arrangements to manage shared competencies and mediate conflicting territorial interests. Whereas in the United States, the relatively larger number of exclusive competencies centers negotiations over resources and allocation at the state *or* federal level, in Russia the negotiations are located *between* the federal and regional governments. This necessitates the creation of institutions to mediate these interests, whether it be political parties, multilateral councils, or other intergovernmental arrangements. With the collapse of the Communist Party in Russia as the principal means of organizing and mediating interests, there was little to take its place. In such a weakly institutionalized environment, preexisting networks and patterns can fill the void, giving some assurance that the state will continue to function. Soviet norms of center-periphery interaction, including informal negotiations and executive decree, continued to dominate federal relations, as regions sought to establish their positions within the federation and President Yeltsin endeavored to maintain his authority. Like orders from the Soviet Politburo, presidential decrees served as the primary tool of convenience for Yeltsin's administration to override preexisting laws and create new federal policy.[16] Nevertheless, regional elites were anxious to find other means of resolving ambiguities and conflicts that limited the scope of presidential power and compelled the center to decentralize decision-making powers—an issue that would focus principally on the economic and fiscal spheres.

FISCAL REFORM IN THE FIRST REPUBLIC

As the federal and regional governments delimited authority through the constitution and other treaties, the federal government struggled to redefine the fiscal system. Public finance touched upon every aspect of the transition to capitalism. The need for tax revenue to fund the state's operations and reforms demanded a completely new relationship among the state, individuals, and enterprises. Expenditure decisions related directly to the question of how and to what extent to dismantle the Soviet system of universal and substantially subsidized healthcare, education, housing, employment, and other features of the welfare state. At the heart of public finance lay the division of authority and responsibility among levels of government. Both regional and national elites had incentives to implement comprehensive fiscal reform to enable their governments to carry out their assigned legislative and executive duties and to provide the economic foundation for federalism. But in the context of constitutionally established joint jurisdictions over many tax and budgetary matters, a new fiscal system entailed intense negotiations between federal and regional leaders. As in other arenas, the center needed to divide its resources between attempting to enact major reform packages, so as to move swiftly from the Soviet system to market capitalism, and ensuring the continued day-to-day functioning of the system. Consequently, central elites relied on informal norms of negotiation and decision making, including informal arrangements with individual regions, while they sought to replace these norms with more transparent authority relations and a functioning legal system. Soon after the formal dissolution of the Soviet Union, the government moved to federalize the tax and budgetary systems with the "Basic Principles of Taxation" and a law on the fundamentals of the budgetary process. The tax legislation attempted to drastically overhaul the centralized system by shifting from revenue-sharing to tax assignment. Revenues from corporate profit and individual income taxes were assigned to regional governments while the VAT, export, and excise taxes became the primary sources of federal revenue (Treisman 1996; Berkenes 1996). The new system was never implemented due to its complexity and the lack of resources, and subsequent legislation reasserted the practice of revenue sharing. In the following year, the revenue-sharing norms depended on even more intergovernmental negotiations than they had under the Soviet regime. Regions arranged to transfer anywhere from zero to sixty percent of the VAT with taxes on corporate profits and excise taxes divided more evenly between the center and the federation subjects (Le Houerou 1996, 17). As a result, regions remitted anywhere from 80 percent to less than one percent of total collected tax revenue on their territories in 1992, creating a wide disparity in revenue sharing across the federation (Treisman 1999, 21).

The growing political chaos leading up to the 1993 "parliamentary coup" and constitutional battles rendered any fixed system of tax collection and revenue transfers futile. The central government had neither the political will nor the resources to implement a new fiscal system. With the republics balking at transferring any revenue and many provinces trying to institute single-channel tax systems,[17] the central government was thankful to receive any revenue from the regions. The problems did not rest only with the regional governments' reluctance to turn over revenue to the federal government. The State Tax Service (STS) became an autonomous agency only in November 1991; until this time, the STS reported to the Ministry of Finance as well as to regional finance departments (Bahl and Wallich 1996, 344–5). As they had under the Soviet government, STS employees received office space, equipment, and other benefits from the local governments, often dividing their loyalties between federal and local officials (McClure 1995). In addition, the STS employees received little training and had few incentives to increase federal tax collection rates, focusing instead on serving regional elites by collecting property taxes and other fees that accrued directly to the regions (Le Houerou 1996, 18; Birkenes 1996).

The emphasis on negotiated revenue-sharing arrangements was only one aspect of the fiscal regime that survived the Soviet collapse. The tax system continued to rely on indirect taxes and the heavy taxation of corporate profits. The ability of the "shadow economy" to escape taxation and government monitoring under Brezhnev and Gorbachev continued in post-Soviet Russia, as the government targeted state enterprises while small private businesses operated outside the official economic system. Despite the initial attempts at decentralization, official state controls over tax rates and local revenue sources continued;[18] as of 1994, only one major tax, the corporate profit tax, included a regional component between zero and 25 percent. Although 1993 legislation authorized four taxes whose rates may be set (with some limitations) by regional governments and another 23 to be set at the local or regional level, these sources—including property taxes and parking fines—provided minimal revenue to provincial and local governments (Hanson 1996, 195; Freinkman and Titov 1994).

Even as subnational governments withheld revenue from the center, they increased their dependence on federal transfers and subsidies. Intergovernmental budgetary transfers increased from 6.7 percent of total federal expenditures in 1992 to 14.8 percent in 1994 (Lavrov 1995). The federal budget allocated transfers to the regions in a number of different forms. The government still granted significant subsidies to specific industries or areas (such as the Far North), with 68 regions receiving subsidies in 1992 (Birkenes 1996, 96). The annual budget also allocated funds for specific (*tselevoe*) mandates, such as environmental or investment projects. In 1994, in an attempt to formalize transfers to the regions and replace some of the sectoral subsidies, the government set up the Fund for Regional Support, which would use a formula to determine the amount of transfers to "needy" and "very needy" regions. The regional fund distributed a percentage of the VAT receipts,[19] and later a percentage of total federal revenue, to financially strapped regions, based on a formula using 1993 as a base year for comparison.[20] Regions needed to apply to the Ministry of Finance to be considered either a "needy" or "very needy" region, continuing the Soviet structure of centralized fiscal decision making and central transfers to compensate for the lack of local revenue sources. The formula-based fund suggests a move away from Soviet-style ad hoc decision making, but the importance of the fund should not be overestimated; according to the World Bank, in 1996 the fund accounted for only 22 percent of budgetary transfers to the regions (Le Houerou 1996).

A significant portion of transfers to the regions, like much of Russia's financial flows, transpired outside of the federal budget and beyond the oversight of legislators. According to one estimate, 63 percent of all federal revenue went into extra-budgetary funds (Kirkow 1996). Some of these funds made their way to the regions through federal mandates, such as the road fund, the employment fund, or nearly thirty other sectoral funds (Kirkow 1996). According to official data from the State Committee for Statistics and the Ministry of Finance, revenues accruing to these funds— enterprises paid into a variety of these funds—exceeded payments out of them, but information on how these funds were distributed is not available (Le Houerou 1996, Table A.4). In addition to the extra-budgetary funds, regions received specific tax credits and loans that made up a significant, but nontransparent, portion of the financial flows from the center to the regions and were subject to the discretion of government and Finance Ministry officials.

The budgetary system of the first Russian Republic mirrored the centralization of the tax system. Although the 1991 "Law on the Foundations of Budgetary Structure and Process in the RSFSR" legalized the independence of federal, regional, and local budgets, it also asserted the unity of the budgetary system, creating a curious contradiction (Birkenes 1996, 100). In practice, subnational governments did not achieve the independence they were promised in the spirit of democratic federalism. By 1991, the Russian government began decentralizing expenditure responsibilities. In the 1980s, subnational governments already held significant authority over social welfare spending, but by the next decade they became responsible for education, housing, transportation, and many other areas. By 1992, regional spending was 40 percent of total budgetary expenditures and increased to almost 50 percent in 1994 (Le Houerou 1996, 22). Despite the financial burden on them, regional governments were initially eager to take on the new responsibilities as it gave them more bargaining power to increase their tax-revenue shares and federal transfers (Martinez-Vasquez 1994). Moreover, greater responsibilities meant more control over how the money would be spent in the region.

Nevertheless, the center was reluctant to decentralize fiscal authority, despite its need for greater subnational accountability for social spending. Even in the absence of federal financial compensation, the central government mandated minimal levels of social welfare spending by subnational governments, thus continuing the Soviet process of expenditure assignment and central oversight (Martinez-Vazquez 1994; Le Houerou 1996, 23). In the 1993 "Law on the Foundations of Budgetary Rights," the federal government went even further in preserving discretion over local budgets by declaring that subnational governments must cover at least 70 percent of regional expenditures with their own-source revenues (Birkenes 1996, 101–2). Whereas the central government saw this as a means to increase tax collection and to control regional spending and rising deficits, subnational leaders viewed it as an infringement on the independence of their budgets and an unrealistic demand in the face of their rapidly increasing responsibility for social spending.

The center's minimal spending mandates and demands for more balanced and self-sufficient regional budgets seemed particularly rigid considering the federal government's own budgetary crises. Whereas subnational budgetary deficits began appearing primarily after 1994, the federal budget was in deficit immediately following Russian independence (OECD 1995). With falling revenues[21] and an enormous social safety net to maintain, rising debt was inevitable. In addition, political pressures, macroeconomic uncertainty, and unrealistic expectations for economic and revenue growth resulted in annual budgets that were impossible to implement. The problems with the federal budgets, compounded by the institutionalized norms of negotiated financial allocations produced "a lack of fiscal discipline in the government decision-making process" (Le Houerou 1996, 70). With the Central Bank balking at emitting more cash, the Ministry of Finance resorted to a process of sequestration, whereby it could withhold authorized payments in the face of budgetary gaps (OECD 1995). The law on sequestration stipulates that midyear spending cuts should focus on capital spending, but the Ministry of Finance was soon forced to withhold or delay payments in more visible areas. Delaying funding—from subsidies to intergovernmental transfers to wage pay-ments and other social spending—became the primary means for the Min-istry of Finance to deal with budgetary shortfalls.[22]

The malleability of the annual budgetary law reinforced the process of ad hoc negotiations for funding allocations and expenditure changes and concealed monetary flows in the economy. With growing debt between the state and Russian businesses and among enterprises, the Russian mar-ket has struggled unsuccessfully to create a cash-based system of financial transactions, exacerbating the informational vacuum.[23] Under Soviet rule, *Gosbank* supervised inter-enterprise accounting, leaving enterprise man-agers with little knowledge of or control over the transactions. In post-Soviet Russia, business owners and managers had more influence over their corporate financial affairs, but transactions still depended on a sys-tem of barter rather than on cash accounts. Many enterprises, especially those still state-owned, did not have enough cash to pay their workers, let alone to pay taxes or for capital goods. As a result, enterprises bartered for necessary goods and worked out deals with the state to survive. For example, a gas company behind in its federal tax payments could agree to provide gas heat "free of charge" to government office buildings. The same gas company might also agree to provide heat without payment to a state-owned factory where the management is behind in its wage and social security payments. The "free" energy would then theoretically free up the necessary cash to cover overdue payments to the workers.[24]

Whereas these arrangements allowed the economy to function in the short-term, particularly as it slowly adjusted to marketization and recov-ered from rampant inflation, the long-term effects were more detrimental. Ad hoc negotiations, a barter economy, and soft constraints on budgetary appropriations created a fiscal system in which monetary flows were difficult to trace or measure. Consequently, central leaders lacked the in-formation to make investment and development decisions and tax au-thorities could not easily sanction lawbreakers. In essence, a "virtual economy" emerged that simply shuffled resources without producing real growth and permitted corruption and extra-legal activities to fill the insti-tutional void (Gaddy and Ickes 1997). Within this context, leaders could not adequately demarcate responsibilities among levels of government nor evaluate the efficacy of the fiscal federal system—the economic foun-dations of a durable federation. Informal negotiations and contracting institutionalized a system of parallel financial structures that weakened federal laws on budgetary mechanisms (Lysenko 1995, 87). This was particularly problematic in a federal system that guaranteed the economic equality of all member states and that was striving toward some measure of redistribution among its unevenly-developed regions. According to Aleksei Lavrov of the President's Analytic Center, "Almost three-fourths of the resources received by the regions from the federal budget came through unofficial and weakly regulated channels, mainly via joint accounts between the different budgetary levels." (Lavrov 1995). Regions received payments and other resources, such as shares of state-owned enterprises, in secret agreements between the executive branches of the regional and federal governments, particularly during election campaigns. The Ministry of Finance then cannot compile accurate statistics on these transactions and the overall balance of payments within the federation (*Segodnya*, 10 November 1996). Without clear information on the total amount of money and credits handed out to the regions, the federal government could not aspire to achieve any redistributional goals, let alone stabilize the expenditure mechanisms of the federal budget. Moreover, in a culture of "backroom deals," numerous channels to negotiate funding, and without transparent financial information, regional leaders had few incentives to rely on formalized mechanisms, such as the Fund for Regional Support, to fulfill their budgetary needs.

Hampered by hazy information, informal bargaining, and fiscal weakness, regional leaders still needed to navigate the complexities of a centralized fiscal bureaucracy. Despite the benefits of post-Soviet decentralizing reforms, principal control over taxation and budgets remained with the federal government. The constitution places considerable authority for fiscal issues under joint jurisdiction, yet regions still had to negotiate with the center to formally delineate fiscal power. In this sense, little had changed since the Soviet collapse; formal documents created the boundaries for change, but the rules for negotiating the specifics of reform were unwritten. As a result, subnational leaders sought to establish their fiscal authority and improve their financial situation using whatever means available. Despite their different approaches and opportunities, Russia's regions, like the Soviet republics, still relied on the central government to allocate funds or transfer fiscal authority, thus placing the intergovernmental relationship at the center of a region's economic development strategy.

Yet the bargaining arena and regional expectations did change under the post-Soviet system. The rhetoric of democratic federalism and the promises of the Federation Treaty and 1993 Russian Constitution created new expectations for decentralization in the fiscal sphere as elsewhere. Whereas Soviet reforms, such as Khrushchev's *sovnarkhozy*, might have given subnational leaders hope for more local control, there was never a sense that they could control local fiscal decision making within the command economy. Instead, local leaders hoped to gain some authority over the implementation of central policies and financial allocations. With Soviet disintegration, Boris Yeltsin's exhortation to the republics to "grab as much sovereignty as you can swallow" became the manifesto of Russia's "First Republic." Yeltsin's political victory and the constitutional referendum in 1993 managed to constrain the impulses toward independence in the initial post-Soviet years, but they did little to formalize the mechanisms of intergovernmental negotiation. Fiscal and budgetary decision making relied on a combination of Soviet norms of negotiated settlements, new and rapidly changing Russian laws, and open conflict between levels of government.

This process continued into the "Second Republic" (1994–1999). Yet the growing fiscal crisis and increasing demands for economic improvement changed the nature of center-periphery relations. The conflict between the center and periphery now centered less on federal principles than it had during the constitutional debates, and began focusing on the substance of federalism—the details of demarcating authority and fiscal resources. For some regions, the potential gains from economic control over their territory raised the stakes for a definitive division of power with the center. For other regions, economic crisis increased their demands for the center to fulfill its fiscal functions. In both cases, regional leaders now had to seek accommodation with the center, whether using long-established norms of negotiation or new, creative approaches, to solve the growing economic problems at home. Central elites realized, too, that Russia's fiscal crisis could not be solved purely by decree or federal law but required new mechanisms of reconciliation and interdependence with the subnational governments.

NOTES

1. Woodruff (1999) argues convincingly that patterns of barter and clientelism among regional and central elites that the Russian government failed to break prevented the successful consolidation of the monetary system under Yeltsin. In a similar vein, Shleifer and Treisman (2000) compare a number of key economic reforms under Yeltsin and assert that the Russian government was least successful in reforming the tax and budgetary systems, in particular due to the intransigence of regional elites.

2. Even with protracted violence and a revolutionary party, much of the previous system may remain, particularly in a country as vast as Russia. Numerous accounts of the Soviet takeover in 1917 and the civil war have shown the persistence of pre-Soviet institutions and elites despite the Bolsheviks' desire to eliminate their dependence on "bourgeois specialists." See, among others, Rigby (1990), Rowney (1989), Jowitt (1992), and many of the chapters in Pinter and Rowney (1980).

3. This was particularly true in 1991. Yeltsin's decree to disband the Soviets

following the showdown between Yeltsin and the legislature in 1993 resulted in more rapid turnover of local personnel. Nevertheless, the local legislative branches saw the most pronounced turnover; heads of administration, other than those forcibly removed by Yeltsin, remained in office. The most gradual turnover occurred in the less-political staff positions (formerly the apparat), where finding trained replacements presented significant difficulties in the provinces (Hahn 1993; Hughes 1997; Matsuzato 1997).

4. Gerald Easter (1996) presents an interesting comparison of state-building in the early Bolshevik period and the post-Soviet transition, arguing that informal personal networks often substitute for fractured political institutions.

5. Throughout this work, I use the term "local" to refer to the oblast level of governance, although occasionally, as here, I use the term to incorporate both the oblast level and the city and village units that comprise it. During the Soviet period, I differentiate between the republic-level and the local (oblast) level.

6. Many scholars have described the ability of local managers to distort information and production data to their benefit. See, for example, Winiecki (1991). Solnick (1998a) explores the principal-agent problem extensively to explain the extensive "bank run" on institutional assets following Gorbachev's reforms.

7. The 1977 Soviet Constitution gave local soviets the right to their own sources of income, so long as the arrangements were ratified by the Ministry of Finance. However, the few local revenue sources, such as small fines, which the Ministry agreed to authorize, contributed little revenue to local budgets (Hutchings 1983).

8. Republics were granted the right in 1990 to add a maximum 23 percent republic-level profit tax on to the federal profit tax of 22 percent (Hanson 1991, 428).

9. Mark Beissinger (2002) uses this phrase to describe the snowballing effect of nationalist movements leading up to the Soviet collapse. He suggests that the success of the initial movements in the Baltics made ethnic groups more likely to organize elsewhere and to press broader demands.

10. Both Woodruff (1999) and Desai and Idson (2002) document the widespread use of barter, to some extent as a "coping mechanism," to deal with the difficult economic environment of the 1990s.

11. Kahn (2002), Beissinger (2002), Brudny (1998), along with many others, detail the dynamics of nationalism within the republics.

12. The treaty is actually a set of three agreements between 1) the center and the krais, oblasts, and administrative cities of Moscow and St. Petersburg; 2) the center and autonomous areas; and 3) the center and the "sovereign republics."

13. Hough quotes the description by a Soviet scholar of the disputed nature of sovereignty even before the collapse of the Soviet Union. According to A. A. Golovko (1991), "...They speak about the sovereignty of individual territories, of individual local soviets, and even of deputies. They speak about the unity of sovereignties of the USSR and the Union republics, about the full state sovereignty of the republics, about the sovereignty of the USSR as a sum of the sovereignties of the republics, about the limited sovereignty of republics, about limitations of the sovereign rights of the republics, and so forth" (Hough 1997, 386). See also Tarr (1999) for a brief discussion of the confusing nature of the term sovereignty in Russian debates.

14. A series of articles in *RFE/RL Research Report* (1993) details the October 1993

events. See, for example, Wendy Slater and Vera Tolz, "Yeltsin Wins in Moscow But May Lose to the Regions;" Elizabeth Teague, "Yeltsin's Difficult Road Toward Elections;" and Vera Tolz, "The Moscow Crisis and the Future of Democracy in Russia."

15. *Konstitutsia Rossisskoi Federatsii* 1993. All English-language quotations from the constitution are this author's translation.

16. Part Two of the constitution, "Concluding and transitional provisions," states that laws and other acts operating on the territory of the Russian Federation before the enactment of the constitution—implicitly including Soviet laws—will remain in force, as long as they do not contradict the constitution.

17. One World Bank observer estimates that thirty oblasts unilaterally instituted such systems in 1993 (Litvack 1994).

18. Centralization should not necessarily be viewed negatively, at least in economic terms. A World Bank survey asserts that the 1991 "Basic Principles on Taxation" tried to decentralize too fast and compromised the power of the central government to collect enough revenue to manage the economy. The authors recommend to continue fiscal recentralization until more stability is achieved and to "help increase the pressure on subnational governments to develop cost recovery" (World Bank 1996, 34).

19. In 1994, 25 percent of VAT revenues was used for the Fund for Regional Support, which was raised to 27 percent the following year. In the 1996 federal budget, the regional fund used a percentage of total revenue.

20. Aleksei Novikov, formerly of the President's Analytic Center, argues that the use of 1993 as a base year favors those regions that still maintained price supports and significant subsidies in 1993, since they had higher expenditure levels (Interview, 30 October 1996). A World Bank survey (1996) concurs, adding that the formula also encourages regional budgets to continue running deficits rather than to cut expenditures.

21. In 1992, total revenues were 16.4 percent of GDP and 11.9 percent in 1994 (Kirkow 1996).

22. Former Finance Minister Vladimir Panskov strongly criticized the reliance on sequestration, calling it "dangerous for the executive branch" and an "abrogation of the functions empowered to the government" (*Rossiiskaya gazeta*, 25 October 1996). See chapter 3 for more details.

23. David Woodruff (1999) provides an excellent analysis of Russia's developing monetary system, including the pervasiveness of barter and the role of subnational elites in sustaining this system.

24. The example is my own, but comes from discussions with Vyacheslav Aronin, the head of the Finance Department of the Samara oblast administration.

CHAPTER 3

The Russian Center and the Road to Bilateralism

With the 1993 Constitution passed by popular referendum and the specter of economic collapse waning, the center now faced the challenge of creating a "politics as usual." President Yeltsin proclaimed the birth of a genuine federation in Russia, yet federalism necessitated the reform and institutionalization of a broad range of political processes and economic relations. As in other transition countries, public finance was tied to every key goal of market reform as well as the process of nation building (Wallich 1996). The Yeltsin government saw no clear path to reforming the fiscal system, with questions of economic redistribution intertwined with more fundamental issues of intergovernmental power sharing. Although leaders at all levels of government agreed that the country needed a more transparent and rule-based system of intergovernmental fiscal relations, their ideas about its organization diverged. The subnational governments focused on issues of decentralization, transparency, and implementation of the budget, whereas the center emphasized central control over the fiscal system with closer monitoring of economic laws, resource use, and revenue collection in the periphery.

Despite the potential conflicts, the center had strong incentives to focus on multilateral solutions to its fiscal problems. National and regional elites, as well as representatives of international monetary agencies, agreed that the tax code and the budgetary mechanisms urgently needed reform. Multilateral legislation could simultaneously address fiscal problems at the national level while tackling the resource and jurisdictional questions between the central and subnational governments. Yet, as reform measures languished in committees, the center pursued negotiations

with individual regions and signed a series of bilateral treaties and agreements with the subnational governments, beginning with the Republic of
Tatarstan in 1994. The bilateral treaties decentralized control over fiscal
resources, potentially threatening the centralization of the revenue system—a basic component of the government's economic program. Not
only did bilateral treaties institutionalize asymmetrical decentralization,
but the system of federation building through "bilateral contracting" was
then institutionalized in federal law. The central government seemingly
chose a strategy that ran contrary to its own interests of revenue maxi-
mization and created the potential for future conflicts between regions.

This chapter seeks to explain this puzzle by examining the center's difficulties in implementing the current intergovernmental fiscal system and
the costs of negotiating multilateral reforms. Following the passage of the
1993 Constitution, the central government put aside larger questions of
reform to the political and economic structure of the federation and addressed the problems of fiscal federalism within the context of multilateral
tax and budgetary reform. Despite the pressures to negotiate comprehensive tax and budgetary legislation, the center could not achieve the collective action necessary to produce multilateral fiscal reform. At the same
time, impending presidential and subnational elections, the center's de-
teriorating fiscal health, and rising subnational demands focused the center's attention on federal instability and its immediate resolution. Given
the institutional context—the informal norms of negotiation carried over
from the Soviet period and the formal rules of the intergovernmental relationship set out in the constitution—bilateral bargaining seemingly offered the most short-term economic and political benefits for the center.
As the final section of the chapter illustrates, however, bilateralism solved
some of the center's problems while creating new ones. The institutionalization of a federal system based upon bilateral ties preserved an asymmetrical system of intergovernmental relations, in which the bargaining
resources of each region shaped its long-term fiscal relationship with the
center.

THE PATH TO REFORM IN RUSSIA'S FISCAL SYSTEM

Following independence, the Russian government confronted three basic choices in managing intergovernmental fiscal relations. It could do
nothing and continue to operate in the current environment; it could attempt to reform the system of fiscal federalism in the context of comprehensive fiscal reform; or it could focus more specifically on reforming and
improving fiscal relations with individual regions. As I will explain, each
of these choices presented different transaction costs to the federal government.[1] In the existing fiscal system, the center could not monitor ade-

quately the complex web of central ministries, subnational agents, and private banks. At the same time, the system performed poorly, failing to generate enough revenue for either the center or the regions to cover their expenditures. The center then had a strong incentive to seek some type of reform. As Eggertsson states, "Given their constraints, actors have an incentive to find ways to lower the cost of establishing and partitioning control because they stand to gain from both lower transaction costs and from an opportunity to put their resources to more valuable uses" (Eggertsson 1995, 49). Nevertheless, reforming the fiscal system demanded that the government consolidate and coordinate its resources to develop an agenda and negotiate it with other central and subnational actors. Even more circumscribed reform, focusing only on intergovernmental fiscal relations, presented greater challenges than simply reducing the uncertainty and complexity of existing relationships. With the weight of seventy years of Soviet economic history and the shifting balance of power between center and periphery, the Russian government could not freely design new rules of fiscal federalism but instead functioned under the constraints of surviving Soviet rules and norms of negotiation and regional demands for change. The center's choices, and the institutions that emerged from the bargaining process, produced a much different picture of intergovernmental relations than any of its participants envisioned.

As chapter 2 describes, the Russian system of fiscal federalism drastically needed reform by 1995. Neither the constitution nor federal legislation had produced the necessary and anticipated separation of powers between levels of government. The emphasis in the 1993 Constitution on shared spheres of jurisdiction—including general principles of taxation, control over land and natural resources, and coordinating external economic relations—put the burden on the federal government to hammer out the substance of Article 72 through legislation. Yet this required the Yeltsin administration to work effectively with a communist-dominated legislature following the December 1993 elections and still accomplish other controversial and urgent reforms such as privatization—a possibly insurmountable task. Meanwhile, ad hoc negotiations for central funds dominated intergovernmental fiscal relations, much as they had during the Soviet period. Regional elites expected to see a dramatic and lasting decentralization of resources and fiscal control in keeping with Russia's new rhetoric of democratic federalism. At the same time, the center sought to stabilize the economy and its hold on power by maintaining the centralization of revenues—a strategy that regional elites strongly criticized.

The need for intergovernmental fiscal reform emerged within the context of a broader crisis in Russia's fiscal system. Although Russia had survived the initial transition period of high inflation, the rising federal debt and budget deficits threatened to bring renewed monetary instability. Other than incurring more costly loans, the government had two principal methods of preventing a crisis: increase the rate of revenue collection and decrease the expenditure burden on the federal government. The budgetary figures for 1995–1997 (see Table 3.1) depict the center's decreasing ability to collect revenues and its inability to implement budgetary expenditures as allocated in the annual federal budget. Tax revenues as a percentage of GDP fell from 29.8 percent in 1992, to 26.4 percent in 1994, to a low of 20.7 percent in 1998 (Treisman 2000). In the face of increasing pressure from international loan agencies, fiscal reform became a primary concern for the federal government.

Whereas the problem of annual shortfalls in revenue collection might have been more acute than expenditure issues in the eyes of many government officials, the federal government had been more successful in institutionalizing the federal tax system than other fiscal areas. In terms of the intergovernmental relationship, the federal government worried most about maintaining the centralization of revenues and the cooperation of regional leaders as agents of the federal government in improving tax collection. The problem of revenue decentralization arose in the immediate aftermath of the Soviet collapse when many regions, particularly the republics, instituted single-channel tax systems, whereby regional heads of administration unilaterally determined the amount of tax revenues to transfer to the federal government. Yet by 1995, the federal government had regained control over the tax-collection system successfully enough to preclude single-channel systems.[2] A series of laws and decrees

Table 3.1
Federal Budgetary Revenues and Expenditures, Planned versus Actual

	Planned tax revenues	Actual tax revenues	Actual tax rev. as % of planned	Planned expenditures	Actual expenditures	Actual exp. as % of planned
1995	224.5*	206.2	91.9	284.8	225.0	79.0
1996	282.5	218.7	77.4	435.7	353.6	81.1
1997	347.6	268.3	77.2	529.8	421.2	79.5

Source: Orlov (1997); Goskomstat (1995, 1996, 1997)

* in trillions of rubles

replaced the dual subordination of the State Tax Service to the Ministry of Finance and regional finance departments with clear subordination to the federal Ministry of Finance and created a federal Treasury system that automatically transferred tax payments from individuals and enterprises into federal accounts.[3] In addition, as chapter 2 describes, the post-Soviet tax laws favored revenue sharing over tax assignment, keeping the control over all but property, tax rates and a few minor taxes and local fees in federal hands. Consequently, the federal government regulated and administered the collection and distribution of the majority of subnational revenues, including the shares of the major taxes such as the VAT and the income tax.[4]

Despite the successes of the central government in institutionalizing and centralizing the tax system, it was still exceedingly inefficient. The tremendous number of tax laws and decrees covering more than two hundred taxes (Levinskii and Patowkin 1997) produced an unwieldy tax system that was impossible to monitor and created absurd sanctions. The federal government lost billions of rubles through loopholes, while the State Tax Service ordered enterprises to pay heavy fines for simple mistakes in calculating their tax payments.[5] The problems between the federal and subnational governments played a small role in the overall defects in Russia's system of revenue collection; the difficulties in monitoring the country's enormous monopolies and wealthy businessmen overshadowed intergovernmental tax issues. Nevertheless, the current intergovernmental tax laws forced the center to rely heavily on subnational and nongovernmental actors to implement the system of fiscal federalism, increasing the center's burden of monitoring so many agents. As in the Soviet system, the center relied on local agencies to supply information on revenue sources and tax bases. Although these agencies, including regional branches of the State Committee on Statistics and even the State Tax Inspectorate and Police, were subordinate to the federal government, in practice they often maintained closer relationships with regional elites. The federal government could independently monitor the flow of funds through the federal treasury but it was poorly equipped to monitor potential revenue sources and tax evaders. The prevalence of cash transactions and bartering in the economy eliminated paper trails, decreasing the ability of the center to monitor financial flows and shifting the regulatory burden to local governments and to regional branches of the State Tax Service. The federal government provided little financial support to local tax agencies, which instead relied on the regional governments to provide offices and equipment.[6] Regional governments, in turn, were often quite happy to equip these agencies in exchange for close working relationships and information. Information on tax evaders could work to the benefit of both the regional and federal government; regional governments had incentives to force local enterprises to pay federal taxes since they would receive a portion of these revenues. Yet, regional officials also had the opportunity to protect local employers who might be unable to pay back taxes and fines. For example, in the Fall of 1996 when the federal government faced a shortfall of approximately one-third of expected budgetary revenues (*Ekspert* 28 October 1996, 4), it formed the VChK (*Vremennaya chrezvichaynnaya kommissiya*), a temporary emergency commission to crack down on major tax debtors. As it threatened bankruptcy to major enterprises such as AvtoVAZ in Samara and Kamaz in Tatarstan, regional governments acted to protect these important sources of regional employment and revenue through rhetoric and private negotiations with President Yeltsin and Vice-Premier Potanin. *Interfax* reported the response of Tatarstan's president, Mintimir Shaymiyev, that "any decision of the central government without prior consultation with the leadership of Tatarstan will without a doubt turn out to not be implemented ... [e]specially if we take into account that the federal budget owes Tatarstan around 300 billion rubles" (*Ekspert* 28 October 1996, 6). In the case of AvtoVAZ in Samara, Governor Titov and the head of the automobile company, Viktor Kadannikov, quietly negotiated a compromise including debt restructuring and new emission of new bonds with the federal government to prevent the company's bankruptcy.[7] Consequently, the VChK produced only minor improvements in revenue collection, with the largest corporate debtors still owing trillions of rubles to the federal government.

The federal government had similar troubles monitoring regional tax legislation. The lack of clear legal boundaries demarcating the authority and jurisdiction of subnational governments in the constitution and in federal tax legislation only increased the costs to the federal government of determining unconstitutional policies at the regional level and enforcing sanctions. The Constitutional Court, a mostly toothless judicial body, offered little recourse, particularly in the short term. Meanwhile, subnational elites declared their authority over regional matters, asserting that the center had little knowledge or understanding of the needs of the provinces. With the majority of revenue controlled by the federal government, many regions created new taxes and added regional components to existing taxes to increase their revenue base, regardless of the burden it placed on local enterprises. The onerous regional taxes only increased Russia's problems with industrial decline and the financial debt of its enterprises (Dmitriyev 1996; Ickes, Murrell, and Ryterman 1997). The government of Udmurtia, for example, legislated a tax on production, creating a negative incentive for firms to produce in the region. Although the Constitutional Court declared the law unconstitutional, the republic did not suffer any sanctions, giving it little reason to comply with the ruling.[8]

The center shouldered the costs of implementing the intergovernmental fiscal system as a result of its complexity and centralization. Enterprises deposited tax payments directly into federal accounts, often in commercial banks specially authorized to act as agents of the federal government. The banks were then responsible for the transfer of the payments into the federal treasury. Two problems arose from this system. First, with an erratic payment schedule, the government could not easily compel banks to promptly transfer the funds. A bank could earn millions of rubles in interest at the expense of the federal government by holding onto tax payments an extra few days.[9] According to the State Tax Service, banks diverted eleven trillion rubles in this manner (Tompson 1997). The center sought to address this problem by limiting the number of banks with the authority to work as budgetary agents and creating a more unified treasury system, yet it still could not monitor the thousands of daily transactions throughout Russia. Second, enterprises deposited the tax payments into federal accounts, regardless of the percentage due to subnational governments. As a result, funds traveled from a shipbuilding factory in Vladivostok to the regional bank and then to the regional branch of the treasury department, finally showing up in the central accounts of the treasury. Based upon the revenue-sharing formulas in the federal budget, the Ministry of Finance would release the transfer of a percentage of these funds on a quarterly basis back to the regional budget of Primorskii Krai. The region's capital, Vladivostok, for example, would receive its share only when the regional government issued a similar revenue transfer. The circular flow of revenues could take several months, involving a vast number of bureaucracies and creating a complex web of financial information in a society where computers were few and outdated. Subnational governments frequently complained about being at the mercy of federal agencies that were often late in transferring budgetary funds. In addition, money due to regional governments often disappeared or was used for other objectives before it could be returned to the regions.

The system's complexity and inefficiencies placed the central government in a quandary as it approached the issue of reform. Although it wanted to maintain control over the revenue system, centralization also burdened the center with the tremendous costs of monitoring and implementing the system. Regional elites hardly behaved as central agents, using their access to information and regional tax agencies as a means to protect local businesses and increase their own financial position often at the expense of the federal government. The inability of the center to monitor the subnational governments meant that any improvements to the system of intergovernmental fiscal relations would result in a loss of centralized control.

The uncertainties of the revenue system, coupled with the yearly revenue shortfalls, hampered the ability of the center to institutionalize the division of expenditure responsibilities in the federation. Since the end of the Soviet period, the center had been steadily transferring responsibility for expenditures to subnational governments. Whereas the consolidated regional budget financed only 23.7 percent of total expenditures in 1992, the total increased to 45 percent in 1995 and almost 48 percent in 1997 (Vazquez and Boex 2001). The majority of regions did not generate enough revenue to finance these expenditures,[10] so the funds had to come from the federal government. By 1996, budgetary allocations for so-called "regionally-oriented expenditures"—funds sent directly to the subjects of the federation for health, education, social spending, etc.—constituted two-thirds of all expenditures in the consolidated budget (Borodulina 1997, 15). Nevertheless, the center did not offset each new decentralized expenditure with corresponding financing (Dmitriyev 1996; Borodulina 1997). According to one estimate, twenty-five unfunded federal mandates accounted for nearly 60 percent of consolidated regional expenditures in the mid-1990s, despite a series of federal laws proscribing the practice (Lavrov, Litwack and Sutherland 2001; OECD 2002). Subnational governments thus became more reliant on other types of transfers to the regions to offset deficits, including the Fund for Regional Support, allocations for federal programs, and loans to regional budgets. The flaws in the Fund for Regional Support (FFRS) underscore some of the problems of implementing Russia's interbudgetary system. The Russian press and western observers have criticized the fund for the lack of equity in its formula since some of the regions receiving transfers, including the Republic of Tatarstan and Orenburg Province, have substantial material and natural resource wealth. The transfer formula has thus become a significant source of conflict among regions, with many of the less-endowed territories complaining about the subjectivity of its formulation. Moreover, because the determination of need is based on each region's ability to cover expenditures with revenues, the FFRS creates incentives to inflate budget deficits.[11] Only 10 of the 89 regions were not considered "needy" of transfers in 1997, down from 14 in 1996 (*Segodnya* 23 January 1997; *The Moscow Tribune* 24 January 1997; *Vlast' v Rossii* October 1996, 8).[12]

At the same time, the size of federal loans to regional budgets continued to increase. The federal budget earmarked most of these loans to cover unpaid wages and pensions to state workers, a growing source of concern for the center.[13] At the end of 1996, the consolidated Russian budget owed more than 9 trillion rubles solely in wages. Some workers, including miners who had played important roles in organized strikes and social unrest in Russia and elsewhere in Eastern Europe, had not received paychecks in two to six months (*Nation* 15–22 June 1998; *Nature* 28 May 1998). Whereas some employers tried to arrange payments in sugar, toilet paper, and other less useful items—*The Economist* (15 March 1997) cites examples of payment in bras in a Volgograd factory and coffins in a Siberian town—others simply shrugged their shoulders and blamed the federal government. State workers had remained surprisingly calm and complacent in the face of financial hardship since the end of the Gorbachev years. During the presidential campaign, Yeltsin promised to find the money to pay the workers, blaming the IMF, the State Duma, and enterprise managers for the problems. When Yeltsin failed to fulfill this promise following his re-election or, having paid some of the owed wages during the campaign, the paychecks again slowed after the votes were counted, workers began to strike throughout Russia, demanding back pay and timely monthly paychecks. The increasing number of strikes in factories as well as in schools and hospitals threatened to shut down key sectors in the economy at a time when Russia was anxious to prove its stability to investors and international loan agencies. Simultaneously, the press—pro-communist papers such as *Pravda* and more reform-oriented papers such as *Nezavisimaya gazeta and Moskovskie novosti*—repeatedly publicized the center's inability to pay its workers and provide pensions for its elderly citizens, raising the specter of social unrest. Strikes and demonstrations presented a threat to economic effectiveness and the electoral plans of elites at every level of government. Although subnational elites still blamed the center for the predicament, they were equally concerned with preventing further instability.

Consequently, the federal government authorized loans to subnational budgets for wage and pension payments. Since the federal treasury did not have the necessary cash, the Ministry of Finance authorized certain private banks to act as federal agents (*upolnamochie banki*) with the Ministry serving as the guarantor of these loans. Despite the much-needed infusion of cash, the center could not monitor the banks adequately to assure timely and accurate payments, similar to its problems with using banks to transfer tax payments. In addition, the regional recipients of the credits lost millions of rubles in the transactions since the banks deducted the interest and fees directly from the earmarked funds (Tompson 1997). Furthermore, the regional governments were often unable to repay the loans, creating multiple levels of debt that were difficult to control. According to Aleksandr Livshits, the Finance Minister until 1997, the regions owed thirty-five trillion rubles to the federal budget in loans and credits (*Finansovie izvestiya*, 11 March 1997). The banks prospered, but the federal government had hardly begun to solve its payments crisis.

The center had a second means of addressing the crisis in budgetary expenditures—sequestration. Even in Soviet times, the Ministry of Finance had sequestered expenditures—freezing spending allocations in the annual budget during the fiscal year—to offset revenue shortfalls or other unexpected economic crises. Russian law continued this practice as a means of reining in the budget deficit. Yet sequestration was an inefficient solution to overly optimistic plans for revenue collection and budgets filled with expensive pork-barrel projects. Sequestering allocations damaged the legitimacy of the federal budget since expenditure outlays did not guarantee their appropriation; interest groups needed to lobby for money throughout the year in order to receive even a portion of what might be in the budget. In addition, despite legislation that only permitted the sequestration of spending outside the social sector, the Ministry of Finance froze allocations for wages and pensions. With the federal debt in this sector rising well above 150 trillion rubles, the treasury did not have the funds to cover current appropriations, let alone unpaid wages from the previous year (Orlov 1997). Sequestration and bank loans to regional governments provided temporary relief for the federal treasury but they did nothing to solve the long-term problems of implementing the interbudgetary system. In fact, these mechanisms only increased the complexity of intergovernmental relations by including intermediaries (the banks) and undermining legislative funding decisions, thus making federal monitoring more burdensome and decreasing the likelihood that budgetary goals would be met.

With no easy solutions to the federal budgetary problems, everyone, including federal officials, regional leaders, enterprise managers, and international loan agencies, agreed that fiscal institutions needed reform. Since problems of fiscal federalism overlapped with larger fiscal problems such as contradictory tax laws and an under-institutionalized budgetary system, the center attempted to resolve the issues simultaneously through a new tax code and budgetary code. Rather than address intergovernmental fiscal relations as an issue of *federalism,* as it had in the Federation Treaty by fusing questions of economic and political control, the center placed fiscal federalism squarely within the context of federal financial legislation. Yet this approach also constrained the ability of the center to quickly resolve intergovernmental tensions over fiscal control and to decrease some of the uncertainty plaguing the relationship. In spite of the tremendous difficulties in implementing and monitoring the current system, the ability to negotiate the tax and budgetary codes proved beyond the reach of the center in the short term. As the legislation fell victim to legislative-executive battles and special-interest lobbying, the center was left to find other means of addressing its intergovernmental fiscal problems.

MULTILATERAL REFORM: THE TAX CODE AND THE BUDGETARY CODE

In the uncertain transitional environment in Russia, there were strong incentives for creating multilateral institutional arrangements to lower transaction costs. Intergovernmental fiscal rules increase the transparency in managing resources and redistributing revenue, and improve the accountability in expenditures and budgetary transfers. In the mid-1990s, the reform of federal fiscal institutions focused on the tax code and the budgetary code. Although both documents addressed issues far broader than intergovernmental relations, they ultimately would determine the core of fiscal federalism: the structure of revenue sharing, redistribution, and expenditure responsibilities, and the burden of implementing this system.

Since late 1991, the federal government had been working on the new tax code, referred to as Russia's tax constitution. The primary goal of the code was to reduce the complexity of the tax system by reducing the number of taxes from more than four hundred to thirty and by eliminating a majority of the tax loopholes and exemptions. The tax code would also ease the burden on enterprises so as to stimulate growth and investment. With a more transparent, simple, and even-handed tax system, the federal government hoped to decrease the costs of monitoring the system and increase compliance. Despite extensive changes to the draft code, however, the government was unable to navigate it through the parliament until 1998, when the Duma approved the first (general) part of the code, suggesting to the government that such lofty goals for the tax system would not be so easily attained.

In late 1996 and 1997, the government constructed a draft that emphasized the unity and centralization of the tax system. It eliminated the right of regional governments to establish local taxes and exemptions and favored revenue sharing over tax assignment. Overall, the draft abolished all but thirty exemptions, creating an uproar among industrial leaders and Duma representatives who complained that such changes would negatively affect growth in their sector or region (Levinskii 1997).[14] In response to the constant political pressure, Vice Minister of Finance Sergei Shatalov moaned that "It is not out of the question that the result could be two hundred [exemptions]" (*Izvestiya*, 19 February 1997). The outlook for the government draft seemed equally grim in the Federation Council. The governors complained that the code trampled on the rights of the subnational governments and contradicted the principles of federalism. If only to emphasize the potential opposition to an overly centralized tax system, five regional governments sued the federal government in Constitutional Court to establish the right of subnational government to set local taxes, which was authorized in a 1993 decree only to be reversed by President Yeltsin in 1996. According to one observer, even if the government could assure passage of the tax code—an unlikely outcome—it remained questionable whether the regional leaders would implement it. "After all, [the federal government's] treasury is empty, transfers from Moscow don't arrive, and the constitution, which authorizes the federal powers to establish 'general principles of taxation,' leaves an endless field for discussion as to what are 'general principles' and what is the right 'to establish local taxes and fees' by organs of local government in accordance with Article 132" (*Izvestiya*, 19 February 1997).

Lacking the political muscle to guide the code through the parliament, the government drafted a new tax code in 1998 with very different goals. According to Vice Minister of Finance, M. A. Motorin, the new draft contained "a new impulse" to develop tax federalism through separate federal, regional, and local taxes. Rather than setting the revenue-sharing norms for the major federal taxes, the draft code left this to annual budgetary legislation. In addition, it established a "grandfather clause" for tax exemptions previously designated by regional governments and allowed subnational governments to add their own tax exemptions and fees in accordance with federal law (*Finansi*, February 1998). Although this draft faced easy approval in the Federation Council, its survival in the Duma was less clear. According to Motorin, members of the Duma were considering several alternative drafts, which "conceptually contradict established international practice . . . of building a system of taxation. . . . If the Duma passes any of these [alternative] drafts of the tax code in the first reading, it will throw the process of tax reform far behind . . . and will make its passage in 1998 problematic" (*Finansi*, February 1998). Without the political capital to push through its version of the tax code, the federal government faced a quandary: either continue to negotiate with parliamentary leaders in the hopes of gaining more supporters of the government's draft code while simultaneously managing the current burdensome tax system, or construct a compromise tax code with political and industrial elites, which might institutionalize the same loopholes and exemptions that plagued the current tax regime.

The central government faced similar hurdles regarding the budgetary code. The draft code addressed the fundamental problems of intergovernmental budgetary mechanisms including the division of revenues, federal transfers, means of stimulating local economies, and the state's redistributive goals. The center and the regions had obvious motives to set the rules of interbudgetary relations, thereby lessening the annual tug-of-war to determine the division of revenue and expenditure responsibilities. Some cost-saving measures, including the publication of budgets and the elimination of numerous extrabudgetary funds, drew strong support from all levels of government. Yet there was little consensus around the core of the budgetary code—the division of revenue and expenditure powers. The central government wanted to create a stronger hierarchy of budgetary authority—a reflection of Yeltsin's vision of executive authority—with subnational budgets remaining subordinate to federal legislation and budgetary decisions. The federal government would control regional budgetary spending through minimal expenditure norms for social services— similar to the norms under the Soviet planning system—and limitations on regional budget deficits. Although the tax code specified some regional autonomy to establish taxes, the budgetary code encroached on this territory by affirming federal revenues and transfers as the primary sources for regional revenues. With a more centralized system, the center contended, the federal government could more easily implement redistributive policies and control the extent of regional budget deficits. As with the tax code, however, regional elites protested against the ostensible infringements on federal principles. The draft code did not guarantee subnational independence in forming and using financial resources. As a result of the dependence on federal sources of revenue, regional leaders argued that the budgetary code contradicted the Russian Constitution, which established the independence of federal, regional, and local budgets (Rodionova 1998). Regional leaders wanted the budgetary code to improve the monitoring of federal fiscal agencies. They demanded that the budgetary code specify the responsibilities of the federal government to fulfill territorial expenditures in the annual budget and the sanctions for violating the budgetary statutes. In addition, they wanted the code to end the circular flows of revenue, which produced long delays and reductions in federal transfers to the regions (Medvedev 1997).

Like the tax code, the budgetary code remained under consideration in the Parliament for several years until it was finally passed in mid-1998. By 1997, the budgetary code had already advanced to the second stage of reading, moving through the negotiation process more quickly than the tax code. In part, the budgetary code's more circumscribed scope guaranteed it greater potential for parliamentary approval. It established the general rules of budgetary formation and implementation, but the most contentious issues—the division of revenues and specific expenditure decisions—were left to the annual budget rather than the budgetary "rulebook." National leaders thus retained the power to alter revenue-sharing arrangements, subject of course to bargaining with regional leaders in the Federation Council. The opposition to the budgetary code rested primarily with the subnational leaders, who hoped to eliminate the process of sequestration, increase the autonomy of regional budgets, and assure adequate financing for subnational expenditures. The final version of the budgetary code failed to address these basic concerns, leaving in place many of the ambiguities of the existing interbudgetary system. According to First Deputy Minister of Finance V. B. Khristenko, the code retained the broadly defined concept of "joint financing" of expenditures without explicitly stating how those responsibilities would be divided (*Finansi*, May 1999). Moreover, the final version did not change the system's heavy emphasis on regulated (federal) sources of revenue versus regional sources—a legacy of the Soviet inter-budgetary relationship.

As the budgetary code moved through the final stages of approval in 1998, the government also chose to circumscribe the negotiations over the tax code. With increasing pressure from the IMF for some measure of fiscal reform, the government decided to focus on only the first part of the tax code dealing with tax administration and tax assignment. In July 1998, President Yeltsin signed Part I of the code into law; the other three sections, which incorporate the substantive tax laws and regulations, remained mired in parliamentary wrangling and interbranch negotiations for another two years. Part One retains the emphasis of the previous draft on federal revenues, but the subnational leaders did manage to win a substantial, if economically questionable, concession: a new 5 percent regional sales tax in addition to the existing 20 percent VAT.[15] Even with the passage of the first part of the tax code after seven years of negotiations, the legislation did little to alleviate the uncertainty in the tax system or improve the ability of the government to collect taxes. With issues of tax exemptions, monitoring, the role of private banks, and the contradictions of current tax legislation still undecided, subnational leaders as well as outside observers saw little hope that the government's fiscal health would improve.

BILATERALISM AND INTERGOVERNMENTAL REFORM

As Yeltsin's administration and the Duma labored unsuccessfully to reform public finance in the mid-1990s, regional leaders continued to pressure the center to fulfill federalism's promise of "self-rule plus shared rule" through further decentralization of authority and improved transparency of central decision making. Despite President Yeltsin's hopes of resolving disputes over the nature of federalism through the 1993 Constitution, political and economic tensions did not evaporate. Lingering conflicts with Tatarstan and Chechnya suggested that federal ideals and documents could not assure political stability—the foundation for Russia's market reforms and the government's political future. In addition, as I will discuss later in more detail, the inability of the center to implement the budget and fulfill its fiduciary promises to the regions resulted in increasing threats by the regions to force the center to yield fiscal control. The slow progress of tax and budgetary reform only gave the regions greater impetus to press their demands. With presidential and then gubernatorial elections rapidly approaching, the center needed a more flexible and immediate approach than multilateral reform to deal with the regions.

Bilateralism emerged as the center's primary approach to intergovernmental reform by 1996 as a response to unflagging regional demands for change and as an alternative to its failing attempts to overhaul fiscal federalism through legislation. Bilateral agreements offered a way of negotiating with regional governments in a more circumscribed framework where the central government could bring more resources to bear on the outcome in an individual region. The center hoped to solve its most immediate problems, particular on the expenditure side, while minimizing the overall gains of the regions. At the same time, to the benefit of both sides, bilateral agreements could improve the availability of information and transparency of fiscal relations, at least between individual regions and the center. Transaction costs would be lowered for both sides: for the regions, by limiting the lobbying costs of obtaining funds and renegotiating fiscal agreements with the center; and for the center, by reducing the need for economic handouts and payoffs as a response to political crises. Intergovernmental fiscal relations thus changed from a problem of national fiscal reform to an issue of federal reform.

The discussion of federalism renewed the debate over the Russian Federation's asymmetrical structure—a legacy of its Soviet past—and how the central government should manage these differences. As the previous chapter discussed, Russia inherited a complex territorial structure from its Soviet predecessor that included provinces (oblasts and krais), republics, autonomous areas, and two "cities of federal significance." The 1992 Federation Treaty incorporated the asymmetrical relationships into its framework, emphasizing the different economic privileges and political rights between the provinces and the republics. The document resulted in enormous conflict and competition among Russia's regions, leading Yeltsin to stress the principle of regional equality in the 1993 Constitution. Rather than deter further discussion of Russia's federal structure, as Yeltsin had hoped, the constitution only added to the uncertainty. It had promised equality, but the republics still possessed disproportionate control over resources and economic decision making (Filippov and Shvetsova 1999; Lysenko 1995). Multilateral fiscal legislation—the equalization of tax and budgetary rights throughout the federation—implicitly sought to implement the pledge of subnational equality in the constitution. With the failure of that goal in the short term and the renewed interest in bilateral negotiations, the center seemingly embraced the Soviet legacy of asymmetrical federalism or at least acknowledged its inability to overcome it.

The Yeltsin administration now recognized bilateral negotiations as a strategy of addressing federal reform rather than simply a mutually understood but unacknowledged mechanism of dealing with the regions. Bilateralism also served key political goals for the president. Since Russia's independence, Yeltsin was forced to work with a communist-dominated, and often hostile, State Duma, even after he disbanded the parliament in October 1993 and hastily arranged new elections. In the case of many crucial reforms, including public finance, privatization of land, civil rights, and budget priorities, Yeltsin had no choice but to negotiate and compromise with national legislators. But bilateralism gave the president a chance to circumvent executive-legislative battles and stalemates and deal directly with regional executives to accomplish federal reforms. Whereas negotiations over the Budget Code, for example, had necessitated simultaneous conflicts with parliamentarians and regional governors, Yeltsin could now eliminate the potentially more dangerous and certainly more antagonistic adversary.[16] In addition, direct interexecutive negotiations served a principal doctrine of the administration—the "presidential vertical." Drawing on historical notions of hierarchical power relations between center and periphery, Yeltsin hoped to tighten the bonds between regional leaders and the president to encourage subnational dependency rather than federal autonomy. Bilateralism appeared both to eliminate legislatures from the structure of state power and to force regional leaders to become beholden to the central government for economic and political rewards.

The bilateral approach to federal reform preserved much of the existing system of intergovernmental relations, making it a more familiar method for solving the center's fiscal dilemmas with the regions. Informal negotiations for funds between central and subnational elites were a hallmark of the Soviet fiscal system. When the Soviet economic system disintegrated, taking the powerful planning and industrial ministries along with it, these informal rules filled the institutional vacuum. Yeltsin had also used promises of financial rewards and resources during his standoff with Gorbachev in 1990–91 as a means to gain the allegiance of Russia's autonomous republics (Filippov and Shevtsova 1999, 70–1). The regions, particularly the more powerful republics, saw these informal agreements as a means of retaining control over territorial assets and revenues, while increasing the amount of federal transfers.

The preservation of purely informal norms of negotiation in the fiscal sphere seemed to offer a number of advantages to the center, yet each of these supposed benefits proved costly. First, a flexible system of fiscal distribution gave the center a powerful tool to reward loyalty to the federation and to the president. Supplemental transfers, tax credits, and federal programs provided a useful "carrot" to promote the "presidential vertical," particularly during the 1996 election campaign. Yet as several studies have shown (Treisman 1996, 1999; Birkenes 1996), these financial benefits did not go to those regions paying homage to the president but to those proclaiming their dissatisfaction the loudest. Both Birkenes and Treisman find a strong correlation between regions that proclaimed sovereignty during the 1993 crisis and the size of transfer payments. Treisman compounds this finding by showing that the number of work days lost to strikes also positively correlates with the size of the transfers. Evidence from the 1996 presidential campaign shows similar results. Payments were used as financial incentives to turn around voters in the most anti-Yeltsin regions, according to the polls, rather than as rewards for good behavior. As a result, although the system gave the president the flexibility to solve short-term problems of infidelity, it simultaneously created incentives to evince disloyalty. No sooner would Primorskii Krai receive funds to settle its strikes than the Republic of Udmurtia would proclaim the impending communist revanchism in the territory if it didn't receive immediate financial support.

Under such a system, relations with federation subjects threatened to dissolve into an unending series of hole-patching with each hole growing larger.[17] Following the presidential election in 1996, however, it became clear that the center lacked the funds to continue such payoffs or even follow through on the financial promises during the presidential campaign. Not only had this informal system become too costly for the center, but its financial promises were no longer credible to the regions since the many of the rewards for supporting Yeltsin did not materialize or quickly dissolved following the election. Yeltsin increased spending by as much as eleven billion dollars in six months to pay back wages of state workers, but the depleted Central Bank could no longer continue paying wages following the second round of elections (*National Review*, 29 July 1996, 2). Without a credible commitment from the central government, and without a sanctioning mechanism, the informal system no longer seemed beneficial, particularly to the most troublesome regions.

The availability of information on regional transfers also became a problem for the Yeltsin administration. Initially, the lack of transparency in the informal system offered some important advantages to the president. Not only did it give him the flexibility to change his allocation decisions, but the dearth of information and attempts to conceal it minimized competition between regions over central allocations. Yet, the role of financial payoffs to the regions during the presidential election became a persistent source of speculation and contention. Journalists used such information to provide evidence of vote trading and other, more corrupt activities such as bribery. Regional elites used this information to complain about the misuse of federal revenue and the need for a new and equitable system of intergovernmental relations. The manipulation of the transfer system to pay off troublemakers particularly irked leaders in regions such as Samara and Orenburg, who had showcased their loyalty to Yeltsin. Meanwhile, Duma representatives, often privy to information on intergovernmental transfers from their political colleagues in their hometowns as well as the media, found the data valuable fodder in their frequent battles with the president. Despite inconsistencies among sources in the specific amounts of the transfers, the availability of the data diminished the asymmetrical control over information that had benefited the central government. Without such control over information, the political costs due to conflicts and regional competition climbed dramatically.

With information increasingly available through the press and the waning ability of the center to manipulate the intergovernmental fiscal system, the move to institutionalize a system of bilateral relations to replace the increasingly unstable informal norms became more likely. The regions rebelled against the ambiguity and uncertainty of the current norms and demanded a system that included incentives to reveal information. For the center, the ongoing bargaining games with eighty-nine different regions, which comprised the intergovernmental fiscal system, grew beyond its capacity. With the center unable to provide a credible commitment to its promises of financial support during the presidential campaign, problems of opportunism threatened to destabilize the federal bargain. If the administration could not follow through on its promises during the campaign, how else might it shirk its responsibilities to the regions? The annual budgetary crisis, with the federal government owing trillions of rubles to the regions, and the regions unable or unwilling to repay loans and credits, only reinforced the idea that the center could not fulfill its fiscal responsibilities.

In response, some regions threatened to take matters into their own hands as they had during the crisis in 1993, increasing the sense of instability in the federation. Some threats no longer held the same credibility: the governor of Tula, Nikolai Sevrugin, warned that he would withhold transfers of federal revenue to the center, despite the fact that such transfers were already firmly in the control of the federal treasury (*Segodnya*, 6 March 1997). Other threats, particularly in the political realm, garnered more serious attention. The Federation Council announced that it would reopen the debate on federalism and seek to renegotiate the balance of power in an effort to circumscribe the powers of the presidency (*Segodnya*, 23 January 1997). At the same time, the senators signaled that passage of legislation favored by the administration, including the budget, would hinge upon the government's financial support of the regions (*Segodnya*, 5 March 1997).

Even though the negotiations of bilateral treaties were already well underway by 1996, the gubernatorial elections in the provinces reinforced the center's short time horizon and the idea that some sort of contracting between the center and regions was essential. In 1991, the parliament had passed a law permitting elections of the Heads of Administration (governors) in the provinces. Yeltsin managed to postpone the majority of these elections until after the presidential election, fearing that elected governors would threaten the authority of the central government and Yeltsin's re-election. First Deputy Presidential Chief of Staff Aleksandr Korzakov openly admitted that he could not find "a single positive element in the very idea of these elections" (Belin 1997, 27). Fearing that the regions would use the gubernatorial elections as a means to increase their independence from the center, the Yeltsin administration sought to influence the outcomes of the elections much as it had during the national elections—through financial promises, donations to specific campaigns, and

visits to the provinces to support incumbents—and through less traditional means, such as the use of political consulting firms (*Moscow Tribune*,
18 October 1996). Yeltsin found other means of offering financial support
to those regions that doubted the ability of the center to follow through
on its promises. For example, in February 1996, President Yeltsin issued
decree 292, "On the transfer to the subjects of the Russian Federation
federal shares of joint-stock properties in the process of being privatized."
The decree, which authorized the transfer of such property to cover federal debts to the regions, lay dormant until the Ministry of Finance and
the State Property Committee began to implement it at the end of 1996 to
"secure the loyalty of regional leaders on the day before the gubernatorial
elections and [to ensure] the ability to help them on a completely legal
level at the necessary moment" (*Segodnya*, 10 November 1996).

Nevertheless, these efforts produced only modest successes in securing
the election of pro-government candidates. Of the fifty regional elections
held between September 1996 and early 1997, fewer than half of the incumbents held onto their jobs (Belin 1997, 24). Not only were many of the
new governors backed by the Communist Party or the Popular-Patriotic
Union, but many of them were the same leaders whom Yeltsin had removed from office in 1993 (Senatova and Yakurin 1996, 17). Despite the
ambiguous outcome of the election, Yeltsin's administration made clear
that it would work with all of the new leaders, including those supported
by the opposition. Yet it would have to develop new ways of integrating
the federation in the face of the governors' newfound local support and
legitimacy. As commentator Vladimir Todress points out,

Earlier, the success of local leaders in their battles with the center was achieved
precisely due to the lack of a uniform regional policy in Moscow. To introduce
general rules and to make heads of administration play according to them could
not even be achieved when they were appointed state officials. Now, to curb the
governors, who were the ultimate crucible in the expression of the people's will
(and precisely in this lies the goal of the Kremlin's 'state-building' projects), will
be decidedly more difficult. (*Itogi*, 21 January 1997)

The center-periphery environment facing the central government thus
appeared much different in 1996 than it had in the beginning of 1994
immediately following the passage of the constitution. Rising intergovernmental debt, wage arrears, and an unofficial financial reward system combined with the increasingly localized base of authority of regional
leaders to make the intergovernmental bonds seem more tenuous than
ever. Informal norms of negotiation no longer presented the same advantages to the center in an environment where regional power seemed at
times to match that of the center. Bilateral treaties, already a means of
integrating the most troublesome republics into the federation, arose as

the easiest solution to the current problems. Even more important, the federal government saw bilateralism as the path toward its ultimate goal—national stability. As Yeltsin noted in a speech proclaiming the rewards of the bilateral treaty process in late 1997, treaties with all of Russia's regions ultimately would produce "a unified, federal state" (*Rossisskiye vesti,* 1 November 1997).

The negotiation of the first "treaty to delimit power," between the Russian Federation and the Republic of Tatarstan, predated the constitution but was signed only after the resolution of the constitutional crisis.[18] Although Tatarstan repeatedly asserted its elevated standing in the federation, from its declarations of sovereignty and Tatar nationalism to the autocratic style of its president, its treaty established a precedent for the other members of the federation. Nevertheless, as Vladimir Lysenko notes, the treaty, negotiated over a period of three years, cannot be dissociated from the conflict with the center over Tatarstan's economic and political inclusion in the Russian Federation, particularly in the context of the growing conflict with Chechnya (1995, 54). The Russian central government, weakened from the unraveling of the Soviet system and the ensuing series of economic and political crises, needed desperately to bring Tatarstan, a large and wealthy region, back into the fold. In the wake of the October 1993 showdown with the national and regional legislatures, the potential costs of a renegade government like Tatarstan to the survival of the federation far outweighed any economic tradeoffs. The Yeltsin administration either dismissed the impact on any future bilateral treaties, or saw it as an inevitable price to pay for the advancement in state consolidation. In retrospect, President Yeltsin acknowledged that "in order to solve some very difficult and divisive problems with Tatarstan ... [the bilateral agreement] served as a kind of emergency first aid. It forestalled the danger of a split in the Federation" (*Rossisskiye vesti,* 1 November 1997). President Shaymiyev used the center's position to negotiate a treaty that both increased its control over the natural resources on its territory and minimized the republic's fiscal responsibility to the federal government, effectively receiving many of the benefits of sovereignty in exchange for sacrificing the rhetoric of independence.

The Tatarstan treaty and its eleven attached agreements included numerous special arrangements,[19] but the economic privileges received the most attention from observers as well as other regional elites. Although the revenue-sharing agreement, primarily through the division of VAT receipts, would continue to be negotiated on an annual basis as with other regions, the treaty granted Tatarstan sole retention of the tax revenue from liquor, natural gas, and oil—very profitable industries in the republic—as well as profits from privatization and the corporate tax to support key national industries. Tatarstan received other "gifts," such as a foreign currency fund and fifty billion rubles credit to the National Bank of Tatarstan.

Regardless of the enormous potential for economic profit to the republic, Lysenko suggests that the real danger of the treaty lay in the political powers granted to the republic, which contradict the constitution.[20] As the treaty did not state specifically that Tatarstan is a member of the federation, the document was essentially "the combination of an international and an intergovernmental treaty of confederal and federal relations" (Lysenko 1995, 54). Unlike other regions, Tatarstan retained authority over judicial appointments, civil and human rights, and the right to conduct international relations. Even the tax privileges raised constitutional questions, since Article 114, part 1 of the constitution gave authority over the budget to the legislative branch, whereas the treaty was negotiated and signed by the executive branch (Lysenko 1995, 54–58).

Although several of the subsequent bilateral treaties—the agreements with Bashkortostan and Sakha-Yakutia, for example—emanated from the same political rationale as the treaty with Tatarstan, most of the treaties, particularly those with the provinces, served different purposes. For the center, bilateral treaties became a means of stabilizing the federation by strengthening the bonds between the central government and the subjects of the Russian Federation (Institute of Law and Comparative Legal Rule 1996, 17–18). As Vladimir Gel'man astutely observes, a treaty-based approach to formalizing federalism serves both national and regional interests better than either "the preservation of a legal base of joint competencies, which has not been divided between the Center and the regions, or the informal mechanisms of receiving specific benefits by regional leaders" (Gel'man 1996, 11–12). As a contract, the treaty provided a credible commitment from both levels of government: from the region to remain a part of the federation and to eschew the rhetoric of sovereignty; and from the center to fulfill its fiscal responsibilities to the regions with clear sanctions for not doing so. In addition, the treaties aimed to reduce the information costs for both parties by demarcating control over property and resources. Not only would the treaties overcome the ambiguities of the constitution, but they would delimit the boundaries more precisely to each specific region than could any multilateral federal document. According to Vice Premier Sergei Shakrai, the head of the presidential commission on the preparation of the bilateral treaties, the agreements could provide an important building block of federalism and help equalize the status of the provinces with the republics—a goal that the constitution was unable to achieve (FBIS-Sov-94–173, 7 September 1994).

In fact, as the treaty negotiations moved from the republics to the provinces—beginning with many of the resource-rich regions such as Sverdlovsk and Orenburg—and gathered steam in 1996, the treaties began to resemble each other. Published in the press upon its signing, each treaty established the broad outlines of joint and unilateral jurisdictions and some of the primary goals of the document. The accompanying agreements, however, which did not become public record,[21] laid out the specifics of the treaty and often included economic privileges that did not comply with the center's rhetoric of equality. Most treaties included close to ten agreements, covering budgetary mechanisms and finance; domestic and international trade; privatization; civil and human rights; the environment; education; public safety; public health and welfare; scientific cooperation; and issues specific to the region. Although the budgetary-finance agreement detailed fiscal responsibilities, each of the other agreements could include a fiscal component, such as the financial responsibility for an environmental clean-up program. In addition, the agreements often reiterated federal programs and their financing responsibilities, already established by presidential decree or governmental edict, so as to create a more binding commitment by the government to its regional development programs and include sanctions for non-compliance.

Regardless of the advantages of bilateral treaties, the center had not simply selected this strategy for federal reform as the best of all possible alternatives. Successive choices and circumstances, including the long-held practice of informal mechanisms of contracting, the short time horizon of the central government, and the initial treaties with the republics of Tatarstan, Bashkortostan, and Sakha-Yakutia, shaped the direction of bilateral negotiations. The treaty process began neither with the goal to create a more symmetrical federation nor to provide an intergovernmental addendum to the constitution, but as a solution to problems with certain troublesome regions. As such, it acquired the mode of more informal intergovernmental mechanisms by "erecting a system of personal interests (dominated by the acceptance of decisions on the regional level) [that serves as] one of the foundations of federalism building in Russia" (Gel'man 1996, 12). Rather than first creating federal legislation to set the boundaries and affix the structure of the treaties[22]—a potentially long and arduous process—the center began negotiating treaties without such limits. Consequently, the treaties took on a more individual character, with each treaty reflecting the interests of the region's elite.[23]

The particularistic nature of the treaties[24] also developed out of the limitations of the bargaining and approval processes to the executive branch. The negotiations incorporated a wide range of economic and political elites from the ministries at the federal level and from the state and private sector at the regional level, whereas the president and governor signed the document as agreements between the executive branches of government.[25] In part, this arrangement originated with the center's desire to limit the negotiating costs. Since the central government chose bilateral treaties as a short-term solution, it sought to minimize the time and collective action costs by limiting the parties to the agreement. Moreover, the position of the executive branch as the foundation for state building has a long history in Russia, starting with the ties between the town governors and tsars in pre-Soviet history,[26] and reemerging under President Yeltsin as the "presidential vertical" (Shevtsova 1996). A strong dependence on the bonds with the governors made sense when the president still appointed the regional heads of administration and, until the 1996 regional elections, a majority of the appointed governors were still in office. In addition, by confining the treaties to the executive branch, the president excluded what he saw as its main opposition, the legislatures, from the negotiations. The Communist Party and other anti-government parties dominated the Duma and the legislatures in most regions. The 1993 crisis, when Yeltsin dissolved both the national parliament and the regional legislatures, reinforced the antagonisms between branches of government, at least in the eyes of the president. Since the constitution gave the president wide latitude in signing and implementing documents without the input of the legislative branch, there seemed little reason to complicate the process by including a potentially hostile group of politicians. Without the processes of legislative approval that might have eliminated some of the differences and discrepancies in the treaties or halted the process altogether in the context of the Duma's conflictual politics, the negotiations took on a more individualistic approach reflecting the resources and relationship between the center and the particular region. Vladimir Gel'man notes that "from the point of view of power relations," the politics of bilateral treaties reflect a "transition from the system of informal contracts, based on personal-clientalistic connections, to a system of 'awarded deeds' according to the principle of status" (Gel'man 1996, 11). Nevertheless, the latter system clearly reflected the previous methods of administration. The long-lasting pattern of informal norms of negotiation, based upon personal relations between elites at different levels of government rather than between government institutions or agencies, conditioned the developing intergovernmental system by emphasizing the particularity of each bilateral relationship. Consequently, the interests of the provincial leaders and the resources they could bring to bear on the relationship with the center held greater sway than in a more uniformly institutionalized system.

The short time horizon of the Russian leadership also emphasized the significance of a region's status and resources in the treaty process. The negotiation of treaties began with the most troublesome republics and moved on to the most important provinces—those with either nationally significant natural resources such as gas and oil, or the most populous regions, whose voting patterns could determine the outcome of the presidential election. Hughes (1996), however, argues that although the process began with three of the most irksome republics and four powerful provinces—Sverdlovsk, Orenburg, Krasnodar, and Kaliningrad—it soon progressed to other regions, regardless of their status. Nevertheless, these first treaties established a model for future negotiations. With the central government anxious to appease Russia's outspoken and influential leaders at crucial points in the political transition—the 1993 constitutional crisis, the 1996 presidential and gubernatorial elections—it focused on the goal of successfully negotiating the treaties rather than on the impact they might have on future intergovernmental relations.

The outcomes of the initial bilateral treaties powerfully influenced the process of bilateral negotiations by raising the expectations of regional leaders for the potential gains of the process. The Treaty to Demarcate Power with Tatarstan successfully reintegrated the republic into the federation—Tatarstan emerged as one of Yeltsin's more loyal regions during the presidential elections—but it came with a price. As noted earlier, the federal government gave up significant control over financial and natural resources on the territory, giving Tatarstan a unique position of economic autonomy in the federation. The treaty with Sakha-Yakutia, the producer of ninety percent of the country's diamonds, also gave that republic valuable control over its resources with the division of diamond revenues determined by an annual agreement between the presidents of the Russian Federation and the Republic of Sakha (*Rossiiskaiya federatsiya*, March 1995, 2–3). The center attempted to conceal the contents of these agreements, particularly the financial aspects, but as with earlier informal agreements, the information surfaced in the press (Balzer and Vinokurova 1996, 119 n. 24; *Segodnya* 25 July 1995). The provinces, seeking a more symmetrical federation, demanded advantages similar to those of the republics.

The first province to negotiate a bilateral treaty, Yeltsin's hometown of Sverdlovsk, had more influence on the demands of the other provinces than did the treaties with the republics. The provinces had long acknowledged the privileged status of Tatarstan, despite their dislike of the enormous benefits awarded to the republics. Yet Sverdlovsk held the same standing in the federation as the other provinces, regardless of the combative stance of its leader, Eduard Rossel',[27] and therefore represented a model for other regions. In a set of fifteen agreements, Sverdlovsk received a wide range of economic privileges, including the endowment of a "substantial" regional investment fund comprised of preferential credits from the Central Bank and revenues from the sale of regional and federal property; the establishment of a free economic zone; and quotas for the sale of natural resources and manufactured goods to be decided by an annual agreement with the federal government (Hughes 1996, 42). In addition, the treaty gave the region the right to use a portion of federal revenues collected within Sverdlovsk to pay for federal programs (rather than wait for the transfer of federal financing), a benefit of growing importance as the center's fiscal health deteriorated. As with the Tatarstan Treaty, both President Yeltsin and Governor Rossel' attempted to conceal the contents of the agreements so as to preclude conflicts with other regions. Again, the press either speculated on the most contentious aspects of the agreements or were leaked information, particularly Sverdlovsk's local newspapers; either way, regional leaders became aware of Sverdlovsk's newly enhanced economic position. As a result, the subject of Sverdlovsk's exalted position supplanted the problem of asymmetry between the republics and the other regions, becoming "no less of a problem for the movement in the direction of an effective federalism and regional democracy (Gel'man 1996, 11).

The success of Sverdlovsk with its treaty, followed by Orenburg and Kaliningrad, whose leaders managed to negotiate free economic zones for their territories, encouraged other provinces to initiate treaty discussions. The privileges granted to the first treaty signatories in the context of short-term political crises thus threatened to spread to the other members of the federation, with each region bargaining for more advantageous terms. The treaty process no longer represented simply a means for the center to solve problems with individual regions, but a "system of relations parallel to the constitutional system" (*Nezavisimaya gazeta*, 13 May 1997). As such, the growing demands by the regions for equity in the treaties, particularly in the economic sphere, indicated that the treaties would become exponentially costly to the central government and endanger the centralization of the revenue system. According to some calculations, the initial signatories pay twenty percent less in tax revenue to the federal budget than other members of the federation.[28] In response, the central government sought to institutionalize the treaty system so as to reassume control over the structure and substance of the documents. Yet as with the process of fiscal reform, the attempt to institutionalize bilateralism and create a foundation to foster a more symmetrical federation through multilateral legislation stalled in the Duma. Although Yeltsin had called on the Duma as early as 1994 to adopt the "Law on the Principles and Procedures for Demarcating Objects of Jurisdiction and Powers Between Russian Federation Bodies of State Power and Bodies of State Power in the Members of the Russian Federation," it took another three years for the legislation to gain passage in the Duma. President Yeltsin did not sign the final version of the law until June 1999. Led by Duma deputy Vladimir Lysenko and the administration's representative, Sergei Shakrai, the new legislation placed the treaties within the context of federal law, outlining the basic structure of the treaties and the agreements along with the possible subjects for their content. The law reaffirmed the supremacy of the constitution and federal laws over the treaties and required that the twenty-six treaties already in force must come into conformity with federal law. Future treaties were required to go through a much more rigid process of negotiation, with the document facing review by a presidential commission and ultimate approval by a majority of members of the Federation

Council. The final document, however, excluded a clause from the draft law requiring the reconfirmation of the prevailing twenty-six treaties. (*Rossiiskaya gazeta*, 30 June 1999; draft law "On the Foundations of Delimiting the Objects of Jurisdiction . . . "). All treaties, as well as the full texts of the linked agreements, would be published in the official acts of the federal and regional governments.

According to Lysenko, the law "formalize[d] the procedure of signing bilateral treaties" by removing the informal mechanisms of negotiation between executive leaders. "Parliamentary control is necessary because we consider that the executive branch is, shall we say, destroying the constitution with these treaties and destroying the solidarity of the Russian Federation."[29] A confirmation process in the Federation Council assumes that regional leaders would not want to endorse further economic advantages to their regional peers, thereby restricting the scope of any future treaties. In addition to limiting future financial costs to the center, the law endeavored to institutionalize many of the advantages of the bilateral treaties by establishing mechanisms for implementing and monitoring intergovernmental agreements and a legal framework for their continued negotiation.

Under President Yeltsin, the center signed forty-six treaties with a wide range of economic privileges, special arrangements, and divisions of resources. Despite the center's use of the bilateral process to solve short-term concerns—Tatarstan's threats of independence; fears of electoral success of anti-government parties and individuals; problems of regional compliance with tax collection—bilateralism substantially transformed the development of federalism in Russia. It emerged from a long-standing method of addressing the country's asymmetries and responding to regional demands. In the uncertainty of Russia's transition, multilateral approaches to fiscal and federal reform offered neither the flexibility nor the speed of bilateralism to manage the center-regional relationship. Moreover, by 1998 bilateralism seemed to have resolved many, if not all, of the threats to federal stability that the 1993 Constitution had failed to quell. Tatarstan gave up its demands for political autonomy; Sakha and Bashkortostan agreed to participate in the federation's tax and budgetary systems. Even Chechnya seemed willing at that time to renew negotiations with the federal government.

Without such an institutionalized procedure and framework for the bilateral treaties, regions that negotiated with the center during the height of the treaty process in 1996 and 1997 were forced to rely on their own resources and abilities to set the bargaining agenda. In the context of the federal government's financial weakness, regional leaders had to develop more creative strategies for reform and seek alternatives to central transfers, loans, and investment. For some regions, the center's weaknesses—its fiscal problems as well as its political cleavages and conflicts—offered tremendous potential to negotiate preferential arrangements. Instead of appealing for federal aid, financially secure regions could seek ways of financing expenditures and investment programs through local resources, using the bilateral treaty and agreements to institutionalize these solutions. Yet for poorer and more fragmented regions, the unstable fiscal environment—rising wage arrears, tax-collection problems, and inter-enterprise, intergovernmental, and international debt—only accentuated the predicament of their situation. These regions also sought some type of rapprochement with the center to ease the financial strain and the burden of everyday intergovernmental transactions. Yet they had to rely on federal transfers and investment to deal with more than a decade of negative growth rates and economic inefficiency. As many resource-rich regions followed in the footsteps of Tatarstan and Sverdlovsk in negotiating advantageous bilateral treaties, the more dependent regions hoped primarily for minor concessions from the center and dreamt of investment windfalls from the West.

NOTES

1. The issue of transaction costs has become a popular subject of debate within the school of new institutional economics. Levi (1988) and North (1990) offer particularly insightful views of the relationship between implementation and bargaining costs (the resources needed to maintain the current system versus the resources necessary to reform the system) and the policy choices of central leaders. In addition, North emphasizes the idea that leaders do not just make policy choices to lower transaction costs. Their choices are also "path dependent"—affected by the existing institutional environment—a point that I assert throughout this study.

2. This excludes the republics of Tatarstan, Bashkortostan, and Sakha-Yakutia, which have essentially negotiated some form of single-channel tax systems in their bilateral treaties.

3. Numerous central and regional sources confirmed the successful centralization of the tax system, including interviews in Moscow with Mikhail Dmitriyev of the Carnegie Center, State Duma representative Vladimir Lysenko, and Aleksei Lavrov of the President's Analytic Center, as well as Nina Zhirnova in the Treasury Department in Samara oblast and Veniamin Alekseev, head of the Vologda oblast Tax Inspectorate. Nevertheless, a number of recent western sources still suggest that the regions retain the capability to withhold revenue transfers (Kirkow 1998), perhaps a result of outdated primary and secondary source materials when single-channel systems still existed and the periodic reports in Russian newspapers of regional leaders threatening to withhold tax payments. See, for example, the report in *Segodnya* regarding the Irkutsk governor's threat of a "tax putsch" (5 March 1997).

4. The OECD (2002, 125–6) estimates that in the 1990s, regional authorities had some substantive decision-making power over the rates and collection of only about 13 percent of all tax revenue, with local authorities affecting only 8 percent of revenues. This included taxes such as the corporate profit tax where regional

authorities had the right to add a regional percentage onto the federal tax within a federally mandated ceiling. Bikalova (2002) similarly estimates that tax sharing with federally determined rates makes up 90 percent of all tax revenue in Russia.

5. At a two-day seminar for accountants and bookkeepers that I attended in Moscow (October 15–16, 1996), State Tax Service officials tried in vain to answer the questions on interpreting the confusing and contradictory tax legislation and calculating the VAT. Many of the participants complained about the heavy fines for miscalculations and that very often, the tax officials, themselves, made the mistakes but were unwilling to reverse the fines.

6. Interviews with Veniamin Yakovlevich Alekseev, Head of the State Tax Inspectorate, Vologda oblast (15 November 1996) and Victor Yakovlevich Filionov, Head of the State Tax Inspectorate, Samara oblast (13 February 1997) confirmed their agency's dependence on the largess of regional governments. Nevertheless, the level of this support could differ tremendously, from Samara's newly constructed and heavily guarded building to Vologda's crumbling facility complete with leaking ceilings and antiquated bathrooms. See chapter 4.

7. Tatyana Veskoboynikova, interview with author, 4 February 1997. See also *Izvestiya*, 5 December 1996.

8. Mikhail Dmitriyev, interview with author, 28 October 1996.

9. The government had similar problems monitoring these banks in the distribution of budgetary funds for wage and other payments of state workers.

10. According to the Ministry of the Economy, only thirteen regions could cover 85 percent or more of their expenditures without transfers from the federal government in 1997 (Laikam and Sharamova 1998, 12).

11. In 1998, with further minor improvements in subsequent years, the Finance Ministry reformed the FFRS formula, significantly improving its ability to base transfers on fiscal capacity rather than on expenditure levels. Yet the lack of accurate data on regional tax bases as opposed to actual revenue collection data means that regions still have a disincentive to increase tax collection rates since that will correspondingly decrease transfer amounts (Martinez-Vazquez and Boex 2001, 58–9).

12. In 1998 and 1999, thirteen regions did not receive transfers.

13. The Russian press and scholarly journals have given enormous attention to the issue of wage and budgetary arrears. See, in particular, the newspapers, *Segodnya* and *Finansoviye izvestiya* and the journal, *Finansi*.

14. Shleifer and Treisman (2000) provide an excellent overview of the failure of tax reform in Russia. They argue that rather than coopting either regional or business leaders, the government angered both groups and "drove them into each other's arms" (153).

15. Observers have decried the addition of the regional sales tax as yet another tax on consumers. Russia already has a 20 percent VAT, excise taxes, and a 5 percent turnover tax (OECD Observer, January 1999).

16. I thank Alan Tarr for emphasizing this point to me.

17. According to Vladimir Pantsirev, a journalist in Vologda oblast, Russians refer to this phenomenon as "Trishkin's caftan," coming from a popular fable in which Trishkin attempts to repair a hole in his jacket by ripping off a piece elsewhere, only to have to repair a new hole.

18. According to Mikhail Filippov and Olga Shvetsova (1999), initial treaty ne-

gotiations with Tatarstan and Bashkortostan began even before the collapse of the Soviet Union.

19. This section on the Tatarstan Treaty draws heavily from Lysenko (1995), Chapter 3.

20. Lysenko's concern for the constitutional, rather than economic, implications of the Tatarstan agreements may, in part, arise from his position as a legal scholar and member of the Russian parliament's committee for the development of federal relations.

21. More recently, the agreements of the 1994–96 treaties have been published in several sources including Guboglo (1997). The Web page, http://www.cityline.ru/politika/reg/dogovory.html, also includes some of the texts of the bilateral treaties and agreements.

22. Spain, for example, first established framework legislation for its asymmetrical bilateral treaties. See chapter 7.

23. See chapter 5 for a detailed discussion and comparison of the Bryansk, Vologda, and Samara treaties and agreements.

24. Vladimir Gel'man (1996) refers to the treaties as "bestowed" (*zhalovannie*) documents as part of a "federalism of advantages" (*foralisticheskii federalizm*). He takes the latter term from Daniel Elazar (1993).

25. More specifically, the president signs the official treaty while the prime minister signs the individual agreements.

26. In her book, *Autocracy in the Provinces* (1996), Valerie Kivelson describes the relationship between the tsar and the town governors that bears a remarkable resemblance to contemporary politics. The governor "was endowed with tremendous power on the local scene as the envoy of the tsar himself and of the central chancellery system, but the governor's ability to abuse that power posed a threat to central control. Fearing the governors' tendency to turn the provinces into their own feeding troughs, the *state simultaneously conferred great authority on them and hobbled them with requirements to refer all decision making to the center* (134, italics my own).

27. In one of the most infamous examples of the administration's flawed regional policy, Yeltsin removed Rossel' from his post as Head of Administration of Sverdlovsk following his apparent disloyalty during the 1993 parliamentary crisis. Two years later, the citizens of Sverdlovsk voted Rossel' back into office, leaving Yeltsin powerless to remove him. Adhering to the adage, "if you can't beat 'em, join 'em," Yeltsin sought a rapprochement with the bellicose governor, hoping to avoid similar embarrassments.

28. Vladimir Lysenko, interview with author, 25 October 1996.

29. Interview with author, 25 October 1996

CHAPTER 4

Institutional Legacies and Regional Choices

Following the completion of the first Treaty to Demarcate Powers between the Russian central government and the Republic of Tatarstan in 1994, the center and the regions tacitly acknowledged bilateralism as the primary, albeit temporary, means to establish the rules of federalism in the absence of comprehensive federal legislation. As the 1993 Constitution had been approved through a popular referendum, bilateral agreements served an important state-building function for the center as a replacement for subnational ratification of the constitution.[1] Moreover, the agreements facilitated the delineation of resources and powers too specific and localized to be addressed in a single federal document.

Yeltsin signed treaties with slightly more than half of Russia's regions in a period of only four years. As such, these treaties represent one period in the ongoing narrative of federal development in Russia. Yet however brief, this four-year period offered the first opportunity for most regions to develop, negotiate, and implement their own ideas for federal reform. Traditional forums for expressing and negotiating regional interests in a federation proved ineffective during Russia's first democratic decade. The upper chamber, the Federation Council, had limited powers and did not meet frequently enough to allow the necessary coalition building and legislative bargaining to actively promote regional agendas; weak political parties only exacerbated this problem. Regional elites were also unfamiliar with the consensus building and multilateral bargaining dynamics associated with the institutions of democratic federalism. Consequently, the majority of regional elites endorsed the center's goals for bilateralism. Many leaders, such as Samara's governor, Konstantin Titov, expressed skepticism about the process as a replacement for intergovernmental reform legislation, but they viewed bilateralism as an opportunity to ease the costs of doing business with the center by institutionalizing their own designs for federal relations and the division of power. Bilateralism also reinforced the regions' belief that since the collapse of the Soviet Union, the center was no longer strong enough to determine the rules of Russian federalism. With the tax and budgetary codes languishing in the Duma, and public sector arrears and debt rising precariously, the center appeared incapable of fulfilling its fiduciary duties to the subnational governments or to its citizens. The successes of Tatarstan, Sakha, and Sverdlovsk in negotiating their treaties signaled to other provinces that the chance to mold the balance of power and resources in their favor had arrived.

Although these initial treaties provided an objective for other republics and provinces, regional elites did not possess a clear road map to formulating and negotiating such agreements. The Tatarstan and Sakha treaties might have established the absolute boundaries of the bilateral process—comprehensive political autonomy was obviously off the negotiating table—but the center had not instituted further ground rules. Without rules to govern the process, regional elites, the majority of whom had received their political education in the Soviet bureaucracy, continued to rely upon Soviet-era strategies and modes of interacting with the center. In fact, regional leaders found that the environment of center-periphery bargaining had changed little since the Soviet collapse.

This chapter examines the negotiating arena for the bilateral treaties. Despite the opportunities to rewrite the rules of federalism that bilateralism and a weakened center offered, not all regions were equally placed to take advantage of them. Even in the Soviet system, regions had varying relationships with the center based on economic structure and clientelistic ties, as I discuss in Chapter 2. Under Yeltsin, these differences across the federation only intensified as the possibilities to devolve power grew. The complex bureaucratic structure, which had hardly changed after the Soviet collapse, and the dominance of the executive branch at all levels of the federation created a playing field in which the economic and political resources of a province determined its bargaining agenda and negotiating strategies with the central government.[2]

The Soviet legacy of bureaucratic complexity produced a costly environment for intergovernmental relations and reform. Regional leaders had to depend on their own capabilities and resources to determine and achieve their reform goals under a system of bilateral bargaining. Local revenue provided funds to pay the costs of negotiations, including information gathering, personnel, and side payments for cooperation. Yet regional wealth, even in light of the fiscal weakness of the center, did not directly confer bargaining advantages. Regional leaders had to develop agendas and strategies that could exploit the economic asymmetries between the federal and subnational government or locate other potential sources of leverage. The primary responsibility for consolidating and exercising these bargaining advantages rested with top regional leadership. The legacy of executive dominance at the federal and subnational levels meant that a governor's durability and effectiveness served as the principal means to translate economic resources into bargaining power through the development of comprehensive agendas and the ability to negotiate them with the federal government. No region automatically received special privileges or authority as a result of its economic resources, size, or political proclivities. Instead, the bilateral system and the complex bargaining environment tested the organization skills of regional leaders, further differentiating between the regional haves and have-nots.

THE REGIONAL RESPONSE TO BILATERALISM

A system of bilateralism meant that the responsibility to improve and consolidate a region's position relative to the center rested on its ability to formulate plans and consolidate its resources. To construct a bilateral reform agenda, regional governments needed to gather and coordinate information from public and private sources, a task that required effective governmental oversight and cooperation among regional agencies and businesses. Answers to the most basic questions that comprised the bilateral agreements, such as development goals, financial resources, economic problems, and influential political concerns, demanded a comprehensive understanding of the socio-economic situation in the province. Consequently, regional elites needed to consolidate a vast amount of information previously unrecorded or dispersed among a variety of institutions and groups. Despite the sizable bureaucracy, Soviet officials were notoriously poor record-keepers, often falsifying or concealing information for political gain or security.[3] Information was often "compartmentalized" by ministries and sectors of the economy, with data rarely consolidated at the central level, let alone at the subnational level (Bahry 1987, 161). Very few regional statistics were published, other than some budgetary and investment data of questionable accuracy (Bahry 1987, 7). The lack of computerization in the Soviet Union did not improve the standards of documentation, a problem scarcely eased by the Soviet collapse. Even in the financial departments of regional administrations, computers were rare, with two and three phones often taking their place.[4]

Without access to computers and functioning regional information agencies,[5] regional administrations had to take a much more hands-on and time-consuming approach in gathering information. Government officials often sought close working relationships with political and economic elites to enhance their access to information and to coordinate and unify development goals and strategies among private and public enterprises. Katherine Stoner-Weiss (1997) convincingly demonstrates in *Local Heroes* that close ties among elites, particularly in concentrated regional economies, produced more effective government policies—including intergovernmental reform plans—and implementation than in more loosely organized regions. For example, regional governments depended on their territorial branch of the State Tax Service (STS), a federal agency, to provide information on revenue collection, tax debtors, and the financial health of regional enterprises, all of which supplied the basis for fiscal agreements for the center. In Samara, this information supported the agreements on interbudgetary mechanisms and defense conversion, among others. The data played a particularly important role in the issue of excise taxes, in which Samara sought to increase its profits from the sale of oil and gas from the region through the bilateral treaty.[6] Viktor Filonov, the director of the STS in Samara, alerted the administration that revenue receipts were falling in the region, primarily because of the Yukos oil company. The company had centralized operations in Moscow, eliminating Samara's access to its tax revenues.[7] Using this information, Samara's administration began a campaign to change the division of profits from oil and gas revenues so as to return Samara's share.

Regional administrations relied on traditional methods of collaboration to ensure STS assistance in increasing revenue collection and monitoring enterprises, including weekly meetings and constant phone calls. Yet regional governments also provided valuable resources to the tax agencies, which are severely underfunded by the federal government.[8] In Khanti-Mansiisky Autonomous Oblast, the regional government used specifically targeted budgetary funds and off-budgetary funds to supplement the STS's federal funding (Treisman 1999). Table 4.1 suggests that Samara and, to a much lesser extent, Vologda devoted significant budgetary resources to support their territorial branches of the federal STS, increasing the interdependence between agency and subnational governmental elites.

The Bryansk branch of the STS received only 60 percent of its federal funding in 1996. With the agency unable to pay its workers on time and in full, many of the specialists left for the private sector, and other employees became prime targets for bribes and corruption.[9] Without the resources and personnel in the STS to monitor local enterprises, the Bryansk government turned to private auditing firms to help the government root out hidden profits. In Vologda, the tax service worked out of a squalid old building with a leaky roof and antiquated bathrooms. Its chief inspector donned a uniform to give the agency an appearance, albeit outdated, of professionalism, bolstered by the Jeep Cherokee that the government provided to him. The Samara tax service offers a stark contrast to that of Vologda and Bryansk. In a sparkling new building with tight security and comfortable offices complete with computers, the STS

Table 4.1
Regional Budgetary Funding to Tax Agencies

	Funding to STS (1996)*	Funding to tax police (1996)*
Bryansk	--------	300,000 rubles
Vologda	6,000,000 rubles	1,200,000
Samara*	22,557,000	4,511,430

Source: 1996 consolidated budgets of Bryansk, Vologda, and Samara *oblasts.*

*Samara funding is from 1995 budgetary figures in 1996 prices.

in Samara reflected the busy, professional air of the regional administration. The head of the tax inspectorate, Viktor Filonov, admitted that since the end of 1995, Samara's government had supplemented the center's payments to the agency for wages and administration, in addition to providing the new offices and equipment. Consequently, he argued, the STS managed to keep the most skilled workers and minimize corruption, enabling the region to rank sixth in Russia in tax collection.

The close working relationships among governmental agencies in many regions extended to private businesses. Although the STS and the administration joined resources to crack down on tax evaders, the regional government also sometimes intervened on the behalf of enterprises to prevent bankruptcy or to reschedule debt payments. A close relationship with businesses, particularly large Soviet-era industries with a powerful impact on the region's economy, provided a wide range of benefits for both sides. For companies such as AvtoVAZ in Samara, the largest Russian automaker, or Severstal', Vologda's metallurgy plant with more than fifty thousand employees, financial and political support from the regional government might spell the difference between survival and bankruptcy, with the potential for enormous social and economic upheaval in the region. Samara's governor, for example, intervened with the STS and the VChK, the emergency committee on tax collection formed in late 1996, to prevent bankruptcy proceedings for AvtoVAZ resulting from its eleven trillion rubles in tax arrears and fines. In Tatarstan, President Shaimiyev successfully negotiated with the central government to remove the region's large automaker, Kamaz, from the official bankruptcy list.

Regional governments also provided guarantees for domestic and international bank loans, a conduit for ties to international investors and Western aid, and specialists to aid a business in the transition to market relations and with new regulations. In return, enterprise directors provided financial support for regional leaders in election campaigns and offered their political support. Enterprise directors could influence the voting preferences of their employees through surviving Soviet-era institutional arrangements, such as on-site union representatives and employee rallies for candidates. Business elites also used their influence in the media to endorse candidates or support government policies. In Vologda, a powerful financial-industrial group of Severstal' and its bank, Metkombank (*Metallurgicheskii kombinat bank*), owned the majority of local print and television media outlets, giving the company an immediate mode of communicating its opinion about the regional government. The control of the media by financial-industrial groups at the regional level matched a tendency at the national level, as with the ownership by Media-Most of the television station *NTV* and the newspaper *Segodnya*, among others. Furthermore, dominant businesses controlled seats in the regional legislature, providing valuable votes for the administration's political agenda and development plans. Because few lawmakers at the subnational level have full-time political posts, they often continued working in their jobs in the private sector or in other professions such as teaching or even in municipal governments. Vologda's Severstal'-Metkombank legislative group consisted of nineteen of the thirty deputies in 1996, with four deputies working directly for Severstal' and fifteen working for organizations or companies that the financial-industrial group owned in whole or in part.[10]

Like the services of economic elites, close cooperation also helped political leaders to establish more comprehensive, detailed, and unified development plans for their region—the starting point for intergovernmental bargaining. Stoner-Weiss (1997) suggests that economic concentration and "the resulting consensus over political goals ... facilitated cooperative relations such that key organized economic interests participated in policy formation and used their authority to ensure the implementation of economic development programs" (189). Regional development plans and the reorganization of key industries were usually inseparable, as these companies produced a majority of the revenue and jobs in the economy. In Nizhny Novgorod, reform plans and investment agreements with the center focused on military conversion programs, whereas in Sakha, plans emphasized the control and reorganization of the diamond industry. In Vologda, the administration's plans for economic growth included the formation of several financial-industrial groups around the major industries, such as the timber processing plants, which would provide the foundation for the eventual incorporation of the region. These conglomerates also facilitated the formulation and implementation of federal programs, such as the bilateral agreement on the forestry sector (Vologda 1996).[11]

Regardless of the benefits of cooperative relations among subnational elites, a region's economic structure still served as the departure point for constructing an intergovernmental agenda for fiscal reform. The emphasis on local resources meant that the wealth and natural resources of a region determined the *opportunities* for fiscal independence and decentralization of decision-making. Elite consensus and interaction, however, enabled a region to forge an agenda that reflected these opportunities by fostering the exchange of information and ensuring a commitment to the regional reform program and the implementation of bilateral agreements. Once the leadership of a region managed to draft its agenda, its economic base again provided the resources with which to guide the plans successfully through the central bureaucracy. At this stage as well, how the subnational government chose to exploit these resources determined the strategies and choices of bilateral negotiations.

NEGOTIATING WITH THE CENTER: NAVIGATING THE BUREAUCRACY

The bilateral treaties and agreements covered a wide array of topics and financial issues. Although the treaties needed only the signature of the regional governor and the Russian president, the bilateral agreements, which specify jurisdiction, financial control, and responsibilities, required a larger number of official authorizations before they reached the prime minister's desk. Negotiation of these agreements sometimes demanded months, even years, of joint committees, drafts, phone calls, and meetings. The bureaucratic complexities and ill-defined rules of negotiation share many similarities with the Soviet bureaucratic minefield. A vast number of central institutions could take up regional appeals and had some measure of authority over their claims, as Bahry (1987) describes. Yet the lack of clarity of jurisdictional boundaries between institutions meant that if no one wished to deal with their claim directly, regional officials would receive conflicting answers or were passed from bureaucracy to bureaucracy. Regional leaders needed time and effort to take advantage of personal connections and to ensure the implementation of any central decision. According to Bahry, the enormous number of potential "patrons" in the center meant that a region rarely gained significant advantage over other regions through a single, well-placed colleague. Success in gaining financial assistance depended more on the persistence of subnational elites and their focus on issues of particular importance to the region.

The convoluted organization of public bureaucracies only marginally improved in post-Soviet Russia. As illustrated in chapter 3, the centralized bureaucracies constituted a complex environment of rules and norms, in which the high costs of negotiating and implementing agreements favored those actors with the resources to overcome these transaction costs. Because the bilateral process placed the burden on regions to develop their own agendas for intergovernmental reform, regional leaders had to rely on local resources to ensure the cooperation of central elites. Moreover, subnational elites needed to decide how best to target their resources: to focus on securing guarantees from the center to implement prevailing fiscal promises, or to attempt to bargain new institutional rules—an even more costly process. The revision of intergovernmental rules required more onerous negotiations, involving a larger number of central officials and bureaucracies and risking stronger opposition. Without the economic and political resources to navigate this system successfully, some regional leaders focused on marginal improvements to the existing fiscal relationship. Other leaders, such as in Vologda, seeing little opportunity for change within the system of bilateral treaties, looked for alternative means of increasing their autonomy from the federal government.

The arduous journey of an agreement on investment activity typified the complexity of the bilateral negotiation process.[12] Once the regional government drafted the document, it went to a variety of federal ministries and committees, depending on the contents of the document. An investment agreement required at least the approval of the Ministry of International Economic Relations (MVES) regarding issues of international investment; the Ministry of the Economy; and the Ministry of Finance regarding issues of fiduciary responsibility and financial flows. If the agreement addressed federal investment in specific areas, federal institutions such as the Ministry of Industry, the State Committee on the Support and Development of Small Businesses, and the Ministry of Construction, for example, might also have had a say in the final document. The draft agreement needed to reach not only these bureaucracies, but also the proper bureaucratic officials. A bureaucrat too low in the institutional hierarchy presented little chance of negotiating and getting final approval for the agreement from the minister or deputy minister. Personal connections and an opportunity to deliver the document personally to the top ministry officials offered the best chance for rapid approval, assuming the agreement did not get lost among the myriad documents awaiting the minister's attention.

The transition to market capitalism, however, created alternatives for regional governments to reach the necessary federal officials. A new breed of lobbyists provided services to guide an agreement through the necessary bureaucratic channels, using personal connections and paying any "fees" to get the document to the approval stage. The lobbyists were often former government elites or even current state employees working in lobbying "institutes" within particular agencies, such as the Security Council.[13] An analyst at the Gaidar Institute for the Economy in Transition describes the process:

A representative from the Economic Ministry of Khabardino-Balkaria came to us at the Gaidar Institute to request help in getting them a particular program. We worked for them as lobbyists,[14] and for that we received a lot of money. This meant getting their official appeal (*obrashenie*) to the right people. It must always follow the same path: from the Ministry of the Economy, to the Ministry of Finance, to the government. There must be a consensus among all three for there to be an official government resolution (*postanovlenie*) and the program to come into being. So this means they—or we, in this case—must know people at each stage and each stage costs money. Of course, the proposed program must have some merit; you must have some basis to argue that it's worthwhile. Maybe this is corruption, but that's the way it is. Nevertheless, there are documents showing each stage of the process in the two ministries and the government. It's just a matter of getting to see them, but it's all official. Sometimes it's purely bribery, with no paperwork, but that's not most of the time and that really costs a lot of money. Basically, this is the way the system is going to be—this type of corruption, personal contacts, et cetera. Until there is real economic improvement, this is the way it will be.[15]

Despite their knowledge of such services, none of the regional officials in my study admitted to availing themselves of professional lobbyists.[16] Whether the cost of employing them was prohibitively high, or the administrations had faith in their established ties and resources to achieve their goals, all of them claimed to rely upon traditional methods of pursuing their intergovernmental reform agendas. If so, regional elites in Samara, Bryansk, Vologda, and elsewhere, confronted equally complex routes through the central bureaucracy to negotiate their agreements and development programs. Relying on their own personnel, regional governments had three options to navigate the bureaucracy. First, regions could establish positions in the administration to focus solely or primarily on the negotiation of the federal programs and bilateral agreements. Although this option offered obvious benefits to the regional government by concentrating efforts in one office, it demanded that the administration steer valuable resources away from other government agencies and programs. Not only did such a position need funds for equipment and wages, but it also required a representative office in Moscow or funds for frequent trips to the capital for meetings. Moreover, the person in such a position had to be a close associate of the governor's, knowledgeable about the primary goals and interests of the region, and trusted to negotiate this agenda on the federal level.

Overburdened with expenditures and bereft of skilled personnel, many subnational governments simply lacked the resources to devote solely to the negotiation of bilateral agreements. Instead, administrations relied on existing positions and departments to handle the bureaucratic complexities of negotiating with the center. Finance departments, which maintained contacts with the Ministry of Finance bureaucrats to handle the daily problems of intergovernmental finance and budgetary relations, helped to form joint committees to work out the specifics of financing the bilateral agreements. In addition, as the bilateral agreements often addressed implementation problems of current fiscal relations, such as the Vologda interbudgetary agreement, the two goals became intertwined. Negotiations between the Vologda finance department and the Ministry of Finance focused on increasing regional revenue share and on the federal debt to Vologda, both of which the interbudgetary agreement addressed.[17] Other agreements—conversion, property ownership, natural resource control—relied on similar intergovernmental bureaucratic contacts to handle some of the specifics.

But as noted, final approval for a bilateral agreement or development program required the attention of more senior bureaucrats and politicians. Regional administrations thus depended on the most senior political officials to handle at least the final stages of the negotiations. The governor and head of the legislature often used their political posts in Moscow as the regional representatives to the Federation Council to advance the regional agenda. An article on the prominent position of Samara's governor in the Federation Council points out that the role of governor and that of senator could often be at odds with one another. Yet in the case of Governor Titov, the author remarks, the governor always won out over the senator (*Samarskiye izvestiya*, 9 March 1996). Committee assignments gave leaders frequent access to top bureaucrats and offered opportunities to present bilateral documents for approval and establish joint commissions to work out any disagreements. As head of the influential budgetary and finance committee in the Federation Council, Samara's governor maintained frequent contact with top finance and economic ministry officials, giving him ample opportunity to address his region's agenda and, as I will discuss, link this agenda with the passage of fiscal legislation. Other posts might have facilitated the negotiation of specific agreements but be of lesser use to the overall agenda, such as the position of Stepan Ponasev of Bryansk on the social affairs committee or Gennadi Khripel of Vologda on the international affairs committee.

Although the governor usually played the leading role in bilateral negotiations, some regions trusted members of the State Duma to promote the their agenda. Unlike the Federation Council, the lower house remains in session throughout the year, giving its members a more constant presence in Moscow during their political tenure. Duma representatives, particularly those serving their second terms, had the potential to establish more enduring bureaucratic contacts, based on repeated and frequent interaction.[18] Vologda's representative, Vladimir Lopatin, used his political ties in Moscow to pursue the region's bilateral agenda with the center.[19] Despite an antagonistic relationship with Vologda's first governor, Nikolai Podgornov, Lopatin continued to negotiate for more funds and to work out a bilateral treaty, a process that became more fruitful with the election of a new governor. Some Duma members' committee assignments provided bureaucratic contacts in addition to those of Federation Council members. For example, whereas Samara's deputies served on the economic policy, budget, natural resource, and defense committees, offering a wide range of contacts, deputies from Bryansk belonged to the veteran's support and labor committees, providing only marginally useful links and still failing to offer access to the crucial finance and economic ministries.

Regional governments called on a wide array of resources—political elites, economic leaders, and bureaucratic networks—for assistance with navigating the complex bureaucracy. The sheer number of potential participants on both sides of the negotiating process necessitated a unified vision and strategy to achieve regional goals, however. Regional leaders had to assess their resources to determine their goals for development and their strategies to achieve them. A region might have a strong tax base of valuable natural resources, but without the support of key interests and the means to harness information and personnel, the economic resources became meaningless to the intergovernmental bargaining agenda.

EXECUTIVE LEADERSHIP

The very structure of the bilateral treaties, signed by the Russian president (or by the prime minister, in the case of agreements) and the regional governor, emphasized the primacy of the executive branch in federal relations. Although many of the treaties addressed budgetary issues, the domain of the legislative branch, legislative approval was not necessary for the bilateral agreements to enter into force. As explained in chapter 3, the dominance of executive leadership derives from the long history of Russian authoritarianism, with new democratic institutions only beginning to acquire some decision-making power. The enormity of the Russian economic crisis, coupled with ongoing ideological and jurisdictional conflicts between the Duma and President Yeltsin, lent support to calls for a strong leader, willing and able to put Russia's house in order. Yeltsin, too, saw the executive branch as the foundation for federal relations and reform. Drawing on the example of the Soviet Communist Party hierarchy, Yeltsin sought to establish a "presidential vertical" between levels of government, empowering regional executives to the detriment of legislative bodies.

Yet Yeltsin based the design for the executive branch hierarchy on appointed regional leaders; elected governors threatened the supremacy of the federal government—the very foundation of the plan. As regions conducted gubernatorial elections through 1996 and 1997, governors combined their institutional powers, which the center bestowed upon them, with a newfound democratic legitimacy. The enhanced powers and expanded aims of regional leaders aside, Yeltsin preferred to concentrate federal relations in the executive branch, paradoxically regarding legislatures as radical threats to democratic and economic reform. Moreover, the problems between Yeltsin and the 450-member Duma also suggested that compromise was more likely among a few individuals within the executive branch than between large and potentially divided legislative bodies.

The concentration of powers in the regional head of administration burdened him or her with enormous responsibilities. The rapid decentralization of expenditures without corresponding revenues[20] and the lack of effective national reform programs meant that the governor was entrusted with stabilizing the region's economy, improving the living standards of its citizens, and negotiating reform plans with the federal government. Clearly, some governors confronted more intractable problems than others owing to differences in economic structure; Bryansk, with its idle chemical-weapons production facilities and farms made toxic from Chernobyl fallout, suffered more acute problems than did Sakha, with its large reserves of oil and diamonds. But the majority of regions shared a desperate need for fundamental economic reforms of outdated and oversized industries and unproductive agriculture and the addressing of environmental hazards. Even Sakha, with its valuable resources, confronted the transportation, food, and social problems associated with a sparsely populated, enormous territory with a harsh climate and an underdeveloped infrastructure. Further, no regional leader could address the problems of reform without examining the issues of intergovernmental relations, regardless of whether his plans placed more emphasis on the federal pocketbook or the rulebook.

Regions without leadership turnover had the best chance of successfully developing reform plans and negotiating with the central government. Some of the best-known cases of successful regional reform and powerful bargaining with the center have occurred in regions with strong leaders who have survived the economic downturns and political windstorms at the center: Yuri Luzhkov in Moscow, Boris Nemtsov in Nizhni Novgorod,[21] Mintimir Shaymiyev in Tatarstan, and Eduard Rossel' in Sverdlovsk. With the support of the electorate and powerful economic interests in their regions, these leaders held strong bargaining chips with the center. As discussed, leaders with tight links to key industries and elites in the public and private sectors gained advantages in collecting information, cooperative problem solving, and generating support for reform plans. Cooperation among elites and popular legitimacy became mutually reinforcing: as political and economic elites jointly confronted issues of wage and pension arrears, unemployment, and investment, the public offered support by backing candidates and programs and by avoiding strikes. Social stability and popular mandate then permitted leaders to remain in office, eliminating the potential costs and dislocation caused by a new government with new policies.

Political longevity and stability had important payoffs before and during negotiations with the center. Access to information and elite consensus permitted leaders to translate development plans into concrete bilateral proposals and agreements with the center without fear of opposition from below. Consensus also provided key bargaining resources to both sides of the talks. The literature on bargaining at the firm level and at the international level asserts the importance of credible commitments and threats to bargaining one's preference successfully.[22] In the case of the governors, their ability to influence regional elites meant a credible commitment to implement agreements and to achieve the primary goal of the center for bilateralism—stability. Implementation of the bilateral agreements often required significant efforts from the regional governments. For example, all three of the agreements on interbudgetary mechanisms in my study required the regions to collect enough federal revenue to cover expenditures such as federal programs or federal institutions on the territory and to target such funds properly to take advantage of a simplified revenue distribution scheme (see chapter 5). Some of the agreements on natural resources obligated regions to establish oversight agencies and bilateral committees, or to collect information on particular areas or resources. Implementation thus required the cooperation of relevant elites and groups whose opposition might have spelled the failure of the entire agreement. Even federal programs on defense conversion, housing, or environmental issues demanded cooperation among private and public interests and usually required local and regional governments to contribute financing to the projects. In Novgorod, Governor Prosak's success in mobilizing local support among political and economic elites translated into valuable federal financial participation in his economic development programs.

Perhaps of greater importance to the federal government, strong regional leaders[23] could offer a credible commitment to political and social stability, thereby contributing to the center's principal objective for bilateralism and for the electoral concerns of the Yeltsin administration. Problems of public sector wage and pension arrears in Russia deepened in the mid-1990s; still, some regions managed to pay their state workers on time and even to provide salaries to unpaid federal workers.[24] In Samara, for example, state employees received their salaries in full and on time, providing support for the regional administration and, as a byproduct, for Yeltsin's government.[25] Adding to the nation's stability, Samara did not have any public sector strikes, even as teachers and health care workers elsewhere in Russia walked off the job in 1996 and 1997.

Luzhkov gained similar social support in Moscow by assuring that some of the tremendous wealth in his city trickled down to state workers and pensioners. In addition, timely payments gave less fodder to leftist parties such as the Communist Party of the Russian Federation during both local and national elections—a key concern of Yeltsin's government. Although communist parties still had strong support in industrial cities such as Samara and Nizhni Novgorod, the popularity of their reform-minded governors also produced electoral success for Yeltsin.

In theory, the power to offer a credible commitment through elite consensus and popular legitimacy also should have translated into the ability to provide a credible threat. Several studies of Russian federal relations from 1990 to 1994 show that threats of regional sovereignty proved very effective in garnering funds from the Yeltsin administration (Birkenes 1996; Treisman 1997). Nevertheless, in this study, regional elites expressed their loyalty to the Yeltsin government, to the unity of Russia, and to bilateral cooperation.[26] Vice Governor Nikolai Kostigov noted that Vologda's top priorities included fulfilling the economic potential of the region and working with the federal government to preserve the unity of Russia as a single state.[27] Many of the most outspoken Russian governors, including Luzhkov and Shaymiyev, also contributed to Yeltsin's success in the 1996 elections, and eschewed any declarations of political independence. This finding does not contest the conclusions of earlier studies but suggests that the rhetoric of intergovernmental relations changed in light of experience. In interviews, the examples of Chechnya and Tatarstan arose as the primary reasons for pursuing cooperative relations with the center; Chechnya represented the outcome of regional extremism and Soviet-style reactions in the center but Tatarstan represented the result of hard bargaining that led to compromise, albeit within a still-conflictual relationship.[28] Despite examples of successful threats against the center, such as when Primorski Krai's governor threatened to foment strikes of coal miners to procure federal money (Kirkow 1995), mutual commitments to national stability and to easing the costs of intergovernmental relations predominated.

The desire for career mobility also promoted cooperation for some regional politicians. In their attempt to create a typology of Russian regions by economic structure and government strategies, Vladimir Mau and Vadim Stupin suggest that regional leaders with wider political ambitions might focus more on economic and political stability and less on their own material well-being. They argue that leaders without promise of or desire for a national political career will be more willing to use their offices to enrich themselves and ensure a comfortable existence after their tenures in office (Mau and Stupin 1997, 12–13). The causal link between political ambition and corruption seems tenuous at best, but the connection between ambition and cooperative strategies appears stronger. Traditionally, national political parties have served as a means to unify the goals of central and regional elites and provide a channel for subnational leaders to move up to national leadership (Riker 1964; May 1970). Outside of political parties, subnational leaders, particularly in the executive branch, gain national recognition from successful policies and from popular support in their home state. Without strong parties to serve as links between the federal and regional level in Russia, subnational leaders could only hope to move into national politics through personal ties to prominent members of the administration, or through their own success at the regional level. For example, Boris Nemtsov, the governor of Nizhny Novgorod, whose reform policies produced economic successes and who worked in cooperation with the central government, represented a prudent choice for a political post in a reform-oriented government. Although political aspirations on a national scale certainly did not produce economic or political success on the local level, they gave a leader incentives to focus on pragmatic problem-solving in tandem with the government, rather than empty rhetoric that might not have yielded results other than the ire of central officials.

As members of the Federation Council, regional governors operated within the national political arena, providing bargaining resources even to those regional leaders without broader political ambitions. A governor's committee assignment in the Federation Council not only gave him access to top bureaucrats, as mentioned, but also offered opportunities to use bargaining strategies such as issue linkage and side payments. As head of the council, Orel Governor Yegor Stroev retained the ability to adjust the assembly's agenda or to hold up legislation as a means to influence bilateral negotiations. Similarly, Titov used his position as head of the budgetary and finance committee to link approval of items in the annual budget with government approval of bilateral agreements with Samara. National elections presented even more opportunities for negotiations and side payments through regional campaigning and participation in political parties. The governors of Samara and Novgorod participated actively in the pro-government party, *Our Home Is Russia* (NDR), that was formed for the 1996 presidential elections, giving them unique access to the party's leader, Viktor Chernomyrdin.

A strong regional executive with the capacity to draw on abundant local resources offered a region a wide range of policy options for intergovernmental reform, including the opportunity to seek more autonomy from the central government. Yet the widening fiscal crisis and uncertainty at the center compelled even those regions without economic and political advantages to reevaluate their relationships with the central government. Forced to rely on local resources, regional leaders responded to the bilateral system by developing and negotiating their own agendas and inter-governmental reform goals, thereby extending the asymmetrical system of federalism in Russia from below.

NOTES

1. Based upon Yeltsin's decree, the 1993 Constitution was ratified by a national referendum rather than legislative approval at the national and regional levels. Although fifty-eight percent of the referendum participants voted in favor of Yeltsin's draft of the constitution, fraud in many areas marred the process (Remington 1999, 46 n. 32).

2. See chapter 2 for a discussion of these institutional practices during the Soviet period and the transition to post-communism.

3. The "moral hazard" problem in Soviet bureaucracies has been well-documented. See, for example, Roeder (1993); Solnick (1998a).

4. An exception was the State Tax Service in Samara, which had computerized tax collection records.

5. The Soviets did establish territorial branches of Goskomstat, the state statistical service, which continue to operate in post-Soviet Russia. The agencies primarily serve the interests of the federal government rather than the regional administration by collecting some basic statistics on agricultural and industrial production, employment, demographics, and prices, that is then published in monthly and annual national digests on the socio-economic situation in Russia.

6. See Chapter 5.

7. Viktor Filonov, interview with author, 13 February 1997.

8. The STS is only one among many federal agencies suffering from budgetary problems. The courts similarly depend on the benevolence of regional governments to pay wages, provide equipment, and pay energy costs, creating the potential for a dangerous symbiosis between the executive and judicial branches of government.

9. Nikolai Zabavo, interview with author, 26 February 1997.

10. Vladimir Pantsirev, interview with author, 26 November 1996.

11. Nikolai Kostigov, interview with author, 2 December 1996.

12. Information about the negotiations comes from government officials in Samara, particularly Vyacheslav Aronin, head of the administration's finance department, and Denislyam Yancheren. Nikolai Kostigov, vice-governor of Vologda oblast, and Vadim Stupin of the Gaidar Institute were also particularly helpful in describing this process. The example of the investment agreement serves as an illustration and does not reflect the exact circumstances of the negotiations of that agreement.

13. Nikolai Kostigov, interview with author, 2 December 1996.

14. Stupin maintained that these individuals were not lobbyists in the Western sense because they acted only as "guides" for the documents rather than advocates of particular issues or ideologies. Lacking a more accurate job title, however, I have kept the term "lobbyist" as its closest English equivalent.

15. Vadim Stupin, interview with author, 21 October 1996.

16. Some regional administrators, perhaps regarding lobbyists as corrupt officials or fearing such conclusions by a foreign interviewer, might have chosen not to disclose their use of such services.

17. Zoya Mayorova, interview with author, 22 November 1996.

18. Robert Axelrod (1984), for example, discusses the importance of repeated, or iterated, interactions for cooperation.

19. Nikolai Kostigov, interview with author, 2 December 1996.

20. See chapters 2 and 3 for more in-depth discussions of these problems.

21. Nemtsov remained governor until 1997, when he was appointed deputy minister in the Russian government.

22. See, for example, Schelling (1960), Young (1975), Hopmann (1996).

23. For lack of better terminology, I am using "strong leaders" to denote governors who can influence the preferences of local economic and political elites so they match, or at least do not conflict with, the preferences of the regional administration.

24. I do not wish to suggest that the ability to pay wages and pensions is purely a measure of leadership qualities; clearly, it relies to some degree on economic resources and the level of economic crisis. Nevertheless, as my discussion of the Vologda case will show, wage and pension arrears also arose as a result of inefficient administration and ill-conceived or poorly implemented budgets.

25. Tatyana Voskoboynikova, interview with author, 4 February 1997.

26. See, for example, Governor Pozgalev's article in the special issue of Federalizm on Vologda oblast (1997, 17–40).

27. Nikolai Kostigov, interview with author, 2 December 1996.

28. Ironically, Tatarstan's president used the threat of non-cooperation (without any declarations of independence) to negotiate a more advantageous treaty with the center (Lysenko 1995). In my interviews, however, elites used the Tatarstan example as a reason for cooperation rather than as a successful use of threats.

CHAPTER 5

Intergovernmental Reform: Setting the Agenda

In 1996, Russian opinion polls depicted an electorate that increasingly blamed President Yeltsin and the federal government for the deepening fiscal crisis in the country. Regional and local officials, however, bore the primary responsibility and capability for addressing the pressing problems of their constituents: wage and pension arrears, employment, housing, and the maintenance of an adequate standard of living. They were presented with the daunting task of creating some measure of stability in their regions in the face of tremendous social and economic upheaval and a chaotic but potentially powerful central government. As regional leaders hammered out plans for local economic reform, they also needed to determine how to delineate rights and responsibilities between levels of government so as to implement these plans. No one wanted to preserve the current system, in which a region's fiscal health depended on unreliable budgetary financing from the center. Yet to negotiate new bilateral fiscal rules, regional leaders had to reconceive the balance of power between center and periphery and determine how a bilateral treaty with the center could accomplish this new conception of federalism.

Chapters 5 and 6 examine three provinces—Samara, Vologda, and Bryansk—and their attempts to reconfigure their bilateral relationships with the center. The center agreed to negotiate with all three regions, yet they emerged from the process with starkly different documents that created unique sets of intergovernmental rules. Whereas Samara negotiated agreements that shifted significant fiscal rights and responsibilities to the subnational level, Bryansk agreed upon a bilateral arrangement that maintained but codified the center's fiscal role in the region's development.

Vologda also sought to increase the region's fiscal rights, yet the balance of power still gave the center a strong role in guiding the future of the region and Russia as a whole. What explains the differences among these provinces?

If we look at the level of wealth[1] of each of these regions in the tables 5.1[2] and 5.2,[3] it seems to correlate to the level of fiscal decentralization the region seeks from the center. Samara, for example, had a level of income and revenue well above Russia's average. It also bargained with the center to decentralize significant fiscal decision-making powers to the subnational level. Yet before we assume simply that the wealthy regions had the resources to get wealthier, we need to understand how regional resources influenced the formation of intergovernmental rules. Putnam (1993) argues for an approach that examines the process, or path dependence, of institutional design and performance, suggesting that the links between socioeconomic factors and outcomes are not nearly so clear. Complex factors, such as social context and historical development, may alter the interaction between variables. In her study of Russia's regional gov-

Table 5.1
Revenue Per Capita (in thousands of rubles)

	1993	1996
Russia Fed.	149,828	2,172.1
Samara	216,137	2,283.4
Vologda	167,504	1,881.3
Bryansk	88,057	1,091.8

Table 5.2
Average Monthly Wage (in thousands of rubles)

	1993	1996
Russia Fed.	102.4	875.9
Samara	116.4	1014.2
Vologda	98.8	955.7
Bryansk	61.4	532.5

ernments, Stoner-Weiss (1997) also looks at the complex relationship between economic development and institutional performance. She
concludes that the level of economic consensus and interdependence
generates opportunities for collective action and improves the effectiveness of regional governments. A variety of economic and political factors
might act as intervening variables and thus affect the relationship between
wealth and institutional outcomes.

The interdependence between fiscal resources and the intergovernmental relationship provides a second caveat to the issue of causality. As regional elites negotiated bilateral arrangements with the center, they were
operating in an institutional environment already structured in part according to levels of income and revenue. By 1994, regions were receiving
federal transfers from the Fund for Regional Support, based upon a measure of revenue and expenditure levels. Only a handful of regions did not
qualify as "needy" or "very needy" of these transfers. Moreover, many of
the regions that qualified for transfers had depended heavily on subsidies
throughout the Soviet period, due to large numbers of failing state industries or a large agricultural sector. As a result, regions did not enter
into the bilateral negotiating process from a *tabula rasa;* they responded to
and bargained from preexisting and diverse fiscal relationships with the
center.

This chapter examines the draft bilateral treaties and regional and federal development programs in Samara, Vologda, and Bryansk as the
"starting points" of the bilateral negotiating process following the 1993
Constitution.[4] These documents, along with observations from regional
administration officials, offer insights into the agendas for intergovernmental reform. How did economic resources and existing fiscal relationships affect the regions' goals of reconstructing the balance of power with
the center? Rather than assuming that all regions sought the same type of
relationship with the center, we need to ask to what extent regions wanted
control over the "rulebook" or "pocketbook" (Putnam 1993, 23), and why
their agendas may have differed. Only then can we address the negotiation processes and investigate the abilities of these three regions to achieve
their goals.

SAMARA AND THE "DONOR" REGIONS

As it entered into bilateral negotiations with the center, Samara strongly
identified itself as one of the donor regions within the Russian Federation.
In 1996, the ten regions, including Moscow and St. Petersburg ("cities of
federal significance"), Tiumen, Sverdlovsk, Novgorod, Volgograd, Nizhny
Novgorod and Krasnoyarsk oblasts, Khanty-Mansiisky okrug, and the
republic of Sakha-Yakutia, generated more than 50 percent of Russia's

total revenue. The profile of most of these regions mirrors that of Samara—oblasts (with the exception of the republic of Sakha and the autonomous okrug, Khanty-Mansiisky), whose economies rely on industry and manufacturing rather than raw materials (excluding Sakha, Khanty-Mansiisky, Tiumen, and Krasnoyarsk). In addition to structural similarities, the donors share a dissatisfaction with their burdensome role as provider for Russia's 79 other regions. In a special section of the magazine, *Rossisskaya federatsiya* (October 1995, 19), entitled «*Region krupnym planom*» ("Region with a major plan"), Samara's governor, Konstantin Titov, compared the role of the donor regions in Russia's economy to that of a freight train's locomotive: "The coal from the fast-moving locomotive is loaded onto another [locomotive], which still hasn't begun to produce steam and is inadequately manned. The result? The first locomotive slows down and the second doesn't gather the necessary speed."

As a small but wealthy group, the donor regions have exercised considerable power in the national arena, particularly within the Federation Council. Within this legislative body responsible for constitutional change, the donors have lobbied for reforms that would grant donor regions fiscal privileges as a reward for their economic productivity and as an incentive for other regions to improve their fiscal health. According to Governor Titov, the donor regions comprise an "elite category," whose members should have the right, for example, to finance federal programs through the local branch of the federal treasury rather than waiting for the funds to go through Moscow. In addition, they should retain 60 to 70 percent of their tax revenue, rather than the 50 percent in the existing revenue-sharing arrangements (*Samarskie obozrenie*, 28 October 1996). The growing federal fiscal crisis in the mid-1990s only increased the power and outspokenness of the donors. As economic problems decreased their numbers—Nizhny Novgorod, once the regional darling of Western investors and economic advisors, began to accept federal transfers in 1997—the donor regions also emphasized local economic efficacy as a counterpoint to the failures of the federal government and as a justification for increased fiscal independence for the donor regions. In a meeting of the Federation Council's committee on the budget, tax policy, and finance to discuss the 1997 draft budget, Governor Titov, the committee's chairman, noted that the donor regions carry a double burden—they must "conscientiously transfer revenues into the federal budget and must support local branches of federal institutions . . . We can't allow that federal workers don't have salaries and social welfare support, that monuments of national cultural significance are falling apart, and therefore we have to spend resources [on federal expenditures] that are intended for improving the lives of the people of our region" (*Vlast' v Rossii*, 44, 1996).

Without explicit sanctions to prevent budget deficits or rewards for fiscal discipline, the redistribution policies of the center gave regions few incentives to reduce federal transfers. Transfer amounts from the Fund for Regional Support were based on the ability of local revenues to cover expenditures, regardless of the size and scope of regional budgetary expenditures. Consequently, the donors continued to proclaim their exploited position at the mercy of greedy and incompetent financial managers. Yuri Luzhkov, Moscow's powerful mayor and the nucleus of the donor lobby, explained,

We need a new principle of formulating transfers which would explain why one region receives them and another doesn't. How are Penza, Ulyanovsk, or Kalmykia better than the position next door in Samara? Among them, the first ones receive transfers, and Samara oblast is one of the donors. Why? There are no gold mines in Samara, the soil is even worse than in Penza oblast, why should it feed its lackadaisical neighbors? Transfers are necessary only in exceptional circumstances, when a region is economically dependent, like Tuva, or is located in extreme climate conditions. In all the others, the leader of each Federation subject is obligated to count only on his own strength and, if things don't work out under him, then he should leave and relinquish his position for someone more talented (*Vlast' v Rossii*, 44, 1996).

Luzhkov's blunt remarks reflected the contention of the donors that their comparatively large tax bases were not simply a result of advantageous economic conditions but of efficient and effective leadership. Although chapter 6 will take up this subject in more detail as it pertains to the negotiation of fiscal rules, the efficiency argument also supported the rationale, particularly of Samara, for decentralizing fiscal control. The editor of Samara's government newspaper, *Volzhskaya Kommuna*, maintained that Titov deserved the credit for preventing the region's collapse.[5] Denislyam Yancheren, the author of Samara's bilateral treaty, agreed, noting that Samara was one of the few regions to pay pensions and wages to state workers on time and that consequently, few strikes erupted. With so much economic and political turmoil in Moscow, he argued, regions such as Samara should receive as much free reign as possible in order to conduct "normal politics" at home.[6]

In December 1996, the leaders of the donor regions issued a list of recommendations for changes to the system of interbudgetary relations. While advocating equality in budgetary matters among regions—particularly between republics and provinces—their reforms proposed to increase the reliance on and access to local tax bases, a change clearly advantageous to the populous and industrialized donor regions. These included the use of differential norms of dividing VAT revenue in the federal budget so that regions might be better able to independently finance their own expenditures, minimizing circular flows of revenues between levels of government, and the right to finance federal target programs using locally collected federal tax revenues. The federal budget should provide compensation to regions, "including the donors," for any financial losses resulting from federal decisions and decrees. In addition, the proposals included stimulating "the interests of the donor territories in the development of their own regional infrastructure and increasing their tax potential on this foundation." Although all regions should have the opportunity to exploit local tax revenues, those that must rely on federal subsidies should be subject to tighter controls. In place of transfers, federal assistance should arrive in the form of grants strictly targeted for budgetary expenditures rather than open-ended transfer payments (*Vlast' v Rossii*, December 1996, 16–17).

The goal of Samara and the other donor regions to reform the system of fiscal federalism reflected the common frustrations of wealthy states that resent the redistribution of their tax revenues to other, less productive areas of the country. Yet Samara ultimately aimed not simply to increase its available funds but to renegotiate the balance of power between center and periphery and reconfigure control over the federal purse strings. For the leadership of Samara, decentralizing control over revenues and the decisions over how to spend them and attract new revenue sources represented the most efficient means of reducing the costs of fiscal management at the regional and intergovernmental level. Federal and subnational responsibilities needed be more clearly defined, with regional expenditures more directly tied to available revenues. Most important, regions should not have to depend on the economic policies or largesse of Moscow to implement their budgets and plans for regional development. Since Samara's tax base afforded it the opportunity to do this through the localization of revenues without additional federal transfers, its reform plans reflected the goal of fiscal independence more than other, less-endowed regions.

Publicly, Samara's leaders derided the bilateral treaty process, arguing that questions of federal relations should be decided on a national level. Even Yuri Baradulin, the presidential representative to Samara, called the treaty process "a false path" from centralization to true federalism.[7] The central government, however, lacked the resources to implement the necessary changes to the system of fiscal federalism on a national level, even if it were willing to relinquish more fiscal control to the regions. Despite the lobbying on the part of the donor regions, few of their changes to the interbudgetary mechanisms were included in the 1997 budget law. Instead, the government and Duma representatives deferred the thorny issues of balancing redistribution with economic stimulation and of revising the Fund for Regional Support to debates on the Budgetary Code. The donors continued to pressure the central government through the Federation Council while they also pursued their objectives through bilateral means, a practice that became standard in the operation of Russia's federal system. According to Denislyam Yancheren, who held primary responsibility in Samara's administration for drafting the treaty, the original intention of the province was to conclude a general partnership treaty with the center. After Tatarstan signed its treaty with Moscow, however, Samara decided to follow the same route and bargain for similar economic privileges.[8] Although negotiating the treaty played a central role in the bilateral relationship with Moscow during the mid-1990s,[9] Samara's leaders used other means of delimiting intergovernmental fiscal control. As this chapter and chapter 6 will show, national legislation and more specific regional development projects were intertwined with the goals of the treaty and its points of dissension. The bilateral treaty served as a means to resolve some of these problems on a broader magnitude than the individual projects but more quickly and easily than federal legislation. As Vyacheslav Ablapokhin, Samara's press secretary for the regional duma, noted, "The treaty is just one knot that might hold back the onslaught of the center and could help to stabilize the [intergovernmental] relationship."[10] Moreover, by reducing the involvement of the federal fiscal bureaucracy through the decentralization of financial management, Samara could address local problems as subnational issues rather than intergovernmental ones.

As of early 1997, the draft "Treaty on the demarcating of objects of jurisdiction and authority between the organs of state power of the Russian Federation and the organs of state power of Samara oblast" included a general treaty and an additional thirteen agreements covering budgetary mechanisms, state property, defense, social welfare, and investment.[11] Although the treaty and the agreements were not signed until the summer, central officials had agreed to their basic terms. As the thirteen agreements worked their way through a variety of joint committees, the financial issues served as the focal point for most of the remaining disagreements. For each of these financial clauses, Samara needed the approval of the Ministry of Finance, described by insiders as a "very conservative organization"[12] and as the dominion of midlevel, inexperienced bureaucrats.[13] The first agreement, "on the demarcating of authority in international and foreign economic ties," addresses many of the same privileges granted to Tatarstan and Sverdlovsk in their bilateral agreements. The agreement assigns to Samara a wide range of rights in the area of foreign trade—an arena once exclusively the center's domain. It gives Samara the right to carry out international trade, attract foreign credits, create insurance and foreign currency funds, and appoint representatives of the oblast to trade organizations in foreign countries, all financed by oblast funds and under the guarantee of Samara's administration. The most likely point of contention in the agreement grants Samara the right to license imports, with the licensing fees going directly to the oblast.[14]

The second agreement, "on the demarcation of authority in the area of the control, use, and disposal of land resources," addresses a significant loophole in the privatization process, including the transfer of federal property to subnational control. Previously, privatization transactions included only the *objects* of state property and did not include the land underneath the state-owned factories or stores. Consequently, the federal government still retained control over the sale and distribution of the property. Privatized enterprises situated on state-owned land could either purchase the land, if they had the resources to do so, or lease it from the state (Wegren 1997, 976). The agreement thus transfers the control over all such property to the regional government, giving Samara's administration the rights to sell or lease it. Moreover, the agreement restricts the federal government's authority over the lands under federally owned buildings or institutions, stipulating that they cannot be sold to a third party.

Agreement Five, "on the demarcating of authority in the questions of budgetary relations," outlines the revenue-sharing arrangement between Samara and the center and represents the core of the bilateral treaty. Similar to earlier treaties with Tatarstan and Sverdlovsk, the agreement grants special revenue-sharing privileges to Samara, which directly contradict federal budgetary laws.[15] The agreement gives Samara 100 percent of the excise taxes from the sale of spirits, including the profitable vodka sales (an increase from 50 percent in the recent federal budgets), and 100 percent of the payments for the rights to extract coal and natural resources, including oil and natural gas. In addition, Samara receives 50 percent of the excise taxes on the sale of oil and gas in the region, whereas the 1997 federal budget law designated 100 percent of these funds to the federal government. The issue of excise taxes presents a significant area of disagreement between the oblast administration and the Ministry of Finance for several reasons. First, excise taxes on vodka and especially on oil and gas resources provide an enormous source of revenue. In 1997, for example, the center projected total revenues from excise taxes to exceed 75 trillion rubles (RF Federal Budget Law 1997). Second, although Samara is not a major producer of natural resources like Tiumen' or Orenburg oblasts, a battle between the oblast administration and the oil company, Yukos, had been growing since the beginning of the privatization process. Like many of the major oil companies such as Lukoil and Gazprom, Yukos bought up many smaller regional companies that were once a part of the state-owned industry, including SamaraNeftegaz and three oil companies (*Samarskoe obozreniye*, 7 October 1996). Whereas previously Yukos paid taxes to Samara, in August 1996, the Moscow bank Menatep acquired Yukos, and it relocated its headquarters to Moscow. Subsequently, Yukos paid its taxes only to Moscow and the federal government, with Samara receiving none of the valuable revenue from oil and gas extraction.[16] According to the presidential representative to Samara, this was costing the region "billions of rubles" every year.[17] The bilateral agreement thus sought to stabilize an important source of revenue by asserting Samara's right to profit from natural resources on its territory. In addition to the excise taxes, the budgetary agreement calls for the allocation of 50 percent of the VAT, customs duties, and excise taxes on imported goods flowing into Samara to finance the purchase of imported medicines and equipment. Here again, the agreement directly contradicts the 1997 federal budget law, which designates 100 percent of import taxes and duties to the federal government.

Another significant area of contention within the interbudgetary agreement focused on reconstructing the time-consuming and inefficient system of financing federal expenditures within the regions. The draft agreement grants Samara the right to finance these expenditures, including federal programs, through the regional branch of the federal treasury, and to finance federal extrabudgetary programs through territorial extrabudgetary accounts. Whereas this method of financing seemed to offer an efficient and cost-effective solution to central budgetary problems, it contradicted the system of centralized control over revenues that developed under the Soviet planned economy and survived its collapse. Moreover, international lending agencies advocated further recentralization of revenues in Russia to manage federal debt and arrears.[18] Nevertheless, Moscow decentralized the system of financing federal budgetary expenditures in Samara in 1995. Under an "experimental program," Samara became the first province to use federal revenues collected within the region to finance federal expenditures, rather than transfer the revenues to Moscow and wait three or more weeks for their return in the form of subsidies and other payments. The money, a total of 1.3 trillion rubles for 1996 (from approximately 6.5 trillion rubles in tax revenue transferred to the federal budget),[19] financed 52 branches and departments of federal ministries, and an additional 1500 institutions that received federal funds.[20] Moscow approved the program in Samara for 1996 and 1997, and extended it to other regions,[21] but it remained an experimental program, subject to the discretion of federal officials. The Ministry of Finance was reluctant to officially decentralize control on a long-term basis through the treaty. In addition, the Ministry of Finance established annual and monthly limits, restricting the percentage of federal revenue available for the program. This system of limits created its own costs and conflicts, with Samara officials seeking to increase the available revenues much as it had under the old centralized system. Despite the expanded local control, Samara still had to rely on federal financing decisions, with bargaining over revenue limits mirroring previous conflicts over transfers and subsidies. In one written exchange between Governor Titov and Vladimir Panskov (the minister of finance in 1996), Titov complained that the Ministry of Finance based the monthly revenue limits on the forecasted total revenues of Russia, rather than on Samara's annual revenues, which exceeded the average for each region.

Consequently, the existing revenues did not fully cover federal expenditures in the region. Titov argued that the system should be reworked, "taking into account that Samara oblast is a region that transfers up to fifty percent of the tax revenues collected on the territory of the oblast into the federal budget. . . ." Panskov's reply reflected some of the political constraints in expanding regional fiscal control:

The decisions made by the legislative and executive branches in the process of implementing the federal budget, which . . . make the situation of mobilizing taxes and other revenues and sources to close the budget deficit very strained, render a positive decision regarding your request [impossible]. In addition, to accept your proposal to sharply expand the practice of unregistered financing of federal budgetary expenditures *would abridge the budgetary rights of the relevant ministries and departments of the Russian Federation—the primary allocators of federal budgetary resources*.[22]

With such routine conflicts over the parameters of control, the treaty attempted to formalize the experimental payment system, eliminating opportunities for the center to recentralize fiscal control. Article seven of the interbudgetary agreement expands the system to create a similar mechanism to cover extrabudgetary expenditures such as unemployment and pension funds. Although the agreement stipulates that after five years it can be renegotiated, ostensibly addressing the reluctance of the Ministry of Finance to relinquish permanent control over federal revenues, the agreement remains intact in lieu of formal requests for modifications by either side. Absent any nagging problems with the system, Samara's elites clearly hoped that the center would be too busy with other issues to renegotiate and the arrangement would become a permanent fixture of intergovernmental fiscal relations.

Several other thorny issues arose in the remaining eight agreements. Agreement 6, "on investment activity and structural policy" restates article 6 of the previous agreement on Samara's right to transfer federal financing of central investment programs directly from the oblast branch of the treasury. The Ministry of Finance had been particularly unwilling to assign control over the financing of federal programs to subnational governments. Not only did the Ministry of Finance wish to maintain the centralization of revenues, but it needed such control to sequester payments during a revenue shortfall. In the 1996 presidential election year, President Yeltsin promised and decreed hundreds of federal investment programs across Russia, many more than the federal budget could finance. Consequently, the central government passed a resolution in the fall authorizing budgetary resources for a small percentage of these programs (RF Government Resolution 1996, 988). As the center increasingly slashed and sequestered investment funds from the federal budget, subnational governments increased the pressure for laws requiring the center to transfer the funds allocated in the budget. The State Duma resisted any law that diminished its control over budgetary revenues, yet the donor regions managed to obtain the right in the 1997 budget law to finance their federal programs with locally collected federal revenues, reflecting the growing power of the donor regions to overcome the opposition of the Ministry of Finance and to link their fiscal interests with other budgetary issues during the joint Duma-Federation Council negotiations.

For Samara, the availability of financing for investment programs granted a significant advantage in the development of the regional economy. Samara participated in more than twenty federal investment programs, including housing subsidies, environmental cleanup, defense conversion, and the construction of a subway system (*Gubernskii informatsionnii bulleten*, 5/17, May 1996). In 1996, Samara received slightly more than half of the 346 billion rubles promised in the federal budget. Of this total, the budget earmarked twenty-four billion rubles to construct Samara's subway. By the end of the year, the region had received only four billion rubles. The minister of finance, Aleksandr Livshits, arranged the remaining financing, but it was done through *vzaimorashchet*, or mutual accounting (tax and expenditure offsets), a system of "creative accounting," in which debts between two or more enterprises and/or the state are canceled out without an exchange of property, cash, or any other monetary instruments.[23] Local control over the revenues for federal programs, as stipulated in the agreement on investment activity, would eliminate the need for *vzaimorashchet*, providing Samara with the designated investment funds and infusing cash into the regional economy.

In addition to reorganizing the system of financing federal programs, Agreement 6 required the federal government to transfer its shares of privatized companies in Samara to the regional government. At the beginning of 1995, Samara's industries were 80 to 90 percent privatized, with less than 20 percent of the shares remaining in federal hands, and an equal amount owned by the regional government (Tacis, March 1996). Despite the fact that the center controlled a relatively small amount of property in Samara compared with other regions (Tacis, March 1996, 67), Agreement 6, as well as Agreement 2 on land resources (see above) and Agreement 9, "on the management of state property," endeavored to reduce federal control of property within Samara oblast to an even greater extent. During the process of negotiating the treaty, Samara's administration pursued other means of shrinking federal holdings in the region. In early 1997, Vladimir Mamigonov, the head of Samara's property committee, negotiated the transfer of federal property into the hands of the regional government to offset interbudgetary debts. The shares, including significant holdings in several automobile-related industries, and a 51 percent stake in Samara's international airport, covered between 60 to 350 billion rubles of the debt. Despite the obvious benefits to the ailing federal budget deficit, the plan met with serious opposition in the center, particularly from the relevant industrial ministries. Any proposal designed to reduce the power of the central ministries—bureaucracies entrenched in the economic system since the height of the planning system—undermined "the very foundations for [their] existence," thus guaranteeing their opposition (*Samarskoe obozreniye*, 27 January 1997).

The remaining agreements in the bilateral treaty cover defense conversion, health issues, education, banking and monetary credit policy, the energy complex, crime and public safety, environmental issues, and agriculture. Each addresses specific jurisdictional questions but also incorporates Samara's fundamental goals of the treaty. For example, Article 7 of Agreement 10, "in the sphere of assuring the functioning of the heat-energy complex," affirms that the federal government must obtain the approval of Samara's government before transferring any shares in the energy complex or making any changes to the management of these shares, thereby subordinating the federal government to the authority of Samara's administration in property and investment matters. Agreement 8, covering banking and monetary policy, revisits the issue of financial flows by empowering the regional branch of the Central Bank to supply government credits. By localizing financial flows—i.e., using federal revenues collected within the oblast to cover federal expenditures and investments in the oblast—Samara reduced the costs of depending on inefficient and unreliable central fiscal institutions by eliminating the waiting period for the release of funds and restricting the opportunities for the Ministry of Finance to reduce or sequester the funds allocated by the federal budget.

Financial independence—the ability to control the expansion and allocation of revenues—represented the primary goal of Samara's negotiations with the center. Clearly, regional elites wanted to maximize Samara's wealth, but they pursued this aim through increasing control over financial decisions and local revenues, rather than through an increase in federal funds from any source available. Its significant wealth thus structured the priorities of the region for intergovernmental reform but less directly than might be immediately apparent. First, Samara's leaders favored an asymmetrical system of federalism, in which efficient and competent regional administrations—defined as the donor regions—received financial control as their reward. According to Samara's administration, the terms of the bilateral treaty compensated the region for its efficacy in comparison to the federal government and other regions, rather than signified the power of the wealthy. Second, its wealth and vast opportunities to increase its wealth allowed its leadership to focus on long-term goals through control over the rules. Despite critical problems in the industrial sector that might have hampered growth in the region for many years, the sizable tax base meant that Governor Titov could forsake short-term monetary gains, such as increased grants, subsidies, or a percentage of the Fund for Regional Support, for future gains through the control over international investments, revenue allocations, and the privatization of federal property.

VOLOGDA

Whereas Samara represents one of the elite wealthy regions, with substantial investment opportunities and a well-developed tax base, Vologda oblast is more difficult to categorize. The economic indicators place Vologda above the mean—its average income per capita in 1996 was nearly ten percent above the average for Russia (Goskomstat 1996)—but its underdeveloped infrastructure, typical of the northern provinces, and lack of energy resources increase the region's economic dependence on the federal government. The financial situation of Vologda was healthy relative to the majority of other regions so that it did not receive federal transfers from the Fund for Regional Support until 1995. In 1996, the Fund allocated 140 billion rubles to Vologda, constituting approximately 5 percent of total revenue in the region's consolidated budget.[24] Nevertheless, Vologda's revenue transfers to the federal government still significantly outweighed its receipts, making it one of the net-payers, rather than one of the more economically dependent debtors.[25]

Unlike the small but powerful group of donors, the net-payer regions do not constitute a unified lobbying group. Whereas the federal budget clearly identifies the donor regions in the article listing transfer allocations, Vologda based its understanding of an unequal financial relationship with the center on its own calculations of revenue transfers and receipts.[26] Whereas the donors exploited the dependence of the federal government on their tax bases and their own budgetary independence as bargaining chips, the net-payers still relied to varying degrees on central transfers, leaving them little room to maneuver. In Vologda's case, its leaders also emphasized the uniqueness of the region and the historical independence of the northern regions, suggesting Vologda's stronger solidarity with its neighbors than with a group of self-identified net-payers. According to Vice Governor Nikolai Kostigov, Moscow paid very little attention to Vologda under Soviet rule since the region played a minor role in the military-industrial complex and in the agricultural sector. Kostigov suggested that, "From one side this was bad, but from another [it was] good. We were able to preserve many things according to our own traditions. We didn't develop our infrastructure but on the other hand we preserved the environment."[27] Vologda's pride in its autonomy and the belief in the region's economic potential influenced its view of federalism. Whereas the donors looked to the republics such as Tatarstan as the models for delimiting authority, Vologda regarded a reform-oriented donor region like Nizhni Novgorod as a model of political and economic success in its local reforms and in its relations with the center.[28] Its leaders, like those in Samara, believed in the sanctity of the Russian Federation, yet they also stressed the need for broader decentralization, particularly in control over regional matters.[29] Vologda's strongest statement on this issue came in 1993 during the constitutional crisis, when it became the first province to declare itself a republic.[30] Vologda's administration subsequently modified its stance on federal relations, regarding the 1993 document as "amusing."[31] As in Samara, the official rhetoric advocated national legislation rather than bilateral agreements to achieve equity but accepted the treaty process as a more efficient and rapid process of demarcating authority.

Two documents, "Fundamental objectives for socio-economic policy of the administration of Vologda oblast for 1997" and "A conception for a regional program of socio-economic development for Vologda oblast," outline some of the basic issues and problems in the region, laying the groundwork for the bilateral treaty. The draft "Treaty on the demarcating of areas of authority and jurisdiction between the organs of state power of the Russian Federation and the organs of state power of Vologda oblast" along with its eighteen agreements address these issues as they pertain to the intergovernmental relationship.[32] The "Fundamental objectives" document, prepared by the regional administration, declares the region to be in a "crisis situation" for 1997, characterized by falling production and revenues, delays in wage and other social payments, and disappearing investment. Compounding this situation, "a double burden encumbers the oblast administration—in addition to our regional duties we must resolve the problems arising from the unsuccessful activities of the federal government." The document then lists the primary goals of the administration: to maintain a sufficient standard of living, to mitigate social tensions by eradicating the payments crisis, to increase production of consumer products, and to stop the growth in unemployment. The "Conception for a regional program" reiterates these problems and expands upon the ambitious goals for Vologda. The report, part of a contract with a senior economist at the National Academy of Sciences to assist the region in creating a plan for regional reform and development, represented a major initiative for the oblast and the basis for a federal program of socio-economic development for Vologda.[33] Although it was only the beginning of a larger project, the document, like the administration's plans, studiously enumerated each problem without formulating explicit reform proposals. The section on budgetary policy, for example, states that chronic deficits plague the regional and municipal budgets. To reverse this situation, the government needs to "increase the tax base in connection with the resuscitation and legalization of production" and implement a "rational" policy of revenue sharing and transfers between levels of government. The report, however, did not specify how the administration might achieve these aims. Moreover, the plan included both market-oriented reforms—lowering corporate tax rates, improving the investment climate—and more statist and parochial goals—equalizing income and expenditures across municipalities, increasing the self-reliance of the oblast, particularly in terms of consumer goods—without acknowledging the inherent tensions between them.

In comparison with the administration's "Fundamental objectives" and the Academy of Science's "Conception," the 1996 draft treaty offered more specific and circumscribed goals, particularly in the fiscal arena. Nevertheless, the treaty still included some vague language and objectives in dealing with the division of authority over resources. This attested to the tensions between the economic potential of the region and the ongoing situation of economic crisis. As with Samara, fiscal issues occupied a central place in Vologda's treaty, with the agreement on budgetary relations and monetary-credit policy coming first in the packet of agreements. Vologda's fiscal agreement manifests both its desire for financial independence and its dependence on federal support. Like Samara's agreement, it decentralizes control over federal revenues collected in the province, "toward the goal of expediting interbudgetary accounting and minimizing the circular flows of financing for federal programs and organizations located on the territory of Vologda oblast and financed by the federal budget . . . " Article 9 extends this system to the collection and distribution of extrabudgetary funds for federal programs. The ability to localize the flows of federal revenues mattered not only as an issue of regional control but as an issue of financial stability. In 1996, the oblast should have received 136 billion rubles in the form of transfers; yet by the end of November, it had received only 64 percent of this sum.[34] In addition, the region participated in twenty-four federal programs, including environmental, housing, and health programs, all of which relied on unstable annual funding from the federal budget.[35]

Nevertheless, the agreement did not completely decentralize fiscal control or responsibility. If expenditures for federal programs and organizations exceed federal revenues collected within Vologda, the Ministry of Finance must finance the remaining sums directly. Moreover, Article 3 stipulates that Vologda can continue to receive financial help in the form of transfers from the Fund for Regional Support and receive federal loans in a situation of economic hardship. In one of the most controversial points of the treaty, Article 3 states that the share of revenues allocated to Vologda cannot be less than 75 percent of all revenues collected in the region. This is a significant increase from the 60 percent of revenues that remained in the region as of 1996.[36]

In addition to authority over fiscal resources, Vologda's eighteen agreements emphasize control of natural resources, particularly in the valuable timber industry and in future discoveries of oil and gold deposits, and intergovernmental cooperation in the development of Vologda's economy, particularly its export sector. Rather than devolving control to the subnational level, the agreements specify the center's role in regional development in an attempt to assure the implementation of federal promises. The agreement on agriculture, for example, denotes the federal programs in which Vologda participates to ensure their implementation over the long term. It also directs the federal government to provide credits for grain production, agricultural subsidies, and payments for federal agricultural procurements. Like many of the agreements, it stipulates that the federal government must provide whatever financial resources are allocated by the federal budget or other federal documents, in the hope of ending years of unfulfilled financing to the region and to prevent the Ministry of Finance from sequestering the designated funds. Agreement 8, on the defense industry, uses the localized financing scheme to address the federal payments crisis. It authorizes that, "In a case of delayed financing from the federal budget for defense orders or [defense] conversion programs on the territory of Vologda oblast, financing can be realized in the established method through the federal treasury department from the accounts of federal budgetary revenues collected in the oblast, with the agreement of the RF Ministry of Finance."

Almost half of the eighteen agreements deal with natural resources and environmental issues, an important part of Vologda's regional development. Although the State Duma has considered legislation on water, land, and forestry resources,[37] the bilateral agreements served as an interim measure while also addressing development issues more specific to the oblast. For example, Vologda's leaders hoped to develop areas such as the Kirillo-Belozerskii monastery and several wildlife preserves for tourism. Since these areas were previously communally owned *kolkhozy*, and the various land and resource codes do not determine specific ownership and decision-making rights, the region's development plans remain in limbo. Similar problems remain for Vologda's vast forests, over 60 percent of its territory (Goskomstat 1996), and the decision to preserve this land or to aggressively develop the timber industry.[38] Nevertheless, the agreements created a mandate for change rather than explicitly delineating the rules of the game. In the agreement "on questions of forestry relations on the territory of Vologda oblast," the Russian government promises to furnish a "specific forestry policy," finance "federal programs on the rational use of forestry resources, increase in productivity, reprocessing, forestry preservation and defense [and] timber production," coordinate international cooperation, and establish a payment system for the use of the forestry fund. The agreement then authorizes Vologda's government to work out regional forestry development programs, establish minimal tax rates and grant tax exemptions for forest lands, and to "make a decision on granting parts of the land fund for long-term and short-term use [and on] the transfer of authority over the land fund from the managers to the state forestry administration." In addition, it stipulates that Vologda oblast should finance the management of the forests with taxes and other payments from the use of forestry resources. Despite the goal of demarcating control over forestry and other natural resources, the agreements only laid out the basic aims and responsibilities, but did not establish the basic rules of authority, clear financial rights, or a time-table for working out these problems.

Agreement 17, "on the control, use, and distribution of the state mining fund on the territory of Vologda oblast," also uses vague language to delimit control over mineral and fossil fuel extractions. In this case, however, the imprecision came from the lack of concrete resources to apportion. The presence of oil and gold deposits in neighboring regions—oil in Komi and gold in Arkhangelsk—located "along the same geological stratum" as Vologda, convinced the administration to organize two joint-stock companies to initiate geological surveys, in the hope that the discovery of valuable fuel or minerals would provide a foundation for economic renewal.[39] The bilateral agreement with the federal government thus addresses the control over potential discoveries by placing potential sites into a state mining fund. Rather than attempting to preserve full control over the resources—a move that would have met with strong opposition—the agreement grants that "to guarantee state needs for strategic and depleted types of fossil-fuel resources, specific portions of these deposits on the territory of Vologda oblast can receive the status of objects of federal significance based upon the joint decision of the federal organs of state power and the organs of state power of Vologda oblast." Other than the unspecified federal share of resources, which includes only fuels and not other minerals such as diamonds, the control and use of the mining fund belongs to the regional government. By establishing a federal stake in future discoveries, however unlikely they may be, without delineating the size of its share, the agreement created the potential for conflict—precisely what it was designed to eliminate.

Despite some similarities to Samara's bilateral treaty—particularly in the role of the regional branch of the federal treasury and the joint control over federal property management—the overall emphasis and tenor of the agreements differ. Vologda's treaty is longer and more legalistic, yet many of the agreements focus on areas of cooperation and federal support in the general development of Vologda's economy, rather than outlining specific plans. Vologda's plans suggest that in 1996, the regional administration was just beginning to formulate its long-term goals while simultaneously trying to focus on solutions to immediate problems. In its bilateral agreements, Vologda needed to balance its current dependence on federal assistance to deal with economic crises with a means to decrease this dependence as the region develops the ability to take advantage of its own resources. Whereas Samara's thirteen agreements stress the spheres of regional jurisdiction, Vologda's treaty highlights the responsibilities, including fiduciary duties, of the federal government, stipulating them in the first section of every agreement. The development of Vologda's economy through federal programs and extrabudgetary funds is incorporated into these obligations or the joint duties of the two governments. Samara's treaty also includes federal programs and federal investment in the development of the region—particularly in the areas of social welfare and defense conversion—yet it emphasizes Samara's right to attract other sources of financing, including from foreign sources. The agreement on international economic ties occupies a central and conflictual place in Samara's bilateral treaty, whereas Vologda's packet lacks such an agreement. The designated guarantor of international credits and investments also indicates the different degrees of dependence on the federal government. As mentioned in several of the agreements, Samara's administration offers itself as the guarantor of any foreign investment. Vologda, in a more precarious economic situation at the time, wanted the federal government to provide its guarantee—a reasonable request, according to Vologda's leadership, considering that the federal government does not have to provide the investment funds.[40] In place of the international economic agreements, the bulk of Vologda's treaty demarcates ownership of specific resources, particularly natural resources such as timber, water reservoirs, and mineral deposits. In Samara, there have been fewer conflicts over the ownership of natural resources, because the Russian government quickly addressed the division and privatization of oil and gas resources after the breakup of the Soviet Union.

BRYANSK

If Samara represents the inclinations of the donor regions toward fiscal autonomy and Vologda displays the need of many regions for balance between fiscal decentralization and continued federal support, Bryansk offers an example of the complicated relationship between the center and the depressed regions of Russia. Since its creation and incorporation into the Russian Federation in 1944, Bryansk has endured a series of economic and environmental hardships. As a key military route between Eastern and Western Europe during World War II, the region suffered tremendous loss of life and property. The Soviets then rebuilt Bryansk as an industrial center for machine-building and defense-related industry, particularly chemical weapons production. After the Soviet collapse, defense orders disappeared and other factories could not compete with the world market and with larger and more productive industries in other Russian regions, such as Samara. Consequently, industrial output declined by 47 percent between 1992 and 1994 (Bradshaw, Stenning and Sutherland 1998). Moreover, in 1986, due to its proximity to Belarus, Bryansk suffered tremendously from the accident at the Chernobyl nuclear facility, with the southwestern portion of the oblast, the region's primary agricultural area, evacuated as a result of radioactive fallout.

The economic and environmental problems in Bryansk affected its financial relationship with the center and its goals for regional development. Bryansk has received transfers from the Fund for Regional Support since its inception; in the 1997 federal budget law, it received a coefficient of .7891 percent, as compared to Vologda's .2583 percent.[41] These transfers, totaling more than 417 billion rubles in 1996, have made up a crucial portion of Bryansk's regional budget. According to the administration's budgetary figures, in 1996, federal transfers accounted for 30.6 percent of the budget, rising to 49.5 percent in 1997.[42] In addition, Bryansk has relied on about 50 federal programs, especially funding for the victims of Chernobyl and housing for the military.[43] With federal funding playing such a key role in regional finances, the fulfillment of the center's fiduciary responsibilities, a perpetually laborious task, dominated intergovernmental negotiations. In 1996, for example, Bryansk managed to attain 90 percent of the allocated transfers, but only 10 percent of the funds allocated in the federal budget for the Chernobyl program (*Bryanskiye rabochii*, 30 January 1997). Concern over the implementation of federal budgetary financing thus provided a major impetus for Bryansk to sign a bilateral treaty with the center.

The leadership of Bryansk wanted to decrease its dependence on transfers, but it also viewed federal programs and investment as a means of strengthening the bonds of federalism. According to Ludmila Tulyagin, the head of the regional administration's finance department, the center needs a variety of measures—not unlike those used by the Soviet planning apparatus—to achieve parity among regions. These include the establishment of minimal social expenditure norms and the equalization of revenue potential through capital investment and tax exemptions for the more economically depressed regions.[44] Among supporters of regional equality, federal investment and even short-term subsidies serve the longer-term goals of equal opportunity and eventual self-reliance for all of Russia's regions. Unlike the donor regions, which blame the depressed regions for impeding the development of the rest of the federation, they perceive threats to Russian federalism as arising from conflict between the "haves" and the "have-nots" at the level of interregional competition and at the individual level (Matveev, 1996). Perceiving economic opportunities in Moscow, Kazan, and Sverdlovsk, individuals in depressed regions might either rise up in protest or move en masse to wealthier regions, creating social tensions that the federation is ill-equipped to handle. To prevent such problems, the center should focus its resources on improving the situation in the disadvantaged areas rather than increasing the division between wealthy and poor regions.

Despite its dependence on federal transfers, Bryansk also wanted more financial independence from Moscow by stabilizing the regional economy. The administration's program "Investment—Employment—Stability" outlined its stabilization plans for 1997. Much of the Bryansk administration's plan originated from a contract with the Gaidar Institute in 1995 to formulate a regional development strategy. Although the administration subsequently canceled the contract, leaving the plan incomplete, Governor Yuri Lodkin revisited the Gaidar Institute's proposals—an ironic source of ideas for a devoted member of the Communist Party of the Russian Federation—after his election in 1996.[45] In the fiscal and investment realm, the stabilization measures included increasing the role of commercial banks and available credit in the region; increasing the use of *vzaimoraschet* (joint accounting measures) to decrease government debts; forming a regional securities fund to provide guarantees to investors; and improving the investment climate of the region. The desire to expand the practice of *vzaimorashchet* provides an interesting contrast to Samara where the administration was seeking to eliminate such accounting measures. Many economists and officials, including the deputy chief of Bryansk's tax inspectorate, agreed with Samara's efforts, noting that *vzaimoraschet* decreases the money available to enterprises and the state and makes profits more difficult to tax.[46] Yet for a cash-starved region that wishes to prevent widespread bankruptcy in its local industries, *vzaimorashchet* might represent the only means to reduce (on paper) enterprise debt and a budget deficit in the hope of future economic stabilization.[47]

The 1997 stabilization program relied on two documents to improve the situation in the region: the bilateral treaty with the center and the governmental resolution No. 1286, "On the state support of the socio-economic development of Bryansk oblast for 1997–2000." The development program for Bryansk is a brief, eight-point document, unlike many of the other, more extensive, governmental resolutions for regional socio-economic development.[48] Its brevity notwithstanding, the program addressed the most important development issues for Bryansk; as with Vologda, however, it established more of a mandate for change than the concrete distribution of power. Similarly, the bilateral treaty focused on intergovernmental cooperation to alleviate the socio-economic crisis in the region, particularly in the agricultural and defense sectors. Despite the secretiveness about the specifics of the treaty documents,[49] administration officials revealed that the agreement on interbudgetary relations occupied a central position in the treaty, much like Vologda's bilateral treaty. The interbudgetary agreement gives Bryansk the right to finance federal programs, particularly the Chernobyl program, from federal tax revenues collected in the region. It also stipulates that Bryansk may finance transfers from the Fund for Regional Support directly through the regional branch of the federal treasury, a system already in place since the beginning of 1996. Yet like in

Vologda, the agreement ensures that Bryansk will continue to receive direct payments from the federal government if the revenue collected in the region does not cover the necessary programs and transfers. As mentioned earlier, the 1996 Bryansk oblast budget relied on transfers from the federal Fund for Regional Support for more than 30 percent of its total revenue and carried more than a 10 percent budget deficit. Although locally collected revenues covered some of the federal transfers and grants, Bryansk depended on additional funds from Moscow to make up for its inadequate tax base and to cover the minimal expenditure norms required by federal law. Moreover, in an attempt to increase subnational fiscal responsibility, subsequent federal budget drafts included a clause to limited transfers to those regions that continue to run budget deficits and carry wage arrears—an enormous threat to Bryansk's financial life-line from Moscow.[50]

The agreement on customs issues was equally important to the region. In lieu of natural resources, Bryansk's geographic position on the border of Belarus and Ukraine is its most valuable resource. The regional administration wanted to profit from this position by receiving a portion of the customs duties and fines, which go directly into the federal budget. In addition, the region sought a percentage of the profits from the transport of natural resources across its territory.[51] In a further effort to exploit its advantageous location, the draft treaty includes the question of a free economic zone in Bryansk,[52] an issue also outlined in the federal development program for Bryansk. In the second point of the program, the Russian government promises to consider proposals to create a free economic zone on the territory of Bryansk. Regional administration officials considered the idea of a free economic zone, which would provide a tax-free and customs-free zone for manufacturing and other industry, as the key to economic prosperity. As an entry point into Russia from Western and Eastern Europe, its airport provided a cheaper alternative to Moscow and St. Petersburg, particularly for transporting goods, and its customs points supplied revenue to the federal government from import and export duties. Bryansk officials hoped to provide a customs-free site for assembling imported manufactured goods within a free economic zone, which would infuse cash and jobs into the struggling regional economy.[53] Yet according to Aleksandr Nemets, an economist and former administration official, the idea of a free economic zone served as a political slogan rather than a realistic plan. Russia, he argued, lacks clear property rights and a law on the status of free economic zones, making any such plans untenable.[54] In addition, without federal investment and support, it is unclear how Bryansk might create the necessary foundations to attract international investment and partnerships.

The development program also addresses Bryansk's losses as a result of the Chernobyl disaster in 1987. High levels of radiation in the southwestern portion of the region all but destroyed potato and wheat crops—staples of the region's agricultural sector. The remaining farms could not find markets for their produce since the high levels of radiation in the area contaminated the goods. The program funnels federal support and loans to organizations that reprocess the harvests to purchase the technology to engineer "clean" produce. The arrangement relies upon Bryansk's private sector—still severely underdeveloped, particularly due to the lack of capital in the region—to build the reprocessing firms, which would then apply for government funding. The bilateral treaty also solicits government assistance for the fall in revenue from agricultural production through state orders for produce.[55] Other arrangements include a provision to allow the region's agricultural firms to pay taxes to the state in the form of produce (*Bryanskiye izvestiya*, 26 November 1996).

In addition to supporting industry through government loans for investment and working capital, the development program covers federal support for defense conversion of Bryansk's industries, an issue also taken up by the bilateral treaty. Conversion programs became particularly controversial in Bryansk since the passage of a federal program law on the elimination of chemical weapons in Russia in early 1996 and subsequent legislation in 1997. As noted earlier, anywhere from 17 percent (*Bryanskiye rabochii*, 30 January 1997) to 30 percent[56] of the nation's chemical weapons supply was located on the territory of Bryansk. In light of significant problems with the receipt of federal funds for Chernobyl programs, Bryansk's administration doubted the ability or willingness of the federal government to adequately compensate the region for the costs of properly dismantling and destroying the weapons. Moreover, Governor Lodkin argued that the process of destroying the weapons posed more of a risk to the region's populace than the status-quo (*Bryanskiye izvestiya*, 22 February 1997). Other regional leaders, such as State Duma deputy Oleg Shenkarov, countered that Bryansk might gain more from federal financing for the program than by maintaining its chemical weapons stock (*Bryanskiye izvestiya*, 13 February 1997). Yet the legislation still required additional government resolutions and agreements to ensure financing for the program. Because it pre-dated the legislation, the socio-economic development program for Bryansk does not directly address the question of chemical weapons, but states more generally that the Ministries of Finance, the Economy, and Defense will review means of financing conversion programs for defense-related industries.

The officially published treaty establishes the basic framework of the bilateral relationship, similar to that outlined in the federal development program. It stresses intergovernmental cooperation through the negotiation of new federal target programs and federal financing to prevent economic collapse in the region. As with earlier documents, the treaty targets the conversion of defense factories, support of agriculture, and the clean-up from the Chernobyl accident for federal assistance. The treaty then reiterates the commitment of the center to fulfill its budgetary obligations to the region in an attempt to halt the mounting federal budgetary arrears to Bryansk.

Similar to Vologda's plans for intergovernmental reform, the treaty in Bryansk needed to balance the demands of economic crisis with hopes for future economic opportunities. In both of these realms, the federal government played a significant role, limiting the means for fiscal autonomy in Bryansk. In the short term, federal transfers serviced basic social expenditures in the regional budget and the prevention of economic collapse depended on the implementation of federal environmental, social welfare, and industrial conversion programs. Consequently, the precarious economic situation served as the principal issue of intergovernmental negotiations. Yet economic problems did not preclude plans for future development and growth. The aspiration of Bryansk to establish a free economic zone on its territory and its desire to increase its control over revenue allocations suggest that the region's leadership envisioned a more self-reliant future. But its plans, only vaguely formulated, were contingent on enormous financial and political support from Moscow, tying the economic future of the region to the direction of Russia's federal government.

The short time horizon of the leadership in Bryansk stands in stark contrast to the concerns in Samara, where leaders focused on gaining long-term control over decision making, even forsaking immediate financial gain in pursuit of this goal. The availability and potential of economic resources structured the agenda for both of these regions in their negotiations with the center. Regional elites viewed the development of intergovernmental fiscal relations based upon their evaluation of their need for federal intervention in and support of their region. Both Vologda and Bryansk saw an immediate need for fiscal support from the center and for written guarantees of this support. Samara, though not yet free from economic worries, charted its course of development based upon its own financial resources. As one of the few donor regions, Samara hoped to decrease the federal government's dependency on the region, as opposed to the goals of Bryansk and Vologda to decrease their reliance on federal transfers. Moreover, each of these regions' financial relationship with the center shaped its view of Russian federalism and how federal relations should continue to develop. Regional elites agreed that Russia's leadership was too beholden to the interests of other regions, but they differed over the relative strength of these interests. Bryansk blamed the wealthy and well-endowed regions for withholding revenues that should be redistributed to equal the playing field for all Russians. Comparatively wealthy Samara, however, argued that the federal government continued to subsidize poor and inefficient subnational governments to the detriment of Russia as a whole.

Despite the complaints of Samara's leadership, the wealthier regions, with the acquiescence of the federal government, have significantly influenced the development of federalism to their benefit. Using the opportunities of bilateralism, Samara—following the examples of Sverdlovsk, Tatarstan, and others—sought to decentralize fiscal decision-making power and control over resources. As the comparison with Bryansk illustrates, decentralization favored those regions that did not depend on the central government for their economic survival. Moreover, Samara envisioned such powers going only to those regions that "earned" them by minimizing budget deficits and renouncing federal transfers, an idea that was tacitly endorsed by the central government in the 1998 budget legislation.[57] Although a system that rewards regional fiscal discipline might eventually benefit some of the poor but more industrious provinces, there were no guarantees that the center would offer such opportunities in the future. Whereas the center faced strong opposition to any attempts to reduce privileges and powers granted under bilateralism, regions forced to forsake decision-making authority for financial support have little recourse if and when the rules of the game change. With wealthier regions able to devolve powers unavailable to other regions, bilateralism reinforced Russia's asymmetrical federalism with parallel systems of fiscal autonomy and fiscal dependency.

Notwithstanding the ambitions of the donor regions, why did the federal government relinquish fiscal authority to its possible future detriment? Our examination of the level of wealth and the corresponding fiscal relationship with the center has elucidated the differences in agendas for intergovernmental reform for the three regions, yet it still does not account for *how* the regions achieved these goals. Samara, in particular, extracted significant long-term advantages from the central government. Once again, we need to ask whether wealth provides a necessary and sufficient basis for improving a region's financial situation in relation to the center. How do economic resources translate into power in intergovernmental negotiations? What other resources can regional leaders rely upon to achieve their fiscal reform goals? Chapter 6 shifts the emphasis to the bargaining process, not only to explain how Samara negotiated its agenda, but also to compare the strategies of Bryansk and Vologda, two regions that focused more on the federal pocketbook. Despite situations of economic crisis, the regions differed in their bargaining strategies and their abilities to construct the rules of the game. These differences, along with the more obvious contrast with Samara, suggest a complex and dynamic process of building federalism, forged from below rather than implanted from above.

NOTES

1. Since I am interested in the dynamic interplay between economic factors and the bilateral relationship and not a quantitative analysis of causal or correla-

tional variables, I use a simple measure of wealth rather than a more complex formula for economic development. For analyses of more specific economic factors and their effects on fiscal federalism, see Treisman (1996, 1997) and Birkenes (1996). For an interesting quantitative analysis of explanatory variables of views on federalism of Russia's governors, see Dowley (1998).

2. 1993 data in 1996 prices from Le Houerou (1996). 1996 data from the Ministry of Finance provided to me by Aleksei Novikov, Institute for Urban Economics.

3. 1993 data based on the month of November from Le Houerou (1996). 1996 data based on the month of October from Goskomstat (1996).

4. Throughout the next two chapters, I differentiate between the bilateral treaty and the agreements. The treaty provides the general outline of the intergovernmental relationship, denoting federal, regional, and joint jurisdictions. Each agreement covers a specific topic, such as interbudgetary mechanisms or defense conversion, and lays out the specific aspects of the division of authority and responsibility as well as the processes to modify or annul an agreement. Although the treaty and agreements are often signed as a "package" (*paket*), this is not necessarily the case, as in the example of Bryansk. The treaty must be signed by the president and the governor (or republic president) whereas the agreements are signed by the prime minister and the subnational leader. Moreover, the treaties must be published by law but the agreements can remain secret.

5. In her discussion with me, the editor Tatyana Veskoboynikova favorably compared Titov's accomplishments with those of his more renowned neighbor, Boris Nemtsov, (now former) governor of Nizhni Novgorod, noting that although "Titov is more energetic, [Nizhni Novgorod's] Nemtsov is nicer."

6. Denislyam Yancheren, interview with author, 10 February 1997.

7. Yuri Baradulin, interview with author, 3 February 1997.

8. Denislyam Yancheren, interview with author, 10 February 1997.

9. In an interview with Andrei Kalmykov, a vice governor who represents Samara in Moscow, he affirmed that he spent the bulk of his time negotiating the terms of the treaty with a vast number of federal bureaucrats and officials.

10. Vyacheslav Ablapokhin, interview with author, 3 February 1997.

11. The following discussion of the draft treaty is based on my notes from the draft supplied to me by Denislyam Yancheren. In keeping with the accepted practice, the signed treaty was published some six months later, but the specific agreements remain unpublished to date.

12. Denislyam Yancheren, interview with author, 10 February 1997.

13. Guri Krilov, interview with author, 3 October 1996.

14. Article 10 of the 1997 federal budget law, for example, states that 50 percent of all customs duties and other fees from international economic activity go to the federal budget.

15. Federal officials and representatives from the IMF and World Bank harshly criticize these types of agreements, warning that they undermine the legitimacy of federal laws.

16. Viktor Filonov, interview with author, 13 February 1997.

17. Yuri Baradulin, interview with author, 3 February 1997.

18. See, for example, *Russian Economic Trends* (1998) and Le Houerou (1996).

19. Data provided to me from the State Tax Service, Samara oblast.

20. Nina Zhirnova, interview with author, 8 February 1997.

21. In 1997, the federal government agreed under pressure from the donor regions to include the right for regions to finance federal expenditures using locally collected federal revenues in Article 29 of the federal budget law (RF, Federal Budget Law, 1997). Nevertheless, the article stipulated that the arrangement depended on an agreement between the regional administration and Russian government, giving the Ministry of Finance plenty of latitude to authorize or refuse it.

22. Letter from K.A. Titov to V.G. Panskov No. 1-11/751, May 3, 1996. Letter from V.G. Panskov to K.A. Titov No. 3-B2-15, May 7, 1996. Author's italics. The letters were provided to me by Vyacheslav Aronin, the head of the finance department in the Samara oblast administration, as an example of the ongoing disputes over fiscal control between the federal and regional governments.

23. Vyacheslav Aronin, interview, 5 February 1997.

24. Calculations of revenue and transfer amounts vary widely among sources. The above estimate is based on data of the Budgetary and Tax Committee of the Vologda Oblast legislature. Ministry of Finance data provided to me by Aleksey Novikov (Institute for Urban Economics) suggests that the weight of transfers in Vologda's consolidated budget may be as high as 10 percent.

25. Since 1998, Vologda no longer receives transfers from the Fund for Regional Support.

26. Some analysts of Russia's system of fiscal federalism, such as Aleksei Lavrov of the Territorial Department of the president's administration, argue that distinctions between donors, net-payers, and debtor regions make little sense since transfers from the Fund for Regional Support—the basis for the categorizations—are only one small part of the myriad funds, credits, and loans that circulate between the center and the regions (Aleksei Lavrov, interview, 4 October 1996). Nevertheless, whether or not the donor regions are actually donors once all of these sources are taken into account—an impossible task, even for Russian economists—they identify themselves as members of an exclusive club that deserves special treatment. I thank Steve Solnick for pointing out the potential problem with using these categorizations.

27. Nikolai Kostigov, interview with author, 2 December 1996.

28. Nikolai Kostigov, interview with author, 2 December 1996.

29. See, for example, an interview with Vologda legislative assembly chairman and Federation Council representative Gennadi Khripel in *Krasnii Sever* (23 November 1996).

30. See chapter 2 for a more detailed discussion of this period.

31. Nikolai Kostigov, interview with author, 2 December 1996.

32. Copies of the "Fundamental objectives" and draft treaty and agreements were provided to me by Nikolai Kostigov, vice governor of Vologda oblast. The regional development program, part of a contract with the Academy of Sciences economist, A. Lvov, was given courtesy of Efim Fayerman, another economist at the Academy of Sciences.

33. Nikolai Kostigov, interview with author, 2 December 1996.

34. Zoya Mayorova, interview with author, 27 November 1996.

35. According to the oblast administration's finance department, the Ministry of Finance owed Vologda 250 million rubles for housing subsidies on January 1,

1996, of which it paid out approximately 77 million by October, 1996 (data provided by Zoya Mayorova).

36. Anatolii Pak, vice governor for privatization, interview with author, 22 November 1996.

37. A forestry code was passed into law on January 29, 1997.

38. Yuri Sudakov, interview with author, 13 November 1996.

39. Anatolii Pak, interview with author, 25 November 1996.

40. Nikolai Kostigov, interview with author, 3 December 1996; Anatolii Pak, interview with author, 25 November 1996.

41. In the 1997 budget, the Fund for Regional Support came from 15 percent of the total revenue receipts, excluding taxes on imports. The regional coefficient determines what percentage of this total sum goes to each region in the form of transfers.

42. Bryansk oblast administration, "Clarification of the oblast budget of Bryansk oblast for 1996" and "Draft Budget of Bryansk oblast for 1997."

43. Aleksey Izotenkov, interview with author, 25 February 1997.

44. Ludmila Tulyagin interview with author, 27 February 1997.

45. Aleksandr Levinskii, interview with author, 22 February 1997.

46. Tamara Zabava, interview with author, 1 March 1997. Non-monetary flows (promissory notes or veksels and mutual offsets or vzaimozaschety) make up 44.7 percent of Bryansk's regional budgetary revenues as compared to 35 percent in Vologda. Figures for Samara are unavailable (OECD 1997, 181).

47. Vzaimorashchet and other accounting measures provide a key piece of the "virtual economy," according to Clifford Gaddy and Barry Ickes (1997). Rather than evidence of economic growth or stability, the canceling of debts only shields companies that should face bankruptcy or some type of restructuring.

48. A federal program for the socio-ecological rehabilitation of Samara covers 27 pages, 16 of which are comprised by the tables outlining the division of financial responsibilities are (RF Government Resolution 1996, 5464).

49. My discussion of the treaty and agreements comes from interviews with administration officials and journalists. Unlike in Samara and Vologda, no one was willing to show me the draft document, claiming that only one copy existed with the governor. The official treaty, which gives the broad outlines of the deal, was published in *Rossisskie vesti* (25 September 1997) without any of the specific agreements (*soglashenie*). The administration's secrecy about the draft agreements conformed to the overall sense of suspicion and mistrust with which many of Bryansk's politicians greeted my visit to their region.

50. The 1998 federal budget law and Government Resolution 441 (May 14, 1998) penalize regions for excessive spending and wage arrears by cutting off federal transfers, including federal programs and loans (*Russian Economic Trends* 2/47, 1998).

51. Ludmila Tulyagin, interview with author, 27 February 1997.

52. Aleksei Izotenkov, interview with author, 25 February 1997.

53. Aleksandr Levinskii, interview with author, 22 February 1997.

54. Aleksandr Nemets interview with author, 3 March 1997.

55. Viktor Kampantsev, interview with author, 24 February 1996.

56. Aleksandr Levinskii, interview with author, 22 February 1997.

57. See footnote 50.

CHAPTER 6

Renegotiating Intergovernmental Fiscal Relations

Regional leaders in Russia were either burdened or blessed with the economic resources of their territories. As the previous chapter illustrates, the agendas for intergovernmental reform in Bryansk, Vologda, and Samara during the mid-1990s reflected their preexisting fiscal relationships with the center. The immediate need for federal financial support determined the region's overall vision of the role of the center in regional development and the time horizon of the regional leadership. Whereas Samara, one of only ten donor regions in the Russian Federation in 1997, used its financial independence to focus on revising the rules of fiscal decision making in its favor, Bryansk and Vologda had to balance their desires for more control with their needs for federal assistance. This level of dependence, combined with the economic structure of the region, created the foundation for the bilateral treaty and agreements. Wealth, in part, structured the opportunities for changing intergovernmental rules; Samara's well-developed tax base provided it with the means to survive more independently of the center, whereas Bryansk lacked such sources of revenue. Nevertheless, wealth only explains one piece of the federal-development story. In Vologda, regional elites focused more on the federal pocketbook and cooperation under the existing rulebook, despite the economic potential for future fiscal independence. Although wealth, either from its tax base or natural resources, might have given a region the opportunity to demand more from the center under bilateralism, it does not explain how regional elites successfully shifted the rules of fiscal federalism to their region's advantage. Instead, we must turn to the political variables—executive efficacy and subnational stability—to understand how these

regions either exploited or squandered economic advantages in negotiating with the central government.

As chapter 4 demonstrates, bilateralism and executive dominance in
Russia placed the burden on regional governors to structure intergovernmental reform agendas and negotiate them with the federal government.
As in other systems of "executive federalism"—Canada, India, and Germany, for example—federal relations and the process of intergovernmental reform depended predominantly on the highest official at each level
of government.[1] Governors could draw on a wide array of bargaining
resources, including the support of local economic elites, clientelistic ties,
and opportunities for issue linkage, to accomplish this complex task. Yet,
it primarily rested with the top leadership of the region to marshal these
resources and direct them toward the goal of improving the region's relationship with the center. In Samara, the powerful and enduring leadership of Konstantin Titov successfully provided a credible commitment
to the center that decentralizing fiscal control to Samara would benefit
both parties to the agreement. In addition, his role in the Federation Council offered additional bargaining advantages, such as opportunities for
issue linkage within the federal budget debate. Despite the government's
foot-dragging and several political roadblocks, Samara signed a far-
reaching power-sharing treaty in 1997. In Vologda, political conflict and
leadership turnover prevented the regional government from exploiting
any economic advantages or potential it might have had at the beginning
of the bilateral process, even as the political situation began to stabilize at
the end of 1996. Instead, a new regional leadership team focused on negotiating a less controversial arrangement with the central government
while pursuing regional ties to improve its economic situation. Even
greater political turmoil and instability limited the already weak bargaining position of Bryansk, eliminating any potential to exploit its geographic
position as a border region. Although Bryansk, like Samara and Vologda,
managed to negotiate and sign its treaty with the federal government,
Bryansk emerged from the process as dependent on the federal government as before the treaty with no new concrete opportunities for autonomous development.

The story of how these three regions negotiated treaties with the federal
government provides a "behind-the-scenes" view of the messy process of
intergovernmental relations in a new federation. But it also raises questions about the future of federalism in Russia. If powerful regions such as
Samara continue to press for more economic autonomy while struggling
and disoriented regions like Bryansk face continued dependence on the
center, how will federalism manage? The negotiation of bilateral treaties
and intergovernmental fiscal reform are but one moment in the process
of constructing federalism. Yet this moment and the political choices that

it contains etch a pattern onto the future evolution of intergovernmental relations, thus giving shape to Russia's asymmetrical federation.

SAMARA

Samara oblast, a heart-shaped province sandwiched between Saratov and Orenburg oblasts on the border of Khazakstan, represents both the potential and the plight of Russia's regions. By some indicators, Samara was one of the most successful regional economies in the post-Soviet era. In 1996, the Russian journal *Ekspert* deemed Samara the fifth most favorable location for foreign investment; Bank Austria listed it as one of three regions with unequivocally favorable investment climates.[2] Based on living standards and aggregate economic indicators, Samara performed well above average. Its per capita gross regional product in 1995 was close to 42 percent above Russia's average (Romanov and Tartakovskaya 1998, 343). As discussed earlier, Samara's financial strength put it among the dwindling number of donor regions, which contribute more to the federal budget than they receive in transfers. In the second half of 1997, Samara placed fourth in its contribution to the federal budget, coming behind the city of Moscow, the oil-rich Khanty-Mansiiskii okrug, and Sverdlovsk oblast.

Despite these impressive results, Samara's economy suffered from the aftermath of the Soviet collapse: bankrupt defense industries, oversized and antiquated companies, and agricultural production resistant to adapting to the market. The destitution of Samara's largest companies highlights the region's problems. AvtoVAZ (*Volzhskii avtomobil'nii zavod*), the region's largest company employing almost 115,000 people, saw its tax debt and fines rise to more than three trillion rubles in 1997, placing it among the country's top corporate debtors and giving Samara the dubious honor of third place in overall debt by region.[3] The economic transition also left Samara's airplane factory, Aviakor (*Mezhdunarodnaya aviatsionnaya korporatsiya*), on the edge of bankruptcy due to the loss of defense-related orders, threatening its fifteen thousand workers with unemployment. The company survived only with the intervention of the regional government and a complex process of incorporation into the financial industrial group, *Rossiyskiy aviatsionniy konsortsium*.[4] Other enterprises of the military-industrial complex faced less optimistic fates. ZiM (*Zavod imeni Maslennikova*), one of Samara city's largest manufacturing companies employing thirty-three thousand people in 1990 faced bankruptcy in 1996; Metallist, a major component supplier of rocket engines, was put into receivership a year earlier (Hanson 1997, 414). By 1997, more than half (59 percent) of the region's enterprises operated at a loss, significantly more than the average (47.6 percent) for Russia (Goskomstat 1997, 383).

The contradictions between Samara's financial successes and trouble-some economic situation do not necessarily predict that regional elites would seek a dramatic shift in the intergovernmental balance of power. On the one hand, Samara's developed tax base gave it the opportunity to survive without the help of federal transfers. This implies that Samara would seek to carve out more fiscal independence from Moscow to gain more control over fiscal decision making. On the other hand, its suffering industries needed debt restructuring and central investment to survive and modernize; the regional administration alone could not cure the en-terprises' ills. The need for federal intervention into the economy implies a more dependent relationship between levels of government, reinforced by preexisting, hierarchical links within particular industrial sectors. The resulting agenda for intergovernmental reform, however, emphasized re-gional control over dependence. To achieve its goals, the administration sacrificed short-term financial gains in order to increase the region's decision-making control and to link these issues with enterprise reform. Samara's governor played the principal role in constructing this agenda and negotiating it with the center, using the resources he had assembled during his six-year tenure in office.

As outlined in chapter 5, Samara's detailed and carefully constructed bilateral treaty served as the centerpiece of the regional government's re-form plans. The administration had set up a formidable team of officials to handle the treaty and navigate it through the complex central bureau-cracy. Denislyam Yancheren, a senior official in Samara's government, fo-cused solely on negotiating the terms of the agreements, setting up joint commissions to handle disagreements, and sending new drafts to senior officials. In addition, the administration kept a vice governor in Moscow with a staff of nine. In 1996, the oblast budget allocated fifteen billion rubles (more than half the amount allocated to child-welfare programs!) to acquire new offices in a high-security building in central Moscow; the sleek, leather furniture and new computers attest to the importance of the office to Samara's government. Although Andrei Kalmikov, the vice gov-ernor in Moscow, did not handle only the bilateral treaty—his office also helps maintain links between Samara's government and economic leaders and Moscow and foreign elites—phone calls to various ministries and departments in regards to the treaty dominated his daily agenda in 1996 and 1997. According to Kalmikov, Samara's treaty required the approval of fifty-five different bureaucratic agencies and departments. The simple gathering of data to construct the agreements and formulate a stronger bargaining position required careful use of connections, particularly in the Finance Ministry.[5] The ministry often refused to give out cross-regional data, even data pertinent to Samara, such as the exact amount of the fed-eral budgetary debt to the oblast (*Samarskoe obozreniye*, 7 October 1996).

Consequently, Samara's government relied heavily on personal connections and business forums in the region to utilize the information and access the interests of regional elites during the agenda-setting stage of the bilateral treaty. According to many observers, Titov managed to gain the support of Samara's economic elite for his policies including the bilateral treaty. The consensus around Titov's agenda was enhanced by the smooth transition in the region from the socialist to post-socialist era: his familiarity with enterprise directors as a result of his previous job as an administrator in the Kiubyshchev Institute of the Planned Economy in the 1980s; the continuity of elites in the administration and in Samara's enterprises from the Gorbachev era; and the reputation of Titov and his deputies as *khozyaistvenniki* (economic managers) rather than ideologues (Matsuzato 1997, 66–7). The only opposition came from directors of former state farm and some enterprise managers in the defense sector—two areas that depend on hefty state subsidies to survive but, consequently, lack the clout of healthier enterprises (Lapshova 1996).[6]

The administration held weekly business meetings with local business leaders and state agencies, which provided forums to share information, discuss development strategies, and address mutual problems such as inter-enterprise debt.[7] More broadly, they also helped to cement the personal and political links between government and business. In addition, the governor and his deputies met regularly with the directors of AvtoVAZ to deal with the ongoing problems of the company's debt, its attempts to find outside investors, and its conflicts with the federal government. In one instance, the administration met with AvtoVAZ directors, other business leaders in Tolyatti, and representatives from local finance institutes to discuss the implementation of a new regional program—entitled "On the strategy of AvtoVAZ operations with industrial enterprises in Samara oblast for 1997–2000,"—an attempt to create a "Russian Detroit" by reinforcing and improving the interdependence between AvtoVAZ and local suppliers (*Samarskoe obozreniye*, 10 February 1997). In informal meetings and phone calls, Titov addressed more conflictual issues, although the administration was not always successful in getting its way. In one of the more publicized examples of the governor's displeasure with AvtoVAZ, the auto company chose LUKoil, a Russian company using Kazakh oil, to supply its service stations, rather than Yukos, an oil company connected to the local Samaratransgaz.[8] Within days of the agreement, Titov phoned the general director of AvtoVAZ, Alexei Nikolaev, to voice his displeasure, remind the director of the administration's help with its budgetary arrears, and suggest he rethink his decision.[9] A formal appeal to the AvtoVAZ board followed this more informal discussion (Romanov and Tartakovskaya 1998, 355).

Outside the realm of public meetings and business forums, political and economic elites had numerous opportunities to reinforce personal ties and conclude backroom deals. As in Moscow, where powerful business tycoons such as Boris Berezovsky rotate periodically through the government, Samara's administration also encouraged close connections between government and business. Governor Titov himself sat on the boards of AvtoVAZ, Aviakor, and Yukos (Romanov and Tartakovskaya 1998, 352). Yuri Logoido, Samara's prime minister—a somewhat fuzzy political position in relation to the rest of the administration—and then deputy governor, also sat on the board of directors of AvtoVAZ (Panorama 1996).[10] Leaders of Samara's companies have also won election to the regional legislature; senior representatives from AvtoVAZ, Volgopromgaz, Samartransgaz, Mezhregiongaz, and the director of the region's airport, all won seats in the provincial duma in 1997. Political campaigns created new opportunities for Titov to improve relations with the region's economic elite, and vice versa. In early 1995, Titov organized the regional branch of Prime Minister Viktor Chernomyrdin's party, Our Home is Russia (NDR) and became second in command to Chernomyrdin. The regional leadership of the party soon included Viktor Kadannikov, the general director of AvtoVAZ until his brief appointment as first deputy prime minister in December 1995; the director of Samaratransgaz and a member of the regional duma, Gennadi Zvyagin; and the chairman of the regional duma, Leon Kovalskii (Lapshova 1996).

Institutional and personal ties between economic and political elites nourished Samara's intergovernmental agenda at the formulation and negotiation stages. Samara's bilateral treaty reflected the regional programs and local development plans created with the cooperation of business leaders. Regional programs developed prior to 1995, such as *Konversiya*, a defense-conversion program that focuses on investment projects in Samara's defense-oriented companies such as Dvigatel' NK, a major producer of rocket engines. Another example was an agricultural stabilization program that provided the basis for the federal power-sharing agreements signed in 1997 (*Gubernskii informatsionnii bulleten'*, March 1996, 13–23). The head of Dvigatel' NK, Igor Shitarev, then showed his support for the treaty by attending the official signing by Governor Titov and President Yeltsin.

In addition to facilitating information exchanges between economic and political elites, the administration encouraged a higher degree of transparency of information than is the norm in Russia, a land where secrecy and control over information are highly valued.[11] Journalists in the region maintain that the government fostered cooperation with the local press, granting interviews and providing information to media sources beyond the government paper, *Volzhskaya Kommuna*.[12] Moreover, the administration published a monthly bulletin that included budgetary and statistical information,[13] new regional and federal legislation, descriptions of the roles and responsibilities of various departments in the administration, and a day-by-day description of the governor's official activities.

During the final negotiation of the treaty, Chernomyrdin's government made a final attempt to take the upper hand in the negotiations with Samara and limit the region's power to demand far-reaching devolution of fiscal authority by focusing its attention on the struggling automaker, AvtoVAZ. The center seemed ready to test the strength of the alliance between Samara's administration and AvtoVAZ, its largest business, by implicitly linking the treaty with the survival of and control over the company. On November 28, 1996, immediately preceding the gubernatorial elections in Samara and at a time when the center had seemingly agreed to sign the treaty[14]—Governor Titov delivered the treaty and thirteen agreements to Prime Minister Chernomyrdin on November 24, 1996[15]— *Izvestiya* reported that the emergency committee on tax collection (VChK) had placed AvtoVAZ on the official *"spisok"*: the list of companies prepared for bankruptcy. The newspaper later quoted the minister of finance as stating that the automaker had "no possible means" of repaying its eleven trillion rubles in tax debts and fines (30 November 1996). According to General Director Alexei Nikolaev, Deputy Prime Minister Victor Potanin had contacted him several weeks before, alerting him that the government would begin bankruptcy proceedings unless the company's board could come up with a means to pay its federal taxes (*Volzhskaya Kommuna*, 14 February 1997). An article in *Segodnya* asserted that the president perceived the VChK and its threats of bankruptcy, in part, as a means to forestall the bilateral agreements and prevent further strengthening of the regions.[16] Yet for Titov, the center's decision to threaten AvtoVAZ during the final stages of the treaty negotiations offered the governor an opportunity to pay back AvtoVAZ leaders for their support as well as assert regional control over a previously centralized industry. The publication of the bankruptcy list produced an angry response in Samara, where a variety of explanations arose to explain the government's decision and the timing.[17] At the political level, the decision seemed to trigger a show of force by the center and Samara as to who could offer the greater threat. Nevertheless, the decision to threaten AvtoVAZ in the days before the gubernatorial election in Samara was ill-timed by the center. Even in a region where the governor was predicted to easily win reelection, the threat of bankruptcy to the region's largest employer and its suppliers might have hurt Titov and other pro-government candidates at the municipal level, particularly in a region where the communist party received fairly strong support. Two days before the election, Governor Titov, the directors of AvtoVAZ, and Russian Deputy Prime Minister Potanin announced an agreement that released the company from the threat of bankruptcy; the center had little reason to carry through with its previous threats. In exchange, the company would sell off shares representing fifty percent of the company's capital stock and begin paying its federal taxes, with much of its tax debts restructured and some of its fines eliminated (*Finansoviye izvestiya*, 5 December 1996).[18] Even with the agreement in place, the governor showed he had little trust in the promises of the federal government, warning that any further threats to the region or its industries would set off a dangerous process of "tit-for-tat." Titov cautioned "his opponents" in the days before the election that he had a number of "powerful strategic options that he could employ should there be any undesired developments on the subject of AvtoVAZ's debt. First and foremost, this related to the federal budgetary debt to the oblast" (*Samarskoe obozreniye*, 9 December 1996).[19]

Governor Titov also employed strategies of issue linkage as the federal government delayed signing the treaty and agreements following the December local elections. During this period, as during other bilateral negotiations, Titov exploited his prominent position as head of the Federation Council's budgetary and finance committee to the region's advantage, holding up government-supported financial legislation in response to Yeltsin's stalling tactics.[20] According to Samara's deputy governor and representative in Moscow, Titov's committee appointment represented the region's most important and effective bargaining resource[21] and "eased the process of opening difficult doors" (*Samarskoe izvestiya*, 7 February 1996). Titov, in fact, candidly admits to the benefits of his central position in the Federation Council, perhaps underscoring the conflict of interest inherent in a national legislative body comprised of regional executives. In an interview, he stated, "To the question of whether a governor in the position of the head of an important committee lobbies for the interests of the oblast, [the answer is] without a doubt, yes" (*Samarskiye izvestiya*, 30 January 1996).

Titov also relied on the organization of the donor regions[22] to increase the pressure on the federal government. In late 1996, Titov and the other donor regions lobbied strongly to incorporate specific fiscal privileges for the donors into the 1997 federal budget. In particular, they successfully argued for the right to use locally collected revenues for federal expenditures in their regions, which would provide a federal legal precedent for a principal aspect of financial control in Samara's bilateral treaty (*Samarskoe obozreniye*, 28 October 1996). As the center postponed signing the bilateral treaty with Samara, the donors issued a list of necessary changes to the system of fiscal federalism that would increase regional control and reward the donors for their fiscal responsibility.[23] The donor lobby became increasingly critical of the center's regional policy and transfer system, arguing that they rewarded regions for poor tax collection and lavish spending. Moreover, they maintained, the overcentralization of revenues created an inefficient system of fiscal federalism, in which the center could not fulfill its financial promises (*Vlast' v Rossii*, October 1996). As one of the most outspoken supporters of the donors' demands, Titov implied that if the center did not sign the bilateral treaty with Samara, he would pursue even greater changes to Russia's intergovernmental fiscal system and on a wider scale.

Despite these games of chicken, both sides had strong incentives to sign the treaty and maintain cooperative relations, limiting their means to use threats and issue linkage in the negotiations. The center had little reason to evoke the ire of Samara's governor, who had been one of Yeltsin's and Chernomyrdin's strongest regional supporters. Moreover, the earlier threat of bankruptcy for AvtoVAZ was hardly credible since it would have produced a wave of economic and social instability in one of Russia's few stable regions and major contributors to the federal budget. For Samara, cooperation with the center advanced overall goals of stability and decreasing the costs of intergovernmental interaction. Unlike other regions during Yeltsin's presidency, such as Primorski Krai and Tatarstan, Titov primarily emphasized cooperation and unity over political threats. According to one observer, "In a bad world, it is better to have nice fights . . . Therefore, Titov will not get into fights with the center. He knows that this might be useful for the oblast for six months but then it will be worse. He is a farsighted [*dalekovidnii*] politician who just says to the center that we must work [together]."[24] The treaty meant institutionalizing a new set of intergovernmental rules that would give the region significantly more control over its own finances, increase its ability to receive financing for approved federal development programs, and negotiate new projects with foreign investors. To achieve these aims, the regional government had few choices other than to negotiate with the federal government; no other strategies, such as multilateral legislation or reform along the lines of the donors' proposals, would achieve the same number of substantive goals so quickly. In addition, the specific rules of the game laid out in Samara's treaty went far beyond the more symbolic proforma treaties that the center had been moving toward since 1996 (Ivanov 1998). According to Vice Governor Andrei Kalmikov, Samara could have agreed to sign the treaty in early 1996 and then waited to negotiate the tougher agreements.[25] Instead, the regional government chose to hammer out the thirteen agreements before signing the treaty, waiting until August 1997 to sign the entire set of documents. As a comprehensive package, the treaty represented a watershed in Samara's relationship with the federal government and the product of critical economic and political resources; Titov had little reason to jeopardize its success.

Despite delaying the signing of the treaty with Samara for almost nine months, the goal of stability provided the center with the incentive to finalize the agreements. Unlike many other regions, Samara's government could offer a credible commitment to contribute to the political, social, and economic stability of the federation and to implement the terms of the bilateral agreements to the benefit of both parties. Titov's administration showed an impressive level of effective economic management even within the environment of growing fiscal uncertainty at the center.[26] According to Deputy Governor Aleksei Kalmikov, Moscow would not have considered transferring the type of financial control contained in Samara's bilateral treaty if the federal government were fiscally healthy.[27] Samara was one of a handful of regions that did not have any wage or pension arrears to public sector workers. In addition, the subnational government subsidized federal budget workers, such as employees of the State Tax Service and federal educational institutions, whose federal paychecks often arrived several months late. Although the regional budget, like the majority of others, frequently ran a deficit (17 percent of expenditures in 1995), it also implemented its budgetary expenditures by an average of just over 100 percent from 1994–1996,[28] financing its deficit through municipal bonds.[29]

Relatively successful budgetary management in Samara had both political and social rewards, a relationship noted by most of my interview subjects. Whereas teachers, doctors, and other state sectors workers began striking across Russia in 1996 and 1997, Samara did not witness a single public sector strike. In a political environment that emphasizes the role of individuals, most state workers and pensioners, two of the more disgruntled groups in the country, attributed their comparative well-being to Titov's leadership.[30] Their satisfaction also affected national and regional elections outcomes. Despite the concentration of industrial workers in the region—often indicating stronger support for communist candidates— both Titov and Yeltsin won reelection in the province, even as the Communist Party of the Russian Federation won the largest share of votes for district seats in the 1995 parliamentary elections.

The ability to function more independently from the federal budget in a stable environment allowed Samara to expand the terms of the bilateral agreements, as in the case of the agreement on foreign investment activity. Samara had the financial resources to provide its own guarantee to investors and thus it would not have to rely on the central government in a case of an investor's untimely departure, and the center would benefit from the increase in revenues from foreign investment. The consensus around Titov's administration also communicated to the center that the region would successfully implement other agreements that depended on cooperation between the administration and local elites. According to one assessment, Samara was one of the only regions with the institutional and legal foundation to implement a bilateral agreement on transfers of federal property (*Samarskie obozrenie*, 20 October 1997). Furthermore, efficient fiscal management and a strong institutional foundation that linked government, corporate, and grassroots groups ensured the implementation of federal programs, such as the environmental program, which relied on a combination of federal and subnational funds and local initiatives to allocate and effectively use the money.

The bilateral treaty and agreements altered the balance of power between the federal government and Samara, creating new opportunities for the region and its leaders. The fiscal autonomy provided by the bilateral treaty along with the some of the bargaining resources that proved effective during the treaty negotiations (such as the unified elite structure of the province) contributed to Samara's rapid recovery following the 1998 economic crisis. By the end of the decade, the economic health of the province ranked well above the national average, putting it in the top ten regions for foreign investment and making it one of only six regions allowed to participate in a World Bank program for regional fiscal reform.[31] Governor Titov also used the success in negotiating the treaty to further increase Samara's power while raising his own national prominence. During the election campaigns of 1999 and 2000, Titov used the donor coalition as a springboard for the creation of a new political party, the Voice of Russia (*Golos Rossii*), and a presidential campaign, both of which put him at odds with the group's other prominent leader, Yuri Luzhkov. As a consequence of Samara's continued financial health, particularly following the 1998 global economic crisis, and its newfound economic autonomy with the bilateral treaty and agreements, Governor Titov began to take a more aggressive and confrontational approach with the center. In addition to continual pressure from the donor lobby for reform of interbudgetary mechanisms, Titov announced potential new strategies for strengthening Samara's economic position. These included the formation of a Volga common market and the establishment of gold reserves in the province (*Nezavisimaya gazeta*, 24 September 1998; *Russia Today*, 7 June 1999). With his ally, Viktor Chernomyrdin, out of office and Boris Yeltsin staggering toward the end of his term, Governor Titov likely perceived few advantages in amiable cooperation with a floundering federal government. His decision to run for president in 2000 also put him at odds with the heir-apparent, Vladimir Putin, and created conflict between the new administration and Governor Titov.[32] Moreover, the decision-making power granted by the bilateral treaty offered Titov the opportunity to focus Samara's economic and political resources on development strategies that circumvent bilateral negotiations with the center. Without the dependence on the federal government for transfers, investment guarantees, or foreign economic ties, Samara could hope for a less costly and interdependent relationship with the center while it increased its financial independence and economic health through multilateral and international relations. Although Samara's development ultimately yielded benefits to the rest of Russia through its federal tax receipts and contribution to national stability, it also gave the region opportunities to retain its wealth and bolster its position unavailable to more dependent regions such as Vologda and Bryansk, which had to rely on an unstable federal government for their economic well-being.

VOLOGDA

In Samara, a powerful governor and substantial economic resources devoted to the goal of intergovernmental reform both provided a formidable bargaining cache. Vologda lacked the economic resources and leadership consensus of Samara, yet it also pursued a less radical bilateral agenda in its treaty, seeking a narrower sphere of regional autonomy in comparison with Samara and employing completely nonconfrontational strategies. Such a cooperative approach to intergovernmental relations seems ironic, given that in 1993 Vologda was the first province to pass a referendum on becoming a republic, beginning the "parade of sovereignties" that would end with the constitutional showdown in October of that year. In the context of the region's unstable economic and political situation, however, a more cooperative strategy appeared the most constructive avenue for intergovernmental reform by the time Governor Pozgalev negotiated the treaty in mid-1996. While Samara and other regions were actively pursuing bilateral treaties in 1995 and 1996, Vologda was mired in political turmoil that threatened its social stability and economic health. As the region stabilized under a new governor Vyacheslav Pozgalev in the summer of 1996, Vologda's administration was finally able to unite its economic and political elite toward the goal of a bilateral treaty and new strategies for reform. Nevertheless, Governor Pozgalev had to temper the administration's desire for greater autonomy from the center with the pragmatic need for federal financial support as a result of the previous administration's mismanagement and corruption.

As the tables in chapter 5 illustrate, Vologda's economic position in the mid-1990s was comparable to Russia's average in terms of revenue and monthly wages. Nevertheless, such basic economic indicators do not reveal the region's more complex economic situation, which affected its ability to negotiate with the center. Like Samara, Vologda's economic picture contained some very contradictory elements. Vologda has a relatively weak tax base, comprising only 15.7 percent of its gross regional product, as opposed to Samara's 25 percent. Financial weaknesses are exacerbated by the region's lack of natural resources and its dependence on outside fuel sources. Yet since the Soviet collapse, the region has suffered a much smaller drop in production than many other regions. This is based in large part on the strength of the metallurgy industry, a sector that has a comparatively bright future in Russia. As a result, the magazine *Ekspert* rated Vologda as one of the regions with the lowest investment risk, particularly for Russian investors (December 9, 1996). Vologda's strong record on privatization also contributed to its positive investment rating. One of the first regions to embark upon a mass-privatization program, the region privatized almost 90 percent of the state-owned enterprises within five years.[33] Other sectors with export potential, such as timber production, gave the region the ability to develop and strengthen its economy independent of central conversion and investment projects. According to one classification of economic potential and income levels, Vologda ranked in the second-highest, or "wealthy" category (OECD 1995). Until 1995, Vologda was economically strong enough to disqualify the region from federal transfers from the Fund for Regional Support.

Despite this promising foundation, by 1995 the financial health of Vologda began to falter. While Samara's government was focusing resources on federal financing "experiments" and investment plans that would form the foundation for the region's bilateral treaty, Vologda's administration was embroiled in scandal that shattered the region's economic and political stability and paralyzed the process of reform. As painstakingly detailed in the 1994 book *Podgornovskiy Milliardi* (Podgornov's Billions), by journalist Vladimir Pantsirev,[34] Governor Podgornov misappropriated 21.7 billion rubles in federal loans intended for the purchase of wheat for the state-run bread factories. Podgornov then used the money, along with other budgetary funds, to purchase cars and build houses for his personal use, and to funnel credits to his relatives and other cronies in business. President Yeltsin removed Podgornov in May 1996 and the state arrested him later that year; still, the political turmoil ended long after the story first appeared in the national press in 1995. From 1994 until mid-1995, the so-called "Bread Affair" (*Khlebnoye delo*) divided the oblast's political and economic elite, with the public feud between the governor and Vladimir Lopatin, a State Duma representative from Vologda and a former member of Podgornov's administration, surfacing in the national press. Lopatin made repeated appeals to the President and Duma to take up the matter, even after a federal commission found no evidence of financial misdeeds. Yet during the commission's investigation, Governor Podgornov dismissed Vologda's public prosecutor, who had hinted that he had collected evidence against the governor. Later, a suspicious fire erupted at the offices of the independent newspaper, *Russkii Sever*, the most outspoken publisher of anti-Podgornov articles, suggesting that the governor was at least attempting to stifle internal opposition.[35]

The conflict virtually halted the political process in the region, eliminating any chance of consensus over economic policies and strategies. From 1994 to 1996, as the governor clashed with the legislature and other regional elites, the administration paid little attention to the need for new intergovernmental rules and the need to develop an agenda for reform to negotiate with the center. As Podgornov's corruption came to light, the agrarian lobby in the legislature began to oppose every move by the governor, particularly in the budgetary sphere.[36] Meanwhile, Vologda's formidable business lobby continued to support the governor as a result of generous tax credits and other financial incentives.[37] In 1995, the legislature managed to pass only forty-three laws and resolutions and had not yet formed any joint working groups between the administration and legislature, a principal means of resolving conflict and developing policy goals (*Russkii sever*, 9 January 1996). The legislature-executive conflict similarly stalled local elections and motivated Podgornov to bring an appeal to the Constitutional Court regarding a disagreement with the Vologda legislature over its local self-government law. The conflict embroiled other regional agencies on which the economy depended. Podgornov tried unsuccessfully to remove the head of the Vologda tax inspectorate, Veniamin Alekseev, after Alekseev refused to implement the governor's decree unilaterally subordinating the tax service to the regional government instead of the federal government (Pantsirev 1996). The governor's opposition to Alekseev did not improve the situation at the tax service, where employees endured dreadful working conditions while managing to collect less than half of the region's expected revenues.

As a result of the political stalemate, the government failed to address the growing fiscal crisis in the region—rising arrears and poorly implemented budgets—that further threatened to undermine both the administration's legitimacy and the ability of the region to regain its former financial independence from the center. The crisis would also set the stage for bilateral treaty negotiations over the coming year. In the first three-quarters of 1996, the government collected only 35 percent of its projected revenue and expected to collect less than half of the total sum by the end of the year. In its annual projection based on measures of the region's tax base and enterprise audits, the finance department estimated that unpaid taxes were over 125 percent of taxes paid; even with new, more stringent tax-collection measures, the administration could only project a percentage of unpaid taxes decreased to 105 percent for 1997.[38] Moreover, the region collected much of its tax revenue through interaccounting measures (*vzaimoraschet*) and non-money surrogates, with only half of its revenue coming in the form of money according to Ministry of Finance data for 1996.[39]

Weaknesses in revenue collection also impaired Vologda's ability to implement the budget, which in turn damaged the social stability of the region. Based on the 1996 revenue shortfalls, the region implemented less than half of the projected expenditures, including wages and pensions to state workers. As a result of wage and pension delays, strikes of teachers and state health care workers began erupting in 1996, increasing the urgency of fiscal and economic reform. Wage arrears similarly afflicted the private sector, dominated by Severstal', the metallurgy factory located in Cherepovets', Vologda's most populous city. Despite the relative health of the metallurgy sector in comparison with other branches of heavy industry, the enterprise still suffered from the problems typical of Russia's transition: enormous employee and social benefits costs, inefficient production, and low quality output. Although Severstal' provided 40 percent of the oblast's budgetary revenue,[40] it also drained significant budgetary resources through tax and investment credits.

The lack of available revenue bore heavily on the administration's ability to modernize and gather data—the foundation for the development of reform plans. In its 1996 budget, Vologda designated less than half of the amount to cover the administration's expenses than was allocated in Samara's budget and it dedicated no funds whatsoever to research and data collection. Although the budget allocated money to computerize the financial department, there were few means or resources for gathering detailed financial information. The administration relied on its own departments for data collection, supplemented by the Vologda branch of Goskomstat, which publishes an annual booklet of very basic regional statistics. The administration also lacked the funds to hire skilled administrators and to provide training to current staff members (Pozgalev 1996, 35). According to one of Vologda's vice governors, the administration was just beginning to hire specialists at the end of 1996, particularly in finance and accounting.[41] With its paucity of information and research resources, Vologda's administration turned to the Russian Academy of Sciences for assistance in compiling economic development and reform plans in 1996 as it looked for a way out of its economic crisis.

The financial problems and rising social strife in Vologda placed the emphasis in the reform plans on crisis management and federal support: helping Severstal' attract foreign investment, increasing the rate of tax collection, and getting the federal government to fulfill its fiduciary promises to the region. The bilateral treaty stressed this last goal, focusing on the center's role in easing the financial crisis and helping the region to reorient itself to foreign investment. Governor Podgornov and his financial misdeeds cannot receive full blame for the economic crisis in the region. Yet they certainly contributed to the lack of attention to the growing problems, the political paralysis, and the subsequent "crisis mode" of Vologda's government. With few attempts to address the budgetary crisis through subnational measures, such as tax reforms or subsidy reductions, or intergovernmental reforms, such as a bilateral treaty, Governor Podgornov bequeathed to his successor an environment of economic turmoil rather than economic potential.

By the time Yeltsin removed Nikolai Podgornov in May 1996, Vologda's economic and political elite strongly supported his replacement, if only to find a measure of political stability. Moreover, Vyacheslav Pozgalev, Yeltsin's choice to replace Podgornov, clearly pleased the region's industrialists. Pozgalev, described by associates and observers as a "Luzhkov-type," and a "pragmatic manager in the 'Cherepovets'-style'"—alluding the pragmatic managerialism favored by the leadership of Cherepovets's largest company, Severstal'—had worked for many years in Severstal', reaching the level of deputy general director. Since 1991, he had served as a popular mayor of Cherepovets and was elected to serve in the Federation Council in 1993,[42] giving him strong ties with the local economic elite as well as central bureaucrats and politicians. With support from the economic elite and the largest city in the oblast, Pozgalev easily won the gubernatorial elections in October 1996, garnering more than 80 percent of the vote. Although he immediately concentrated on improving tax collection and paying state workers (*Segodnya*, October 2, 1996), he also focused on improving the economic position of Severstal' and other local companies and maintaining their support by sponsoring new probusiness tax legislation for the region.[43]

Pozgalev began to "prepare [Vologda] to meet the twenty-first century" (*Federalizm* 1997, 33) by creating a new relationship with the center that would balance intergovernmental cooperation with Vologda's historically independent spirit.[44] Yet the fiscal crisis created by Podgornov's economic mismanagement constrained the governor's choices. The governor used his new office, his membership in *Our Home is Russia*, and strong voter support in Vologda for Yeltsin in the June 1996 presidential elections to gain access to central officials, such as Minister of the Economy Evgenii Yasin. At first, Pozgalev followed Podgornov's modus operandi of intergovernmental politics: request increased federal funding and investment in the region.[45]

The dearth of federal funding, however, necessitated a new type of politics to replace the existing policies under Podgornov of federal and subnational handouts. According to the editor of the newspaper, *Krasnii Sever*,

[With Pozgalev] some hopes and programs and projects appeared, communication with ordinary people and also ties with the Northwest [regional economic] Association. These were more realistic contacts, not just simply 'you give me and I give you' with the center, but already some realistically thought-out economic projects. . . . It no longer pays to go to him with an outstretched hand as many are used to doing, [saying] "give me money," as it used to be until now. Pozgalev isn't accustomed to working this way and never will be. He now clearly says, "It's not going to be like before. Don't come to me, don't ask. But come and say, 'Here is my business plan and this is what I need to achieve it. To get results, I have to do this and this.' If you come to me without this, the conversation will be fruitless." Exactly this type of pragmatic approach will create the tone for the entire regional environment. In my opinion, this is particularly promising during difficult economic times.[46]

Thus, while Pozgalev sought more money from the center, he also engaged the Academy of Sciences to develop a business plan for the region, using the economic and financial analysis in the program to serve as the foundation for the bilateral treaty.[47] For three months in late 1996, Governor Pozgalev used the ties to the center that he had also cultivated during his two-year tenure in the Federation Council as well as his new position on the budgetary and finance committee with Samara's Governor Titov, to shuttle the treaty through the necessary bureaucracies. Unlike the more contentious agreements with Samara, which required numerous joint committees to resolve differences, Pozgalev could concentrate solely on getting the necessary approvals. According to First Deputy Governor Nikolai Kostigov, the most difficult issue was getting President Yeltsin and Prime Minister Chernomyrdin to sign the final version.[48]

As the regional government worked belatedly to develop reform strategies, the political fragmentation in the region under Podgornov was replaced by a new consensus. Pozgalev no longer had the opportunity to translate this support into more extensive bilateral agreements. Instead, it gave Pozgalev valuable resources to consolidate his control over the region, ensure the signing of the existing set of agreements, and to offer a credible commitment to the center to implement them. The powerful Severstal-Metkombank group solidly supported the governor and his new policies, financing his gubernatorial campaign and endorsing him in the media outlets under their control. Moreover, the Severstal' lobby in the regional parliament—controlling 19 of 30 deputies following the elections in 1996—voted for Pozgalev's probusiness budgets and legislation. The Severstal' group also communicated its support for the bilateral treaty through parliamentary review of the documents and private meetings with the governor.[49]

In exchange, the government strengthened its relationship with the business community by increasing its involvement through the exchange of information, providing specialists and advice, and continuing regional credits and investment despite budgetary pressures. In addition, the regional government agreed to act as guarantor for bank loans by enterprises and for foreign investors, meanwhile negotiating with the central government to provide that service for Vologda's government. Anatolii Pak, Vologda's vice governor in charge of privatization, also stressed that businesses such as Severstal' particularly depended on the regional government in dealings with foreign investors because the government still owned the land underneath the private enterprises.[50] Pozgalev's administration sought to appease a variety of groups that had been at odds with the previous governor, reestablishing a cooperative working relationship with the State Tax Service and increasing the number of meetings and transparency of information between the two offices.[51] In addition, Pozgalev tried to smooth over tensions with the agrarian lobby, although a new "bread affair" somewhat hampered his attempts.[52]

Pozgalev's landslide election in October 1996 gave the regional government a legitimacy that had been absent the previous several years. In addition, it raised hopes among the Vologda's elite that economic reforms could finally move the region away from its dependency on the federal government. Pozgalev sought to ease some of his constituents' mistrust by improving the relationship of the government with the media and opening the government to broader scrutiny.[53] In addition, the governor increased his visibility through such measures as a weekly "Ask the Governor" column in one of the local papers. Nevertheless, the economic crisis, and the wage and pension arrears in particular, limited short-term opportunities to improve the administration's legitimacy.

The mostly futile appeals for money from Moscow (particularly after the presidential and gubernatorial elections)[54] and the new consensus in the region propelled Pozgalev to find new strategies for intergovernmental reform. With few of Samara's resources to bargain for advantageous decision-making power, Vologda's administration focused on negotiating a treaty that would ensure the implementation of the center's fiduciary responsibilities by allowing the region to use locally collected federal tax revenue to cover transfers and federal programs[55] and get the Ministry of Finance to act as guarantor for foreign investments and loans. Vologda's administration then turned to improving foreign and multilateral ties within the Northwest economic region as an alternative economic strategy to negotiating fiscal autonomy. The Northwest Association, which includes St. Petersburg and the wealthy Komi Republic, provides an important economic network for Vologda by providing new outlets for trade, enhanced access to energy sources in Komi and Kostroma, and an institutional basis for interregional ties among private enterprises and state agencies. In addition to a ruling body of its members' governors, the Northwest Association operates a legislative assembly—the first interregional parliament—comprised of the leaders of the regional dumas.[56] The association's structure also includes multilateral committees on finance, forestry, industry, information, and intergovernmental cooperation, as well as forums for interregional business ties.

These institutional links helped Vologda to pursue its development agenda with limited involvement from the federal government. By providing alternative means of obtaining investment, loans, and assistance with economic reform, regional ties de-emphasized the importance for Vologda of the bilateral treaty and the intergovernmental relationship in general. Whereas Samara's leadership stressed the need to wrest control from an overly centralized federal government, and threatened to retaliate when the center stalled in signing the treaty, Vologda's leaders maintained that the treaty served only to establish the basic rules of the game, allowing the region to pursue its goals through a variety of means. According to Vice Governor Nikolai Kostigov:

We should all be together in Russia in order to be Russia. But I already said that we cannot wait, we do not have time for that. We cannot wait for anything. It is necessary to give us the rules of the game, we will play by these rules, and if there are new rules, we will play by those. . . . We are now working on long-range programs and are trying to develop it so that we don't have to go to the government to ask for money. We go to the government and say, "Support us in this and that question. Act as a guarantor." Nothing more is necessary.[57]

In part, alternative development strategies provided an important bargaining resource for Vologda, which lacked the political muscle of Samara. As with Samara, the center postponed signing the treaty after Pozgalev won reelection in the fall of 1996. Rather than push to sign the treaty without the specific agreements, Vologda's government simply waited while pursuing other avenues in its economic development plans. As a result, it concluded a treaty that met its fundamental goals: federal guarantees to implement its financial promises, federal guarantees for foreign investment, and the establishment of the basic rules of the game for intergovernmental relations.[58] Within a context of cooperation and greater dependency than Samara, Vologda still altered the intergovernmental rules of the game. As one observer noted, using as a point of comparison the infamous example of exceptional privileges won through bilateralism, "Without a doubt, the Treaty with the Republic of Tatarstan and the Treaty with Vologda oblast differ from each other in content. But conceptually they are identical" (Ivanov 1998, 164).

Alternative development strategies also allowed Vologda to emphasize loyalty to the center and intergovernmental cooperation. Without the capacity to link the passage of the treaty to other issues at the national level, Vologda's leadership placed the bilateral agreements in the framework of an intergovernmental partnership, regarding them as a means to prevent conflict by establishing the rules of the game.[59] Thus, they presented the treaty as a resolution of uncertainty, rather than an attempt to gain special privileges. According to one legislator, the treaty would resolve issues specific to Vologda; the province would await federal legislation to solve broader questions of national importance and pursue bilateral agreements to address individual points of conflict.[60] The leadership stressed that the primary interests of the region—economic reform and stabilization—coincided with those of Russia. Moreover, with Pozgalev's membership in *Our Home is Russia* and Vologda's strong support of Yeltsin in the 1996 elections, Pozgalev presented the region's political interests as linked to those of the central government. In an interview preceding the gubernatorial elections, Pozgalev noted that votes for Yeltsin were also votes in support of his appointment as governor and reform policies (*Segodnya*, 5 October 1996). Russia's unity, intergovernmental cooperation, and regional development outside the micromanagement of the center all fit within Vologda's ideas for federal reform. According to Governor Pozgalev,

Today it is obvious that to achieve the stabilization of socio-economic development and [to find] a way out from the oblast's economic crisis, collaborative work between governments at every level . . . is essential. Without cooperation, ongoing problems will not be resolved. A measure of political-economic freedom toward which we, like all regions, are striving, dictates the need for the resolution of still one more problem. An organization of administrative structures, which would ensure the autonomy, initiative, and responsibility of all levels of government is necessary. . . . Most important [toward this goal] is the delineation of powers between the federal Center and Vologda oblast [and] between organs of state power of the oblast and organs of local self-government. (*Federalizm* 1996, 40)

After Vologda signed the bilateral treaty and agreements with Moscow in mid-1997, the region's fiscal situation steadily improved, with foreign investment and revenue collection increasing and budgetary arrears disappearing. Whereas much of the economic improvement can be attributed to growth in two major sectors of Vologda's economy—metallurgy and timber processing—the institutionalization of intergovernmental rules also contributed to Vologda's development. By establishing the balance between dependence and autonomy, bilateralism structured the range of policy choices available to Vologda's leaders and the role of the federal government in those policies. The political disarray and fiscal consequences of the Podgornov administration constrained the region's ability to seek the type of autonomous development evident in Samara, but they also created the opportunities to find alternatives to bilateralism as a reform strategy under the newfound conditions of political stability. Yet, alternative development strategies also necessitated the consolidation of political and economic resources to devise new programs and present credible commitments to partners. Without the ability to harness these resources, as will be evident in the case of Bryansk, few alternatives existed to financial dependence on an unreliable federal government.

BRYANSK

Bryansk, with its defense-oriented industry and struggling state farms, epitomizes the immense hurdles facing Russia's poorer regions in the economic transition. According to one World Bank survey, Bryansk has the potential to raise only half its needed revenues without federal transfers.[61] In 1996, its industries' profits barely balanced out their losses, producing only 129 billion rubles in revenue in the first nine months as compared to over 3.5 trillion rubles in Samara (Goskomstat 1996, 233). The largest employers in Bryansk, Bryansk Machine-Building Factory (BMZ) and Bryansk Automobile Factory (BAZ), which produces trailers for missiles rather than cars, operated on the edge of bankruptcy, as did the chemical weapons production facilities. Its agricultural sector, particularly potato farming, needed substantial government assistance, with most of the farms located in the southern part of the oblast that was evacuated after the nuclear accident at Chernobyl. Yet, there were still a few areas of optimism in Bryansk's economy. Its chemical industry and glassworks witnessed increases in production after 1995 (Panorama 1996). In addition, the region's advantageous geographical position on the borders of Belarus and Ukraine offered the potential for revenue from trade and customs duties and for the development of the region's economy as a supplier of inexpensive construction materials and even food products.[62]

Numerous plans emerged in the 1990s to resurrect Bryansk's economy, including the creation of a free economic zone, the expansion of the regional airport to serve as the southern alternative to Moscow and St. Petersburg, and the courting of Moscow's largest banks to invest in the region. In the context of the political turmoil that plagued the region, however, these plans had no chance to come to fruition and lacked realistic strategies for financing and implementation. The bilateral treaty and plans for intergovernmental reform, as outlined in the previous chapter, included proposals to develop the region's potential as a border state with only vague promises by the federal government to explore the issue. Assurances by the center to continue financial support and provide loans with no means for the region to apply sanctions for noncompliance offered little hope of economic improvement. Whereas in Vologda, the political conflict caused by Governor Podgornov delayed serious reform efforts and constrained the options for his successor, in Bryansk, governmental chaos and more intractable economic problems precluded opportunities for change. Not only did leadership turnover and governmental corruption strain Bryansk's limited financial resources and increase the region's need for federal financial support, but they also restricted the region's ability to create and implement development plans and to envision the center's role in these plans.[63] Bryansk's bilateral treaty and plans for intergovernmental reform reflected the high level of instability and uncertainty in the region.

Between 1991 and 1996, Bryansk endured five changes of leadership, with each one ushering in new administrations and policies but none having the time or resources to address the federal relationship.[64] Bryansk's governors alternated between the status quo of seeking federal handouts and popular but unrealistic reform proposals. In 1991, President Yeltsin appointed Vladimir Barabanov as head of the Bryansk administration over the objections of the majority of the oblast soviet. Barabanov created a sense of panic throughout his term in office with his lack of economic policies, other than advocating free lunches for the poor.[65] In April 1993, Bryansk held gubernatorial elections and Yuri Lodkin, a member of the Communist Party of the Russian Federation and a former correspondent for Itar-Tass, took over the leadership post. Lodkin advocated programs that symbolized the economic security of the Soviet system—increasing transfers from Moscow while subsidizing bread during the economic crisis (*Bryanskoe vremya*, 4 December 1996). Yet, his tenure was short-lived; five months after the election, Yeltsin removed him from office for supporting Ruslan Khasbulatov and the anti-Yeltsin forces in the October 1993 parliamentary coup.[66] He replaced Lodkin with Vladimir Karpov, a pro-Yeltsin "democrat" and a corrupt careerist who would splinter an already disintegrating region. During Karpov's two years in office, the mayor of Bryansk and the head of customs were both arrested for misuse of office. The head of the regional state property committee was also indicted in 1996 for illegally transferring state property into the private ownership of his friends and allies (*Bryanskoe Vremya*, 16 October 1996). Karpov established close relationships with several powerful business elites in the region, giving them government contracts, tax privileges, and substantial budgetary funds. His closest ally, Oleg Kibalchich, fled the country in 1995 after the federal government's antiorganized crime unit began investigating him for allegedly misusing budgetary funds allocated for Chernobyl victims and for illegally importing goods (Panorama 1996). Two of Karpov's senior officials, including the deputy governor, had been employees in Kibalchich's firms, strengthening the links between Karpov and regional corruption.

Notwithstanding the turmoil, a bilateral treaty still surfaced as the anchor for reform. With little time or financial resources to devote to research and data collection, Karpov's administration, like the government in Vologda, turned to outside specialists to draft a development plan for Bryansk. The first part of the development program, drafted by Moscow's Gaidar Institute, based the recovery in the region on a bilateral treaty with the center and financing from Moscow's largest banks (*Bryanskoe Vremya*, September 4, 1996). Governor Karpov's policies painted him as reformer in comparison with his predecessors, but like Governor Podgornov in Vologda, he focused principally on enriching himself and his associates rather than addressing the region's economic crisis.

The political strife in the region undermined public and elite support for any reform plans, such as the Gaidar program, and eliminated any hopes for their implementation. In addition to corruption and local conflicts, Yeltsin also spoiled any possibility of stability through his emphasis on short-term political goals. In mid-1995, a majority of the region's political organizations and elites, including both communists and pro-Yeltsin democrats, appealed to the president to remove Karpov, signaling the level of antagonism between his administration and the rest of the regional elites. Yeltsin finally replaced him in August of 1995 with the former governor, Barabanov, who was then serving—and continued to serve—as the president's representative in Bryansk. Despite their previous opposition to Barabanov, the communist-dominated legislature supported the change and the new governor's desire to "clean up" the administration and bring stability to the region. Barabanov focused on completely overhauling regional and local administrations while abandoning Karpov's economic reform plans.[67] Yet, Yeltsin reversed his decision less than a year later, removing Barabanov in June 1996 for "improperly fulfilling assigned responsibilities, breaking the laws of the Russian Federation, misusing federal budgetary resources, delaying wage payments, and also worsening the socio-economic situation" (Panorama 1996, 273). Underlying this litany of accusations, according to observers, was an allegation by the local branch of *Our Home is Russia* that Barabanov lacked sufficient loyalty to Yeltsin during the presidential election campaign. Ironically, by removing Barabanov, Yeltsin squandered an opportunity to stabilize the political situation in Bryansk and to achieve his long-term goal of enforcing the "presidential vertical" in a staunchly pro-communist region. Barabanov's allegiance to and strong connection with the Yeltsin administration, evidenced by his position as the presidential representative in the region, assured Yeltsin a means to control and monitor a region otherwise dominated by anti-Yeltsin groups. Moreover, Barabanov's pledge to rid the regional government of corruption gave the center some hope, at least, that federal funds might occasionally reach their intended destinations. By removing Barabanov, however, the Yeltsin administration once again threw the region into political turmoil, leaving little chance that the economic situation would improve.

The beginnings of a bilateral treaty surfaced only in mid-1996 under Bryansk's fourth governor, Aleksandr Semernov, a local city boss and former member of the corrupt Karpov administration. As the first leader to advocate reducing the region's dependence on Moscow, he also initiated the concept of a free economic zone in the region, an idea that the subsequent administration would take up with even greater enthusiasm. Taking advantage of the center's support from Moscow as a Yeltsin appointee in a communist-dominated region, Semernov negotiated a program for the region's socio-economic development that laid the basic foundations for a bilateral treaty (*Bryanskaya gazeta*, 16 January 1997; *Sobraniye zakonodatel'stva*, 30 October 1996). But with little experience during his previous years in politics in constructing pragmatic reform plans, Semernov focused on Bryansk's long-suffering agricultural sector, giving large advances from the budget for grain harvests while delaying wages for state workers (*Bryanskoe vremya*, 10 December 1996). For the bulk of his six months in office, Semernov prepared for the gubernatorial elections scheduled for December, in which he was opposed by two previous governors, Vladimir Barabanov and Yuri Lodkin. With the fledgling democratic organizations divided among candidates and Yeltsin's representative unwilling to support the incumbent, Semernov had little chance against the communist candidate, Yuri Lodkin, who was the sentimental favorite due to his earlier illegal removal from office.[68]

Lodkin's election with more than fifty percent of the ballots in the first round of voting marked the first chance for political stability and the development of an agenda for economic and intergovernmental reform in Bryansk. Only Vladimir Karpov in his twenty-month tenure served long enough to develop plans for regional reform. Yet the corruption that dominated his administration limited any chances for reform and left even more massive financial problems for future leaders. Furthermore, all of the pro-Yeltsin governors (Barabanov, Karpov, and Semernov) had to deal with a legislature controlled not only by members of the communist party and the leftist Patriotic bloc (*Patrioticheskaya Brianshchina*), but dominated by directors of failing industries and Soviet-era apparatchiks (now local bosses), most of whom advocated continued state subsidies and price controls (*Bryanskoe vremya*, 25 December 1996).[69] Frequent conflicts with the leadership, along with internal strife seemingly halted activity in the Bryansk duma. From its election in 1994 until the beginning of 1996, the legislature managed to pass only six laws, one of which was declared illegal by the court. As of early 1996, the duma had not scheduled elections for new representatives, marking the end of its two-year term, or local self-government elections, as decreed by Yeltsin. Only in December 1996 did the legislature manage to hold elections for all levels of government, including the governor (*Bryanskiye izvestiya*, 25 January 1996).[70] With the regional governing bodies unable to address the most basic issues of governance, more complex issues of federal reform and intergovernmental fiscal relations remained beyond their grasp.

Governor Lodkin, a member of the leftist-nationalist coalition, National Unity, had greater hope of bringing a new consensus among Bryansk's mostly communist political elites and building support for his development policies. Lodkin had already served three years in the Federal Assembly (first in the Federation Council and then in the State Duma), providing him with connections in Moscow unavailable to previous administrations. Yet, the economic and political constraints of the region limited both the bilateral treaty and Lodkin's socio-development program, based on the reforms developed earlier by the Gaidar Institute. Even more than Vologda's leaders, Lodkin lacked a strong foundation for reform programs due to the constant political and economic turmoil in the region. With a declining tax base burdened by substantial expenditures—high poverty rates and the aftermath of Chernobyl strained the regional budget—the Bryansk administration did not have the money to pay for research, computerization, or the training of specialists (Bryansk oblast budget 1996, 1997). Previous administrations did little to analyze the economic situation, failing to establish institutions and forums for gathering and exchanging information among the region's elites. Even the Chernobyl program, which infused state and private funds into the region to decontaminate Bryansk's southern half and to compensate victims from the accident, failed to devise clear goals and provide for proper oversight to prevent the misuse of funds.[71]

Furthermore, the government could not subsidize federal agencies, like the State Tax Service, or provide substantial technical or financial support to businesses, both of which would have enhanced the ties and transparency of information among elites within the oblast. In early 1997, employees at the State Tax Service had not received salaries for four months (*Bryanskaya Vremya*, March 1997). Despite the federal government's responsibility for paying their salaries, the regional government suffers when it cannot subsidize the agency as in Samara and Vologda. The tax service managed to collect the majority of its planned revenues in 1996, but the administration's finance department had lowered its projected revenues by one-third during a mid-year audit, thus reducing the burden on the tax agency to fulfill its plan. In addition, wage arrears caused the agency to lose specialists and other agents became targets for corruption,[72] a situation only exacerbated by the government's inability to regulate the region's financial institutions. In 1995, the arbitrage court overturned 70 percent of the decisions by the Bryansk tax service in audits of company and individual tax receipts, a record for territorial branches of the State Tax Service (*Bryanskoe Vremya*, 14 August 1996).

Political instability also undermined the development of a regulatory system that would safeguard the allocation of Bryansk's limited financial resources and might provide a credible commitment to the center to implement federal programs and bilateral agreements. An administration audit for 1995 found that Bryansk had misused three hundred million rubles for the Chernobyl program and 227 million rubles for social welfare payments and that two Bryansk banks had failed to properly turn over six billion rubles to the federal treasury (*Bryanskiye izvestiya*, 20 February 1996). A federal treasury department audit of federal funds at the end of 1997 found that the situation had not improved in the region. The agency found widespread examples of the misuse and ineffective allocation of federal funds by the Bryansk administration, including funds for housing, Chernobyl, and agricultural programs. The report stated that Bryansk municipalities misused more than 6.9 billion rubles in federal allocations and Bryansk banks had held up at least 8.6 billion rubles in federal transfers to enterprises in order to profit off the interest (*Guberniya*, 10 December 1997). The Chernobyl program gained particular notoriety when the treasury department uncovered that the regional government had funneled funds into its own pockets to purchase expensive foreign automobiles and into construction companies that used the money to build fancy offices.[73] Despite the tremendous need for investment and renewal in the region, Bryansk was becoming a "black hole" for Moscow, where its money disappeared without apparent results. The inability of regional elites to ensure the proper use of federal investment funds may have contributed to

Moscow's decision to sequester the designated funds, particularly to the Chernobyl program, so that Bryansk received only 10 percent of the allocated sum in 1996 (*Bryanskiye Rabochii*, 30 January 1997). In addition, the federal government temporarily halted payments from the extrabudgetary road fund as a result of financial mismanagement in the region.[74]

With so little foundation for advantageous and comprehensive bilateral agreements, Lodkin chose to sign the bilateral treaty with broad outlines for intergovernmental reform without signing all of the more detailed agreements. Although he signed the treaty in July 1997, he did not finalize a pivotal agreement with the Economic Ministry on industrial policy and conversion until almost two years later (*Guberniya*, 25 June 1999). Lodkin's ability to negotiate the agreements may also have been hampered by a rift in Bryansk's communist coalition that emerged even before the gubernatorial elections. In an article in *Bryanskiye izvestiya* (15 November 1996) entitled "Lodkin: Communist or Careerist?" a State Duma deputy and former leader of the regional communist party (CPRF) organization accused Lodkin of disloyalty to the communist faction and his constituents during his tenure in the Duma. The author, Oleg Shenkarov, refused to support Lodkin in the election, setting the stage for future conflicts following Lodkin's victory. In addition, Shenkarov, an outspoken opponent of President Yeltsin and reform members of the government, was unlikely to support Lodkin's attempts to meet with Anatolii Chubais, Boris Nemtsov, and other members of the liberal reform team in the government in early 1997.

Consequently, Lodkin chose a route similar to that of his predecessors and many other regional governors: to continue the status quo of requesting money from Moscow while promoting unrealistic development plans. Although outside observers, from journalists to economists to politicians, have emphasized the continuing need for pragmatic reform plans in the region, the creation of a free economic zone emerged as the pet project of the Lodkin administration.[75] The idea of a free economic zone in Bryansk, which the federal development program and bilateral treaty pledged to explore, lacked a sound plan for how the region would create the necessary infrastructure to support foreign investment and define the role of local enterprises.[76] One former administration member scoffed at the notion of a free economic zone in Bryansk, contending, "I don't know of such plans, I only know such slogans. In addition, property rights are not clear enough. . . . One can evaluate an idea, but if it is simply a name then it will remain a name."[77] Lodkin's reforms rested upon a plan for Bryansk to profit from the customs duties across its international borders, a source of income the center was unlikely to relinquish to a debtor region.[78]

The five years of political chaos in Bryansk limited Lodkin's resources to negotiate with the center. They have intensified the economic crisis in the region, leaving Lodkin little choice but to continue the region's financial dependence on the center. According to journalist Aleksandr Levin-skii, "I think our governor is in this position right now because if he does not bring home money from Moscow, he does not know how to make the region work. When he came to power, he had ten principles and this was all that he had. He said that he would support agriculture, construction, medicine, schools. Where is he going to get the money? He never told [us]."[79] As with Vologda, guarantees of federal implementation of finan-cial promises remained one of Bryansk's primary goals for intergovern-mental reform. Estimates by the regional government in early 1997 show 136 billion rubles of federal debt to Bryansk, including transfers from the Fund for Regional Support, payments for federal housing, and Chernobyl programs (*Bryanskiye izvestiya*, 4 February 1997). By the end of 1996, the federal government owed 344 billion in pension payments and even more in wages for federal employees; teachers, for example, had not received their salaries in almost six months (*Bryanskiye izvestiya*, 8 February 1997; 20 February 1997). Even the strategy of focusing on the implementation of the current system of fiscal federalism raised new problems for Gov-ernor Lodkin. Despite his conflict with President Yeltsin and his criticism of the government's free market policies, Lodkin had to request help from his ideological adversaries, such as Anatolii Chubais, while risking the opposition of communist elites in the Bryansk legislature and Bryansk's representatives in the central legislature.[80] Nevertheless, the need for fed-eral assistance also created the foundation for cooperation between the center and a resolutely communist region that the bilateral treaty further institutionalized. The implementation of agreements on defense conver-sion, agricultural development, and the environment demand intergov-ernmental collaboration, not just on the issue of federal financing, but in terms of developing reform programs that the federal government is will-ing to support. Whereas the specific terms of the bilateral treaty might pale against those of the treaties with Tatarstan, Sverdlovsk, or Samara, the existence of the treaty furthered Yeltsin's state-building goals. The short-term economic objectives of the regional government, however, were in greater doubt.

The uncertainty in the region continued to limit Lodkin's ability to ne-gotiate better and more secure financing for the region. First, the support for communism by the region's leaders and their constituents provided little basis for Moscow to reward Bryansk for loyalty. With frequent lead-ership turnover and splits within the leftist coalition, however, Lodkin also lacked the power to offer a credible threat of opposition that might convince Moscow to pacify the leadership with funding.[81] The numerous financial scandals in Bryansk also strongly hinted that increased federal funding might not reach its intended targets, thus doing nothing to ease the social tensions in the region. Based on the federal audit in 1997, Mos-cow had little reason to direct its meager resources to a region that would likely misuse the funds. As a result, most of the Ministry of Finance's allocations to Bryansk in the late 1990s were on paper, rather than actual financial transfers. With Bryansk enterprises more than 425 billion rubles in debt to the federal budget by the end of 1996 (*Bryanskiye izvestiya*, February 4, 1997), the Ministry of Finance and the Bryansk administration negotiated a complex system of interaccounting (*vzaimoraschet*), whereby the federal debt, enterprise debt, and regional debt to energy companies such as Mosttransgaz cancelled each other out without any exchange of money (*Bryanskiye izvestiya*, February 7, 1997).[82] Only under strong domestic and international pressure to address its wage arrears in late 1997 did the Ministry of Finance finally begin transferring billions of rubles in back wages and Chernobyl payments from its 1996 budgetary allocations (*Guberniya*, 26 December 1997).

For Bryansk, financial dependence was not a short-term solution to a fiscal crisis but a long-term strategy to bring revenue into the region. Although this dependency originated with the structural problems of Bryansk's economy—heavy defense-related industry combined with an agricultural sector ravaged by the Chernobyl accident—it also resulted from the weak institutional development in the region. Despite an economy similarly dominated by heavy industry and inefficient agriculture, Boris Nemtsov managed to achieve radical economic reforms during his six-year tenure in Nizhni Novgorod (Mau and Stupin 1997, 22). Moreover, Nizhni Novgorod's bilateral treaty with the center, signed in 1996, addressed the division of federal and subnational power very specifically, including an agreement that transferred specific pieces of property into regional hands (Guboglo 1997). In Bryansk, however, constant leadership turnover and political instability prevented the development of an economic system that could create the foundation for intergovernmental reform. Neither Lodkin, nor any previous leader, had the opportunity or resources to exploit the bilateral process or explore alternative development strategies. Interregional ties, which provided an important option and bargaining resource for Vologda, were not explored in Bryansk until the end of 1997, when Governor Lodkin signed a bilateral agreement with Kemerov oblast (*Guberniya*, 10 November 1997). In part, this is due to the overall weakness—apart from Moscow—of the central economic zone, which includes other depressed regions such as Smolensk and Ivanovo. But Bryansk's leadership also failed to utilize cross-regional ties, even to exchange information and ideas, as a means to explore new options for development and reduce its dependence on the federal government. Whereas Samara needed cooperation with the center to ensure future opportunities for more autonomous development, Bryansk had to rely on the shaky finances of the federal government to ensure the region's economic survival. One observer summed up Bryansk's intractable position: "Today, without the support of the center, the oblast is unlikely to find its way. We are a subsidized oblast and depend very heavily on the center's financing. Then there is also the Chernobyl catastrophe that powerfully affected our region. Of course, in today's conditions, it is not advisable to count on the center . . ."[83]

The center's acceptance of bilateralism as a means to address federal reform presented the opportunity for Samara, Vologda, and Bryansk to structure intergovernmental mechanisms in their favor. Nevertheless, the three regions were not equally equipped to take advantage of this opportunity. Bilateral negotiations demanded that each region assess its economic potential and need for reform and determine how the center and subnational governments should divide responsibilities and resources. After establishing the agenda, the regional government had to develop strategies and tactics and dedicate resources to navigate the agenda through the central bureaucracy and to the final stages of approval by the president and the prime minister. Above all, the development and success of the treaties depended on the abilities and leadership of the governor. Russian governors, particularly in their joint role as regional executives and representatives to the Federation Council between 1995 and 2001, held the primary responsibility for setting the agenda for federal reform and harnessing the resources to bargain successfully with the center.

In comparison to Samara and Vologda, Bryansk's governors were least equipped to address the task of intergovernmental reform. The economic consequences of the Soviet collapse and the accident at Chernobyl certainly limited the choices for reform plans of Bryansk's government; the level of financial autonomy sought by Samara's government would not have served Bryansk's needs. Yet the political instability in the region—constant leadership turnover, executive-legislative conflict, financial mismanagement, and corruption—eliminated any potential to capitalize on Bryansk's principal resource: its geographic position. The political turmoil exacerbated the economic problems in the region, reducing the resources available to address the issue of intergovernmental reform and the ability of the government to offer the center a credible commitment to implement any changes. With each new governor, new reform plans emerged with different ideas for establishing economic and social stability. Each change in direction meant less time and resources to negotiate with the federal government.

Vologda's political crisis yielded similar results, although its more promising economic situation and eventual political stabilization produced more opportunities for fiscal autonomy than in Bryansk. As in Bryansk, corruption and mismanagement by the governor paralyzed politics—including the ability to take up intergovernmental reform—and deepened the budgetary crisis in the region. Even after a new, popular governor, with strong ties to the region's economic and political elite, stabilized the political situation in Vologda in mid-1996, he still faced the consequences of the previous regional administration. Samara's government had already developed the infrastructure and assembled the resources to negotiate a comprehensive and detailed bilateral treaty when Vologda's governor was only beginning to establish the basic framework of an agenda for intergovernmental reform. Although the region had existed independent of federal transfers less than two years earlier, Vologda now had to depend on federal support to ease its payments crisis. Nevertheless, Vologda's newfound political stability in 1997 produced opportunities unavailable to Bryansk's ailing government. Bryansk had little choice but continue its dependence on the federal government. Meanwhile, Vologda began to develop its ties with neighboring regions to improve its economic situation as an alternative to negotiating for federal funds. Although Vologda's bilateral treaty managed to establish the basic parameters of federal responsibilities to the region and intergovernmental cooperation, interregional ties offered another means of aid and development in response to an unreliable center.

Whereas Vologda's leaders saw their bilateral treaty as a tool to improve future intergovernmental interactions, Samara's governor envisioned the region's treaty as a means to reduce federal involvement in Samara's affairs. Instead of establishing the center's responsibilities to the region, Samara's treaty laid out the region's autonomous sphere of rights and responsibilities and the rules of federal *nonintervention*. Bilateralism offered Samara's government the chance to negotiate from a position of strength with a financially weak federal government. Based on the financial health and political consolidation in the region, Governor Titov could offer the center a credible commitment that fiscal autonomy would benefit both the federal and regional governments and a credible threat that failure to sign the treaty and agreements would result in Titov's opposition to government budgetary bills in the Federation Council.

Although structural factors determined the range of options for intergovernmental reform available to the leaders of Bryansk, Vologda, and Samara, regional governors still made choices within that context that determined the outcome of the bilateral bargaining process. Governor Titov could have used Samara's substantial resources to bargain for a larger share of revenue from the center and to increase the number of federal programs, employing more confrontational strategies similar to those of Tatarstan or Primorskii Krai. Vologda's second governor, Vyacheslav Pozgalev, might have preserved the bilateral relationship that existed under his predecessor and opted for a broader role for the center in Vologda's development in place of multilateral ties. Institutional factors structured the opportunities for autonomy or dependence, but regional leaders still selected the goals and strategies and determined how to consolidate the region's resources toward these aims.

These leaders' choices, however, had a broader impact on the development of intergovernmental institutions. Yeltsin used bilateralism as the principal means to address the uneasy center-periphery relationship at a time when the central government had few economic or political resources to ensure federal stability. Bilateral agreements, particularly in the financial sphere, brought unruly regions back into the federal fold; even Chechnya signed a treaty following the end of the first round of war. Bilateralism provided the center with a flexible, if not always successful, tool of addressing short-term crises: the position of Tatarstan in the federation; demands by donor regions for changes to the system of fiscal federalism; concerns during presidential and gubernatorial elections; and provincial anger over the special privileges of the republics. For a large and asymmetrical federation such as Russia, the center required a strategy of individualism to manage regional differences.

Yet by 1998, as chapter 7 will explore in more detail, the Yeltsin administration could no longer perceive the gains from bilateral treaties and halted further negotiations. As the door closed to the forty-three regions that had not yet signed treaties, the long-term consequences of the short-lived and half-completed process became more apparent. In his quest for a unified federation comprised of loyal regional leaders, Yeltsin had replaced a short-term crisis of stability with the long-term predicament of supporting weak regions without the aid of stronger, more independent regions. The successes of regions such as Samara, Sverdlovsk, and Tatarstan in negotiating a wide degree of economic autonomy and capitalizing on it in the face of a financially and politically weakened central government contrasted starkly with the ongoing financial dependence of impoverished areas such as Bryansk and Ivanovo. Without extending the treaty process to the full 89 regions, the existing bilateral treaties assumed a more ambiguous status, at least for the central government. As the Russian government regained its economic footing in the transition from the Yeltsin to the Putin administration, it looked for ways to reclaim some of the powers it decentralized. Even before Yeltsin's departure from office, the Russian government proposed a reorganization of Russia's federalism by reducing the number of regions in order to eliminate or diffuse existing regional privileges (*Nezavisimaya gazeta*, 24 February 1999). President Putin has focused considerably more attention on this goal.

But earlier choices conditioned future opportunities for federal reform. Bilateralism borrowed two significant arrangements from the Soviet era and institutionalized them as part of federal relations in the new Russia. First, Yeltsin consolidated a type of executive federalism that drew upon Russia's long tradition of executive power. Yet in the context of bilateralism, power was no longer simply in the hands of the central leadership but within the grasp of subnational executives as well. Regional politics became a story of how well leaders could unify and consolidate power and then translate this power at the intergovernmental bargaining table.

At the same time, central leaders hoped that executive federalism would solidify the "presidential vertical" and alleviate the burden of negotiating with potentially hostile or fractured legislatures. Leaders at all levels of government rarely seek to increase checks on their power or enlarge the federal bargaining table, thus suggesting that intergovernmental reform will remain principally in the arena of executive federalism.

Second, bilateralism cemented Russia's existing asymmetries—the differences between the ethnic republics and other regions—as laid out in the 1993 Constitution and then widened and deepened those asymmetries. In the context of political uncertainty under Yeltsin's presidency, when the rules of federalism remained in question, central strategies to deal with asymmetries had a much broader impact on the structure and operation of federalism than simply the distribution of resources. Asymmetrical federalism in Russia now consists of a hodgepodge of different fiscal and legal arrangements. Although the central government might now strive to level those differences, it cannot do so without directing substantial resources toward that goal. Regions such as Samara and Tatarstan—that have benefited from asymmetrical devolution of power—will continue to devote their resources toward maintaining many of their gains and toward differentiating between republics and oblasts, between donors and recipients, or whatever other asymmetries they see as essential to Russia's future development. The final chapter of this study examines the future of asymmetrical federalism by comparing the strategy of bilateralism in Russia with two other countries that have used bilateralism to manage intergovernmental relations: Canada and Spain. Their capacity to balance subnational demands in asymmetrical federations and central goals for unity sheds light on the implications of bilateralism for the future of federalism in Russia.

NOTES

1. In Russia, the system of executive federalism reflects Yeltsin's vision of a "presidential vertical," except that subnational executives do not rely on the largesse of the president for their positions.

2. *Kapital*, 21–27 August 1996, p. 2. Cited in Hanson (1997).

3. Viktor Filonov, interview with author, 3 February 1997.

4. Samara's government did more than provide the company with credits and tax deferments. It also intervened when Aviakor's holding company rejected attempts to join the financial industrial group (Panorama 1996; Hanson 1997, 415). For more information on Russia's growing financial industrial groups, see Johnson (1997), Gorbatova (1995), and Starodubrovskaia (1995).

5. Andrei Kalmikov, interview with author, 17 March 1997.

6. Tatyana Voskoboynikova, interview with author, 4 February 1997.

7. Viktor Filonov, interview with author, 13 February 1997.

8. Despite the governor's defense of Yukos in this situation, the administration

has had an antagonistic relationship with the company ever since the locally based Yukos merged with other smaller oil companies into a Moscow-based conglomerate and was bought out by the mega-bank, Menatep. Since the takeover, Yukos has lost out on bids with the region to mine new oil fields and struggled with licensing arrangements as the government attempts to "show who's boss" (*Samarskoe obozreniye*, 20 January 1997; Konstantin Lange, interview, 5 February 1997). In order to reclaim some of the lost revenue from the company, Titov has worked to come to an agreement with Yukos and the federal government, including a provision in the bilateral treaty to increase its share of revenue from oil and gas extraction.

9. Konstantin Titov, interview in *Volzhskaya Kommuna*, 14 February 1997.

10. By 1997, the position of prime minister was eliminated from Samara's governmental structure and Logoido became a deputy governor.

11. Stoner-Weiss (1997) and Putnam (1993) include informational and statistical services as an element of governmental performance since they produce better-informed constituents. Information may play an even broader role in previously closed societies such as Russia by providing a foundation for constituents' trust and creating at least the appearance of openness and accountability in the political process. Despite the tranformative effects of *glasnost* at the end of the Soviet regime, access to government information, particularly financial information, has improved only marginally in the Russian Federation, a result of both political opposition and technological deficiencies (Bellows 1993).

12. Konstantin Lange, interview with author, 5 February 1997.

13. The Samara branch of the State Statistical Department (Samara Goskomstat) also publishes economic and financial data.

14. President Yeltsin promised to sign many of the bilateral treaties in 1996 during the campaigns of gubernatorial incumbents in the hopes of increasing their electability. Yeltsin then postponed many of the signings when these incumbents were reelected, particularly in seemingly stable regions, since he no longer had any immediate incentive to follow through on his campaign promises (Nikolai Kostigov, interview, 2 December 1996; Andrei Kalmikov, interview, 17 March 1997).

15. Andrei Kalmikov, interview with author, 17 March 1997.

16. The author of the article, Dmitri Badovskii, focused particularly on the example of Kamaz, an auto factory in Tatarstan, noting that the Tatarstan government had successfully managed to remove the company from the bankruptcy list (*Segodnya*, 10 November 1996).

17. Viktor Kaddanikov, the general director of AvtoVAZ, suggested that the center wanted to bankrupt the company so that an unknown buyer could then "incognito get the sweetest piece of Russian industry and the last of the still working factories" at bargain-basement prices (*Izvestiya*, 28 November 1996). The editor of *Volzhskaya Kommuna* speculated that some enemies of Kadannikov, who briefly served as a deputy prime minister under Chernomyrdin, wished to avenge a particular decision during his short-lived stint in Moscow. She also noted that the decision was announced while Prime Minister Chernomyrdin, a close ally of Titov through his political party, was not in the country (Tatyana Voskoboynikova, interview, 4 February 1997).

18. The agreement would be drafted as a presidential decree, emphasizing the importance of the decision to the central government.

19. AvtoVAZ won a lawsuit against the Ministry of Finance regarding allegations that the firm had underpaid its 1994 taxes. The ministry was required to return 800 billion rubles to AvtoVAZ, which was worth less than half that amount by the time the company received it. According to company directors, this dramatically reduced the firm's ability to pay its 1995 and 1996 federal taxes and thus further fueled the ire of company and regional elites over the threat of bankruptcy (*Russian Regional Investor*, 7 September 2000).

20. Alexei Kalmikov, interview with author, 17 March 1997; Vyacheslav Aronin, interview with author, 5 February 1997.

21. Aleksei Kalmikov interview with author, 17 March 1997.

22. Samara's membership in the donor region coalition plays a much more important role in intergovernmental relations than its participation in *Bolshaya Volga* (Great Volga) association, the regional economic association of Volga provinces and republics. *Bolshaya Volga* serves primarily to resolve regional issues, such as agricultural reform and ecological problems, coordinate joint development programs, and attract foreign investment to the Volga region rather than to lobby the federal government. This provides an interesting contrast to Vologda and its membership in the Northwest Association, a group that plays a much more significant role in conveying regional interests to the federal government.

23. *Vlast' v Rossii*, December 1996, 16–17. See chapter 5 for a more detailed description of their suggestions.

24. Tatyana Voskoboynikova, interview with author, 4 February 1997.

25. Aleksei Kalmikov interview with author, 17 March 1997.

26. Samara's economic and fiscal health continues even after the Russia's economic collapse during the summer of 1998. Despite a fall in industrial output by 12 percent immediately after the August crash, the region quickly regained its previous output levels, attracting new investors such as Nestle and the Sibirsky Aluminum Group, which relocated to Samara from Moscow. In addition, Titov continued to pay state workers and pensions on time throughout the crisis (*Russia Today*, 10 June 1999).

27. Aleksei Kalmikov, interview with author, 17 March 1997.

28. Budgetary figures provided to me by Vyacheslav Aronin, head of the administration's finance department.

29. Gruppa monitoringa fondovogo rinka, 1996. Samara was also one of the few regions prepared to issue Eurobonds (*Central European*, 14 April 1998).

30. Yuri Baradulin, interview with author, 3 February 1997; Tatyana Voskoboynikova, interview with author, 4 February 1997.

31. Information obtained from the official Website of the Samara oblast administration (www.adm.samara.ru).

32. The conflict between Titov and Putin flared up during the summer of 2000 when the government initiated criminal proceedings against AvtoVAZ, accusing it of selling more cars than it was reporting on its federal income tax statements. Putin's administration subsequently dropped the case in August, citing a lack of evidence (*Russia Newsline*, 4 August 2000).

33. Anatolii Pak, interview with author, 22 November 1996.

34. As a principal figure in the controversy—Governor Podgornov attempted

to remove Pantsirev and destroy his newspaper after it published the allegations— Vladimir Pantsirev certainly holds strong opinions about Podgornov's misdeeds and his leadership that might have biased some of the book's conclusions. The book, however, is primarily a collection of documents—local, national, and international newspaper articles on the subject, official documents, and letters between Vologda and federal officials—rather than pure commentary.

35. According to an article in *Izvestiya*, the arrested arsonist turned out to be the driver of a well-known Vologda businessman who had received 400 million rubles in "wheat credits" from the governor (29 November 1996).

36. Igor Efimov, interview with author, 25 November 1996.

37. Vladimir Pantsirev, interview with author, November 26, 1996.

38. Budgetary figures provided to me by Zoya Mayoreva in the administration's finance department.

39. Data provided to me by Alexei Novikov.

40. Severstal', not surprisingly, also owed significant tax payments to the federal and subnational budgets. Although the State Tax Service in Vologda would not provide specific information on tax obligations, the projected 28 percent fulfillment of the profit tax for 1996 hints at Severstal' sizable tax debt to the oblast.

41. Nikolai Kostigov, interview with author, 2 December 1996.

42. Regions elected two representatives to the Federation Council in 1993 until the passage of a 1995 law that automatically appointed the leaders of the regional executive and legislative branches to the Council.

43. Vladimir Pantsirev, interview with author, 26 November 1996.

44. According to Nikolai Kostigov, Vologda's image is that of a northern outpost that survived more or less independently from Moscow and the country's military machine during the Soviet period (interview, 2 December 1996), save the creation on Vologda's territory of tens of labor camps for exiled "kulaks" and, during World War II, Soviet Germans (Pohl 1997).

45. Vladimir Pantsirev, interview with author, November 26, 1996; Zoya Mayorova, interview with author, November 27, 1996. In a letter dated 19 November 1996 to Deputy Prime Minister Viktor Ilushin, Pozgalev detailed the decrease in federal funding as a result of legislation via transfers, federal housing programs, customs duties, and excise taxes, concluding that Vologda would lose at least 855 billion rubles in federal funding in 1997. As a result, the governor requested that the government review the oblast budget, raise the region's share of VAT from 25 to 50 percent and the income tax from 90 to 100 percent, and increase the amount of transfers from the Fund for Regional Support. Letter No. 04–3/DP. Copy provided to me by Zoya Mayoreva.

46. Interview with author, 21 November 1996.

47. Nikolai Kostigov, interview with author, 2 December 1996.

48. Nikolai Kostigov, interview with author, 2 December 1996.

49. Igor Efimov, interview with author, 25 November 1996.

50. Anatolii Pak, interview with author, 22 November 1996.

51. Veniamin Alekseev, interview with author, 15 November 1996. Elite circulation also enhanced transparency between the tax agency and the regional government. Venyamin Alekseev, the former head of the agency, now serves as an advisor to Governor Pozgalev while the head of the administration's financial department took over Alekseev's position at the tax service.

52. This time, however, the scandal involved a large shipment of rotten wheat from Kazakhstan rather than financial mismanagement. Nevertheless, the shipment raised questions about Pozgalev's choice of firm to handle the lucrative grain contract for Vologda's bread production and whether there was any corruption involved in the decision. Pozgalev claimed that the Kazakh firm was suggested by "someone in the Russian government," raising the level of intrigue over the matter (*Izvestiya*, 4 February 1997).

53. Vladimir Pantsirev, interview with author, 26 November 1996.

54. Before the elections, Pozgalev managed to get federal money—approximately 10 percent of the total projected investment, or almost 1.5 trillion rubles over 13 years—for an environmental program to clean up the city of Cherepovets (*Sobraniye zakonodatel'stva*, 3 October 1996). Other requests, particularly for increased transfers, went unheeded (Zoya Mayoreva, interview, 27 November 1996).

55. The treaty also stipulates that the federal government will transfer any amount that the tax revenues do not cover—an important provision given the state of Vologda's tax collection. See chapter 5.

56. Although supportive of the regional associations, the center has been less sympathetic to the Northwest parliamentary association. In early 1997, the Ministry of Justice refused to register the group. Despite the association's goal to conform legislation in the members' regions, the center seemingly feared the lobbying strength of the group in the Federation Council and its potential to subordinate national legislation to regional laws and interests (*Rossiiskiye vesti*, 26 February 1997).

57. Nikolai Kostigov, interview with author, 2 December 1996.

58. Nikolai Kostigov, interview with author, 2 December 1996.

59. Nikolai Kostigov, interview with author, 2 December 1996.

60. Yuri Sudakov, interview with author, 13 November 1996.

61. Unpublished data. Provided to me by Mikhail Dmitriyev of the Carnegie Foundation.

62. Aleksandr Nemets, interview with author, 3 March 1997.

63. I also suggest that political chaos and economic crisis have made regional elites more guarded in their willingness to answer questions from an outsider and to analyze the situation in Bryansk. Although some of their wariness may be attributed to a communist administration's distrust of westerners common under Soviet rule, it extended to elites outside the government. One interview subject, an economist and director of a private auditing firm, insisted that I turn off my tape recorder halfway through the interview, fearing that he was offering too negative a picture of Bryansk that might somehow cause harm.

64. This section draws heavily from Panorama (1996) as well as articles from *Bryanskoe vremya* and my interview with journalist Aleksandr Levinskii.

65. Aleksandr Levinskii, interview with author, 22 February 1997; Aleksandr Nemets, interview with author, 3 March 1997.

66. Lodkin first tried to blockade himself in his office and then decided to sue Yeltsin in Constitutional Court. In 1994, the Court determined that Yeltsin's action was unconstitutional and ruled that Lodkin should be reinstated. The central government along with the Bryansk administration blocked the implementation of the decision. Lodkin and the Court had no recourse or means to sanction the executive branch and Lodkin remained out of a job.

67. According to one journalist, Barabanov treated the Gaidar Institute consultants "like animals, and chased them out of the region. And, for a long time, they were not even paid for the work that they did" (Aleksandr Levinskii, interview with author, 22 February 1997).

68. Viktor Kampantsev, interview with author, 24 February 1997.

69. According to one study, local bosses and enterprise managers comprise two-thirds of the legislature (Slider 1996, 245).

70. Mau and Stupin (1997) suggest that structural factors may play a larger role in impeding the work of the administration and legislature: "The administration of Bryansk is in a rather unpleasant situation, because it has to stand heavy joint pressure of lobbyists from the agricultural-industrial and military-industrial sectors. . . . The most meaningful policy for the administration in this situation is trying to divide the joint front of these lobbyists" (24, n11). With enterprise lobbyists dominating the legislature, however, a divide-and-rule tactic may also create political gridlock.

71. Aleksandr Nemets, interview with author, 3 March 1997.

72. Nikolai Zabavo, interview with author, 28 February 1997.

73. Aleksandr Nemets, interview with author, 3 March 1997; Aleksandr Levinskii, interview with author, 22 February 1997.

74. Ludmila Tulyagin, interview with author, 27 February 1997.

75. For more information on free economic zones in Russia, see Kushnirsky (1997) and OECD Economic Surveys (1998, 192–97).

76. Akhnaf Zakirov, interview with author, 26 February 1997.

77. Aleksandr Nemets, interview with author, 3 March 1997.

78. Aleksei Izotenkov, interview with author, 25 February 1997; Aleksandr Levinskii, interview with author, 22 February 1997.

79. Aleksandr Levinskii, interview with author, 22 February 1997.

80. A national meeting of the Communist Party of the Russian Federation in 1998 illustrates the fancy footwork required by Lodkin's precarious position. Before attending the convention, Lodkin, along with numerous other communist governors, contacted Yeltsin to indicate that his participation in no way indicated opposition to the government (*Moskovskie novosti*, 4–11 May 1997).

81. An example of a credible threat might be Primorskii Krai, whose defiant governor threatened to encourage extended strikes among its miners if the federal government didn't come through with increased financing, which it did (Kirkow 1997). Aleksandr Lebed's strong support nationally as well as in his own region also gave him the political power to offer a credible threat to the center.

82. See Chapter 3 for a more in-depth explanation of interaccounting measures.

83. Akhnaf Zakirov, interview with author, 26 February 1997.

CHAPTER 7

Defining Federalism

The development of federalism is not simply a matter of implementing an efficient and clear institutional design to delineate authority and jurisdiction. It is a process by which actors actively bargain over the definition and shape of the institutional environment. New circumstances challenge preexisting norms and rules, and actors must choose between maintaining the status quo or devoting resources to change the rules of the game. Since federalism is essentially a contract between the center and subnational units, it demands constant negotiation and adjustment, resulting in shifts between periods of greater decentralization and centralism. This dynamic process characterizes all federations, but each nation's institutional arrangements create a matrix of opportunities and constraints within which subnational units may shape the rules of federalism. In Russia, the center's use of bilateralism to address problems of federal unity and intergovernmental conflict eliminated the utility of collective action by the regions to affect the rules of the game. Instead, regions actively developed and pursued their territorial interests based on their abilities to negotiate with the federal government, giving some regions tremendous opportunities to bargain with the center for extensive economic autonomy. Yet the prevailing economic crisis limited the advantages of autonomy for many regions dependent on federal transfer funds and investment for their economic survival, despite the unreliability of these financial sources. Furthermore, the costly process of negotiating intergovernmental treaties and agreements benefited those regions, like Samara, with the economic and political resources to develop comprehensive agendas and the leadership to navigate them through the convoluted bureaucracy.

This chapter addresses the broader consequences of "bilateral federalism" in Russia and other federal states. I argue that there exist significant constraints to eliminating bilateral bargaining as a means of defining center-regional authority relations, even after this strategy has outlived its usefulness for the federal government. I first examine the intergovernmental relationship in the Russian Federation at the end of the Yeltsin era and in the first year of Vladimir Putin's presidency to see how the Russian government has sought to eradicate bilateralism and its effects on the structure of federalism. As this study has shown, bilateralism created the potential for persistent intergovernmental and inter-regional conflicts by establishing asymmetrical rules and resources among Russia's regions. With bilateralism no longer serving the same short-term goals as in the initial years of post-communism, Russia's leaders have questioned the validity of bilateral bargaining as the bedrock of intergovernmental relations. After signing treaties with forty-six regions, Russia's government halted negotiations with the subnational governments in mid-1998. President Putin has since attempted to reduce federal asymmetries through new centralizing initiatives. Despite these well-publicized actions, however, Russia's institutional structure offers few alternatives to bilateralism for intergovernmental negotiations and reform. Consequently, the center must choose between maintaining the existing rules of federal interaction or devoting vital political and economic resources to altering the status quo.

To better understand the consequences of bilateral federalism in Russia and some of the constraints to reforming it, the second part of this chapter looks at two other countries, Spain and Canada, that used bilateralism as a strategy for dealing with regional differences and demands during the process of intergovernmental reform. Cross-national comparisons, particularly those that traverse regional, cultural, and temporal lines, risk "conceptual stretching" and similar methodological pitfalls (Sartori 1970). But they can also draw attention to explanations and implications that go beyond the trajectories of individual countries. As in Russia, national elites in Canada and Spain relied on bilateral negotiations to achieve federal unity under conditions of political uncertainty and instability. As interregional conflict and competition increased in response to federal asymmetries, national leaders endeavored to eliminate or restrict the use of bilateralism to delineate authority relations between the center and regions. Canada sought unsuccessfully to replace bilateral bargaining with multilateral negotiations to resolve the "Quebec question" and other federal tensions. In Spain, the comprehensive use of bilateralism to decentralize the state gave the central government important tools to integrate a fragmented multiethnic state but did not adequately settle the balance of power between the center and the regions. In both of these countries, federal institutions failed to offer credible alternatives to bilateralism to address subnational demands and diminish federal tensions. The barriers to reforming bilateralism and asymmetrical federalism in Canada and Spain provide cautionary guidance to Russia's leaders as they reconsider the rules of federalism. But the institutional foundations for federal debate, however weak, also provide reason for optimism that Russia can limit interregional conflict in the future.

BILATERALISM IN THE POST-TREATY ERA

By 1996, bilateralism had emerged in Russia as the dominant strategy to address intergovernmental problems. Contrary to its role in the Soviet system, where bilateral relations manifested themselves through personal connections and clientelism, bilateralism became a more institutionalized and officially sanctioned process under President Yeltsin. The center had signed forty-six treaties and hundreds of bilateral agreements as part of the treaty process by the summer of 1998. Nevertheless, the status of these agreements in relation to federal legislation remained uncertain. Russian Duma representatives and many subnational leaders, many of whom had not yet negotiated their treaties, decried the unequal privileges contained in the agreements and the lack of legislative oversight of the process. Central officials complained that the agreements contradicted federal laws, particularly tax and budgetary legislation, yet there were few attempts to unify the documents. Like the 1993 Constitution, the budgetary code, passed in mid-1998, proclaimed the equality of the subjects of the federation in relation to the central government; the bilateral negotiation process resulted in regions that were anything but equal.

In 1997, Duma representatives drafted a law entitled, "On the principles and order of delimiting areas of jurisdiction and authority between organs of government power of the Russian Federation and organs of government power of the subjects of the Russian Federation," to establish the framework and limits of the treaties and agreements and subordinate them to federal law, requiring past treaties to be brought into accordance with federal legislation. Whereas the Constitutional Court resolves specific conflicts in the implementation or revision of the treaties and agreements, it is the responsibility of the executive branches to bring existing documents into accordance with the current legislation. The law, passed by the Federation Council in July of 1999, reaffirms the equality of the federation subjects. It requires the Federation Council to approve all treaties, shifting the ratification stage from a bilateral to a multilateral forum to create incentives for Council members to reject special privileges for their neighbors. The bilteral agreements, which contain specific financial arrangements such as revenue-sharing formulas and control over revenue flows and extrabudgetary funds, need only executive approval, thus limiting the impact of legislative oversight on the bilateral process.

Even before the passage of the bilateral treaty law, the Russian government had suspended the negotiation of new treaties with the remaining forty-three regions. In June 1998, the center signed a treaty and agreements with the federal city of Moscow, in what would turn out to be the final treaty of the Yeltsin administration. Although the treaty law institutionalized and circumscribed the bilateral negotiation process to the center's benefit, bilateralism had already ceased to serve the center's needs. Initially, the treaty process served as a means to integrate Russia's "wayward" republics into the federation, officially beginning with the Tatarstan treaty in early 1994. The expansion of the bilateral process advanced a variety of short-term goals for the center, including unifying the state, delineating property rights, and providing economic payoffs for political loyalty, particularly during the 1996 presidential campaign. In some regions, such as Samara, the treaties increased the efficiency of the fiscal system by permitting the regions to allocate a portion of locally collected federal tax revenues to social expenditures and federal programs, thus eliminating time delays and intermediaries from the process. All of the bilateral treaties defined the mechanisms of the interbudgetary system, establishing the center's responsibilities in the regional economy and, at least on paper, the ramifications for failure to implement them.

Although the center employed bilateralism as a short-term solution to intergovernmental problems in lieu of federal legislation, it did not abandon multilateral legislation. In mid-1998, the Federal Assembly passed the budgetary code, which detailed the mechanisms of the interbudgetary system and the budgetary process at the federal level, as well as the first part of the tax code. The Assembly had already passed water and forestry codes, delineating control over many of the resources covered in the bilateral agreements. Even some of the specific privileges contained in the agreements made their way into federal legislation, although not on a permanent basis. In 1997, the federal budget included a clause that gave donor regions the right to keep a percentage of locally collected revenue to cover federal expenditures, similar to the terms of the Samara agreement; the 1998 and 1999 federal budgets, however, eliminated this right. With multilateral legislation on the intergovernmental fiscal system and resource issues finally enacted, the central government no longer needed the bilateral agreements to resolve jurisdictional questions. Issues relating to specific territorial resources, outside the scope of federal legislation, could be resolved with very limited individual agreements, rather than by incorporating them into the expansive treaty process.

In addition, after 1996, treaties no longer offered the center effective payoffs during election campaigns. During the 1996 presidential election, Yeltsin promised to negotiate treaties with many regions, including some of the more nationalist and communist-oriented regions, in exchange for elite support. Most of these hastily negotiated treaties included few special privileges, replicating the form but not the substance of earlier treaties (Ivanov 1998). Regions such as Samara and Moscow that held out for more advantageous or explicit terms fared better the following year. Faced with hotly contested gubernatorial elections in the majority of regions, the center was once again willing to promise economic payoffs and advantageous treaty terms to garner support for pro-Yeltsin candidates. Moreover, as the financial crisis deepened in the country and the center was seen by regional elites as unable to implement its financial promises from the 1996 campaign, President Yeltsin and Prime Minister Chernomyrdin were forced to offer other incentives for political support, such as greater control over finances, resources, and property. But the promise of such payoffs failed to produce the anticipated windfall of support for pro-government candidates in the regions. The enlarged representation of opposition members in the Federation Council only served to remind Yeltsin's administration of this failure.

With bilateralism no longer needed to address major jurisdictional questions and no longer successful in overcoming electoral obstacles, unity—the original purpose of the treaty process—appeared to be a distant, and perhaps unattainable, goal. In many respects, the initial attempts to prevent disintegration of the federation from sovereignty claims by Tatarstan and from unilateral seizure of resources, such as through single-channel tax systems, proved successful. Tatarstan eschewed any claims of political autonomy and, along with other republics including Sakha and Bashkortostan, agreed to establish revenue-sharing agreements in cooperation with the central government. Yet complete control over the federation's borders remained illusive for the Russian government. The war in Chechnya, which resurfaced in 1999, and outbreaks of violence and ethnic strife in Dagestan and elsewhere in the Caucasus, slowed the consolidation of the Russian state. The treaty process, which had successfully integrated Tatarstan, Sakha, and Bashkortostan into the federation, could not deal with the more intractable political and ethnic problems, particularly in Chechnya. Despite signing a bilateral treaty that granted Chechnya a financial stake in the oil pipelines connecting the oil-rich Caspian Basin with Russia through its territory and provided extensive federal investment in the region's infrastructure, the Russian government faced renewed demands for independence and violent opposition from the Chechen leadership. With bilateralism no longer fulfilling the goal of federal integration, the process lost its legitimacy as the foundation for national unity.

During the final years of Yeltsin's presidency, the context of center-regional bargaining shifted as well. Forty-six regions negotiated their bilateral treaties in the midst of profound financial weakness and political discord at the center. The burden of initiating, developing, and advancing the treaties and agreements thus rested on the shoulders of regional leaders. By the end of 1998, following the financial crisis and subsequent currency devaluation in August, the financial position of the federal government recovered dramatically. Boosted by higher world oil prices and more competitive exports, the government saw its revenue projections exceeded for the first time and real economic growth top 3.2 percent by 1999 according to the World Bank. The government still relied on regional leaders to use their political influence and resources to improve revenue collection, but the federal budget no longer depended on their compliance. With the sudden resignation of Boris Yeltsin at the end of 1999, and the hasty election of the heir apparent, Vladimir Putin, the shift in the balance of power toward the center accelerated. Putin's active support for the renewed war against Chechnya as Prime Minister in 1999 and then as President foreshadowed the return of the center's initiative.

Since his election in March 2000, President Putin has asserted his commitment to regional equality and federal authority. Whereas Yeltsin promoted bilateralism to realize national unity, Putin's administration argued that the process and the resulting "self-sufficiency of certain governments" threaten domestic security (*RFE/RL Newsline,* 9 June 2000). Vowing to rein in insubordinate regional leaders, Putin has focused on reversing some of the decentralization achieved under bilateralism while limiting the power of regional governors in federal decision making. He has drawn on the widespread support for a return to law and order and a strong state to rapidly push through legislation that alters the institutional framework of federal relations. Putin's offensive against the bilateral treaties and regional inequalities signifies a new federal strategy in dealing with subnational leaders. Yeltsin successfully co-opted defiant regional leaders, using economic incentives to obtain political loyalty and to prevent interregional cooperation against the center. President Putin has seemingly abandoned his predecessor's nonconfrontational strategy with the regions, seeking instead to expropriate their political power.[1] Notwithstanding the considerable changes to the formal powers of regional leaders and to the balance of power between center and periphery that began at the end of the Yeltsin regime, the informal resources and powers of subnational leaders persist. The outcome of Putin's federal reforms thus far illustrates this point.

Using the support of the conservative and centrist majority in the Duma and public support for stronger central authority, Putin sought to diminish the power of regional executives and bolster the "presidential vertical" through three significant pieces of legislation. First, Putin created seven "super-districts" as intermediaries between the center and the eighty-nine regions. An appointed presidential representative leads each district, replacing the representatives in the regions who often behaved as political lobbyists for the regions rather than as federal administrators. The new presidential appointees, the majority of whom served in the KGB with Putin or in the military, serve as gatekeepers to federal authorities, severing some of the clientelistic ties under Yeltsin. In addition, they coordinate the implementation of federal policy and the use of federal budgetary funds in the regions and oversee the unification of regional laws with federal legislation through appointed inspectors in the regions. The institutional reorganization, which bears a striking resemblance to the political reforms under Khrushchev that attempted to break the power of the government ministries, exists parallel to the current bureaucratic and territorial structures. As under Khrushchev, the change only adds another layer of bureaucracy—albeit one that has had some successes in unifying the Russian legal space—rather than creating a new model for federal relations.

New legislation also enhances the power of the President to restrain rebellious regional elites. Despite a veto by the Federation Council, the Duma passed a law in the summer of 2000 allowing the president, with the consent of the court, to dismiss regional leaders for violating federal laws. In addition, with the consent of the Duma the president may dissolve a regional legislature for similar violations.[2] Although President Putin and regional leaders have pledged to harmonize regional and federal laws and reinforce Russian unity through cooperative negotiations, the center now holds a powerful bargaining chip. In fact, during the first two years of his presidency, Putin did not implement his power of dismissal, but instead used it as a threat against stalwart regional opponents. The case of Primorskii Krai illustrates the president's newfound power as well as the limits of this power. Governor Nazdratenko, who had been equally as vexing to Yeltsin, had ruled his Far Eastern fiefdom with a praetorian fist outside the purview of federal law and thus presented a perfect test case for the new federal legislation. Instead, the two leaders negotiated a compromise: Nazdratenko resigned from the governorship but gained a new position as the head of the Ministry of Fisheries and escaped prosecution for corruption. Although Putin successfully eliminated a powerful regional boss from a strategic province, he also gave Nazdratenko a new source of bureaucratic power and funds from which to potentially enrich himself.

In changes to the formation of the Federation Council, the Putin government has also reduced the power of regional leaders in federal decision making, limiting their ability to link regional demands with the passage of federal legislation. Responding to the president's threat to dissolve the Federation Council altogether, members of the Council negotiated with the government to reform the body by replacing the regional governors and chairs of regional legislatures with one representative appointed by the regional executive and one by the regional legislature from each subject of the federation. In theory, regional leaders would continue to affect voting and negotiating in the Federation Council through their proxies, but without direct contact with government elites, their influence would be weakened. Yet the long-term effects may be the reverse. Whereas in the first two years of Putin's presidency, the Federation Council has shown enormous deference to the federal government, there exists much more potential for institutional independence.[3] By creating a full-time upper chamber, Council members have more opportunities to develop the necessary bonds for collective action to advance the interests of some or all of the regions—precisely the function of an upper chamber in a federation. At the same time, regional governors and republican presidents can now devote more energy and resources to shoring up local support and using it as a resource to lobby and bargain with the center. Many regional leaders have used their appointments to the Federation Council to select Muscovites rather than local elites, with the expertise to navigate the federal bureaucracy and act as lobbyists for regional interests (*Izvestiya* 10 July 2002; McGrath 2002). In addition, Putin has shown his willingness to bargain with regional leaders despite his centrist rhetoric, permitting some subnational leaders to run for a third or forth term of office in exchange for continued support of his administration (*RFE/RL Russian Political Weekly*, 17 July 2002).[4]

Clearly the most direct attack on bilateralism has been the move to abrogate the power-sharing treaties and agreements. In the context of building a unified and symmetrical legal space, Putin has negotiated with regional elites to annul the treaties or to revise their terms to conform with and subordinate to federal law. By July 2001, six regions, including Nizhni Novgorod and Orenburg, had announced their unilateral withdrawal from the power-sharing agreements, stating that the federal government was not observing their terms, rendering them meaningless (Smirnyagin 2001). By the following year, twenty-eight treaties had been annulled (*RFE/RL Tatar Bashkir Report,* 19 April 2002). But the treaties that established the benchmark of regional autonomy—those with Bashkortostan, Tatarstan, as well as Sverdlovsk and Samara—remain in place as of mid-2002. With Putin free from the political and economic dependence under Yeltsin on dominant regional leaders, the central government currently has the power to demand revisions to the bilateral arrangements to bring them into compliance with federal law.

Yet if these treaties and agreements remain in force, the changes may ultimately give them more significance in the long term. First, the revised treaties, having conformed to federal law, gain new legitimacy as constitutional acts rather than as furtive products of a corrupt and weak administration under Yeltsin and opportunist regional leaders. Second, they solidify the asymmetrical framework of the Russian Federation, legitimizing bilateralism as a means to secure individual arrangements with the federal government. The federal government faces the same bilateral bargaining process to alter the agreements as with the original ones, albeit with expanded authority and resources. Rising tensions between Tatarstan and Moscow over the bilateral treaty suggest that President Shaymiyev will eventually test the credibility of the threat of removal and force Putin to resort to more cooperative bargaining strategies or confront stronger and more united opposition from the periphery.

Under the existing federal system, the center, like its Soviet predecessor, must find a means to deal with the uneven needs and demands of its constituent units. Russian leaders have continued to depend on ad hoc arrangements and bilateral negotiations that emphasize regional differences rather than uniformity. The 1992 Federation Treaty incorporated three separate agreements to recognize the differences among the various territorial units; the special addendum for Bashkortostan added yet another distinction to the document. The bilateral treaties and the fiscal and resource agreements with individual regions suggest an understanding by Yeltsin's government that a highly diverse federation requires individually tailored intergovernmental relationships. This acceptance of unique regional identities and the need for some type of asymmetrical federalism suffuses federal relations. Regardless of lofty proclamations of regional equality in the Russian Constitution and in presidential speeches, the central and subnational governments have displayed a stronger interest in and reliance on bilateral bargaining than multilateral reforms to address Russia's asymmetries. Institutional reforms and a renewal of the debate over the demarcation of responsibilities under Putin signal a revived interest in multilateral legislative solutions to federal reform. This shift, however, warrants two caveats. First, multilateralism works to the benefit of the center only in the context of a politically and economically strong federal government and a submissive Federation Council. As Thomas Remington notes, this describes the current conditions, but the Council might readily change its posture in the future. Second, many members of the Federation Council continue to provide their support for legislation in exchange for specific financial or political concessions to their region (*Russian Political Weekly*, 8 August 2002). Thus, the informal norms of negotiation between center and regions—those that reflect earlier relationships and remain more resistant to change—preserve bilateral bargaining, even within the arena of demarcating power.

In the post-Yeltsin era, the center is likely to continue to reap some rewards from bilateralism. Although this system might generate perpetual conflict between the center and particular regions, it also produces more interregional competition, which often benefits the federal government. Resentment by some regions of the special deals and privileges of others limits the potential for collective action and "all-against-one" strategies against the center. The long-standing emphasis on central-regional hierarchical ties rather than inter-regional horizontal cooperation, coupled with the under-institutionalization of multilateral forums, further limit the potential for regional collective action to alter the balance of power in the federation.

The search for alternatives to bilateralism in Russia reflects the experiences of other federal systems that have utilized bilateral bargaining to delineate center-regional relations. Canada and Spain, two countries with significant ethnic and resource asymmetries, have employed direct negotiations with individual regions to determine the balance of power. Although the extent and goals widely differed, bilateralism transformed the development of federalism and the opportunities for subnational elites to affect this process in both states. As central elites in Spain and Canada sought to replace bilateralism with less costly and more centralized strategies for intergovernmental reform, they faced institutional environments that offered few workable alternatives. The difficulties of altering bilateral federalism in Spain and Canada suggest that not only can powerful regional elites fight to maintain this system but weak federal institutions can bolster bilateralism and undermine the ability of the federal government to curb the autonomy of wayward regions.

SPAIN AND INSTITUTIONALIZED BILATERALISM

As an emerging federation and a new democracy, Spain provides an instructive comparison with Russia in its use of bilateralism to institutionalize intergovernmental relations. Although Spain is not technically federal—the authors of the 1978 Constitution did not designate its democratic institutions as federal—most experts categorize it as "federative" or "quasifederal" (Watts 1999a; Linz 1989, 272). Robert Agranoff notes that "federal compacting can be evolutionary, through a set of negotiated agreements, along Spanish lines, as an alternative means of creating a federation" (Agranoff 1996, 386). The Spanish Constitution establishes many of the foundations for building federalism—regions with powers exclusive of the central government and a framework to decentralize authority—but the choice of the post-Franco government to pursue bilateral negotiations with the regions hastened Spain towards de-facto federalism. As in Russia, in the absence of strong federal institutions such as a senate or federal council, bilateral bargaining over fundamental intergovernmental rules increased the opportunities for individual regions to negotiate preferential arrangements and limited the ability of the center to control the process of decentralization.

In designing democracy, the new leaders of Spain faced significant ethnic cleavages, from the cultural and linguistic differences in Catalonia and Galicia to the sometimes violent nationalism in the Basque region. Although the 1978 Constitution emphasized state unity and integration, its founders also recognized the need for special relationships between Spain's ethnic territories and the center.[5] All three of these "historical nationalities" had experienced periods of autonomy prior to Franco's regime, based on the idea of the *fueros*, or charters, established in the medieval period to protect local customs and limited self-rule (Moreno 2001). Thus, their support of the new democracy rested on the resurrection of their autonomous status most recently experienced under Spain's Second Republic (1931–39). The negotiation of the *preautonomías*—an accelerated decentralization of administrative and fiscal control—with Basque, Catalonia, and Galicia predated the constitution, giving Prime Minister Suarez an opportunity to meet the demands of the nationalist parties in Catalonia and Basque in exchange for their loyalty to a democratic Spanish state. Like the Federation Treaty in Russia, however, the pact failed to achieve its desired goal. In the 1978 Constitutional referendum in Spain, the Basque nationalists withheld their vote, leaving the unity of the state in doubt.

Yet the agreement to allow regionalization to newly established autonomous communities (ACs) as part of the 1977 Moncloa Pacts had enormous implications for the balance of power in Spain. As Juan Linz observes, the Moncloa Pacts illustrate "something that those studying transitions from authoritarian regimes to democracy should never forget: decisions made during the transition period by a government that is either weak or not fully institutionalized become irreversible at a later stage" (Linz 1989, 271). Through its preconstitutional bargaining, Spain established bilateralism as the principal means to decentralize the state. Its leaders may have originally intended to limit the process to Catalonia, Basque, and Galicia—the regions presenting the greatest immediate threat to the integrity of the Spanish state—but the government quickly extended it to the other fourteen ACs. Bilateralism initially offered the center a flexible strategy for responding to subnational demands and allowed the decentralization of power on a case-by-case basis. In this way, the center could prevent the regions from collectively calling for a radical devolution of power. Asymmetrical relations seemed an acceptable framework for ethnic diversity in Spain, supported by the outspoken Basque and Catalan nationalist parties and the centrist parties. Rather than the bargaining power that the center hoped bilateralism would give them, however, subnational demands for the administrative powers of Basque and Catalonia rapidly overwhelmed the national government. Moreover, despite Article 138.2 of the constitution, which prohibits the unequal distribution of economic and social privileges to the ACs, the center granted Basque and Navarre the right to establish single-channel tax systems based on nineteenth century fiscal arrangements.[6] Subsequent bilateral negotiations decentralized control over health, education, and policing to only a handful of regions (Agranoff and Gallarín 1997).

The fiscal privileges achieved by Navarre and the widening and seemingly unstoppable process of decentralization shifted the support at the center for bilateralism. The national government sought to contain the process and its inherent discord by extending autonomy to a total of seventeen regions, transferring administration and some limited fiscal functions, and homogenizing electoral laws. The resultant 1981 Organic Law for the Harmonization of the Autonomic Process (LOAPA) gained tremendous support among centrist parties following an unsuccessful military coup in early 1981 that sought, in part, to return firm control to the center. Even opposition party members, who argued for further decentralization supported stabilizing measures, including the provision in the LOAPA to allow the national parliament to overturn AC laws. Yet the center could not easily replace *principio dispositivo*—ad hoc bargaining by regional elites to gain maximum advantage—with "coffee for all" (Linz 1989). Several regions appealed to the Constitutional Court, arguing that national laws should not prevail over all AC laws. In 1983, the court overturned much of the LOAPA and ruled that autonomy meant an AC had the right to the final decision in certain domains (Colomer 1998). The Constitutional Court also validated bilateralism by declaring that all competencies not included in Article 150 of the constitution must be transferred through bilateral agreement rather than a blanket transfer of powers. Nonetheless, Article 150 allows the parliament to harmonize the decision-making powers of the seventeen subnational governments through broad transfers of power when it advances the "general national interest" (Agranoff and Gallarín 1997, 4–5). This gives the central government a somewhat ambiguous mandate to pursue equalization among the ACs. Consequently, the center has vacillated between bilateral and multilateral transfers of competencies, depending on the prevailing perception of the balance of power. In 1993, the parliament approved a blanket transfer of thirty-two competencies, primarily to even out control over health and education. In the mid-1990s, Catalonia negotiated a fiscal agreement to retain fifteen percent of income taxes; the center subsequently extended the same arrangement to most of the other ACs (Colomer 1998, 48). In 1996, the Catalan nationalist party successfully bargained for an increase in the income tax-sharing rate to thirty percent and new transfers of power to Catalonia including ports and traffic.

The aggressive bargaining by Catalonia and Andalusia, in particular, has propelled the decentralization process and highlighted the difficulties of regulating bilateralism. Whereas Catalonia could claim to belong to the category of historic nationalities to support its demands for autonomy, Andalusia, a large and populous region, had no ethnic basis for special status. Instead, the Socialist Party (PSOE), the majority party in Andalusia and at the national level in the 1980s, successfully appealed to the sense among its voters of "relative deprivation" in comparison with Catalonia and Basque to pass a referendum in 1982 on rapid autonomy for the region (Colomer 1998). As Andalusia negotiated the transfer of administrative powers, other nonethnic regions demanded similar arrangements. Meanwhile, Catalonia continued to demand further decentralization to the province, including fiscal powers to match those of Basque and Navarre. Andalusia followed with its own demands for fiscal autonomy. The central government soon realized the potential political and economic costs of bilateralism. The approach to decentralization succeeded in holding the fragile state together at a critical transition point, yet bilateral negotiations also produced tremendous interregional and center-periphery conflict. By 1983, only small groups of Basque separatists threatened the integrity of the Spanish state but there still existed broad disagreement between the historic nationalities in the Basque, Catalan, and Galician ACs and the other regions over the nature of the state. In July 1998 the leading regional parties in the three historic ACs issued the 'Declaration of Barcelona' which declared a confederal relationship between the center and the three communities and introduced the notion of shared sovereignty (Moreno 2001, 65). Taken by most observers as a political move by opposition parties rather than a demand for any specific changes to the balance of power, it nevertheless underlined the fact that regional and central elites have yet to definitively resolve Spain's federal identity.

As in Russia, the lack of strong multilateral institutions in Spain strengthens the need for and the asymmetrical effects of bilateralism. Spain's upper chamber duplicates the role of the lower house in a watered-down form, thus creating a second debating chamber for political parties rather than a means for regional representatives to shape national policies. Direct elections of most senators—208 senators are directly elected and an additional forty-four senators are appointed by the seventeen AC parliaments—give the major national parties an additional means to shape and influence the upper house. Consequently, regional leaders focus far more attention and resources on the multitude of sectoral and bilateral conferences that handle the bulk of intergovernmental relations and conflicts. The conferences occur on an irregular basis and lack many of the institutional norms of a Senate: frequent and reliable interactions; compromise; and public accountability.

Unlike Russia, however, party politics permeate center-periphery relations and give some regions more power in bilateral negotiations and at the national level. As Moreno notes, "Intergovernmental relations are very dependent on the colouring of the political party in charge of different levels of government. Consequently, most of the conflicts are political rather than policy-oriented. That is why 'bilateralism' is still the preferred manner of reaching political agreements rather than the institutionalization of multilateral intergovernmental relations" (Moreno 2001, 140). In the absence of strong multilateral institutions, regional parties can play the role of representative for the ACs.[7] In Catalonia, the moderate nationalist party (CiU) has ruled since 1980, giving the region both continuity of governance and bargaining power in the parliament as a key "swing vote." In 1996, for example, the CiU along with two other regional nationalist parties helped the Popular Party gain a parliamentary majority. In exchange, the CiU received new decision-making powers for Catalonia from the central government (Agranoff and Gallarín 1997, 33). As Colomer points out, "the intermediate, moderating role that the Catalan nationalists can play on some issues on the left-right dimension is not duplicated on the decentralisation issue, on which they are located at a more extreme position in relation to the major state-wide parties. The pivotal position of the regional nationalists in Spanish politics [gives] salience to the decentralisation issue. . . . " (Colomer 1998, 49). In Andalusia, a nonethnic AC that has aggressively bargained with the central government to obtain control equal to that of the historic territories, the regional party joined with the PSOE to form a majority government in the Andalusian parliament. In addition, regional leaders of the PSOE in Andalusia and several other ACS are known as 'barons' due to "their control of regional constituencies and their capacity to negotiate with the party's national leadership in favour of their regions' interests" (Colomer 1998, 46).[8] Using this power, Andalusia successfully negotiated the first autonomy statutes for a nonhistoric territory in 1982, during the majority control of the central government by the PSOE.

In its basic contours, bilateralism has produced similar institutional outcomes in Spain and Russia. Asymmetrical federalism has continued to generate conflict among regions for extended control over decision-making powers. The initial commitment in Spain to a two-tiered system of intergovernmental relations, with a few ethno-territories receiving broader powers, was subsequently weakened by extending these powers to other regions. Given the power of the Basque and Catalan nationalist parties in national politics, however, the center could not simply replace asymmetrical relations with regional equality; earlier arrangements held lasting consequences for future negotiations. Bilateralism has also sustained an unstable relationship between the center and regions, curtailing the possibility of recentralization but not eliminating it. As Colomer concludes, "If a disciplined political party were to gain an absolute majority control again, the temptation to introduce institutional and legal restrictions on the regional governments would be likely to reappear. In spite of the relatively high rates of financial and political decentralisation which have been attained in Spain, the future of the Spanish State of Autonomies is more uncertain than federalism in more formally institutionalised states" (1998, 51–2).

Nevertheless, the barriers to dismantling the asymmetrical effects of bilateralism are much higher in Spain than in Russia. The 1978 Constitution makes a firm commitment to safeguarding Spain's regional differences and does not place the same emphasis on subnational equality that appears in Russia's 1993 Constitution. The Constitutional Court—a legitimate and authoritative political institution from the beginning of Spain's transition to democracy[9]—has anchored the bilateral arrangements in the law through a series of decisions, particularly the 1983 decision that annulled much of the LOAPA (see above). The Court served as a neutral arbiter during the early years of the decentralization process, receiving 960 challenges to regional or federal laws in 1981–1997. In the past decade, however, such challenges have decreased significantly, suggesting that the basic parameters of the center-periphery relationship have been fixed (Moreno 2001, 142–3). Unlike in Russia, where implementation of Constitutional Court decisions remains sporadic and the central government must resort to threats and political negotiation, such arm-twisting is unnecessary in Spain's more effective judicial system. As a result, bilateralism presents less of a long-term threat to the integrity of the Spanish state, despite the likelihood of persistent regional conflict and competition.

Even in more mature federal systems, however, bilateralism can produce instability in the central-regional relationship. In Canada, a federation since 1867, both central and regional leaders condemned the underdevelopment of federal institutions and avenues for provincial representation. In the 1960s, the federal government chose to address the most pressing of its federal problems, the demands for autonomy by Quebec, by negotiating bilaterally with the province. Consequently, when the government sought to reform federalism through multilateral forums in the 1980s and 1990s, it faced a split between provinces demanding bilateral deals and provinces calling for equal treatment, similar to what we see in Russia.

CANADA AND THE PROSPECT OF FEDERAL REFORM

Although Canadian federalism emerged from a different institutional tradition than the Russian Federation, it faces many of the same tensions in relations between the center and subnational governments. Canada's provinces differ substantially from one another, well beyond the distinction between francophone Quebec and the English-speaking ROC (Rest of Canada). The Western provinces, particularly the natural resource-rich Alberta and British Columbia, as well as the agricultural prairie provinces of Manitoba and Saskatchewan, hold a substantial economic advantage over most of the more industrialized provinces to the east. The Atlantic provinces—New Brunswick, Newfoundland, Nova Scotia, and Prince Edward Island—have suffered from economic competition with the United States and elsewhere, forcing them to depend heavily on government subsidies, social programs, and investment. Ontario and Quebec[10] have maintained a more positive economic outlook than their provincial neighbors, although they, too, have had to adjust to a more competitive economic environment. Based in part on these economic differences, the Western provinces have been the principal lobbyists for broader devolution of power to the provinces during the federal debates of the 1980s and 1990s, supporting Quebec in many of its conflicts with the federal capital, Ottawa (Lusztig 1995). The Atlantic provinces, however, depend on the center's financial equalization programs to survive and therefore can expect to receive few benefits from further decentralization. Despite similarities to Russia's mechanisms for addressing center-periphery conflicts—executive dominance and underinstitutionalized forums for intergovernmental negotiation—the emphasis in Canada on equality and cooperative federalism minimizes the power of individual provinces, such as Alberta, to gain control over the federal rulebook.

Canada's system of federalism integrates, albeit uneasily, institutions drawn from its British ancestry and its disparate provincial interests. The British parliamentary system serves as the foundation for the political structure, endowing the Prime Minister[11] and the House of Commons with legislative and decision-making power at the center. Similar to Britain's House of Lords, Canada's upper federal chamber, the Senate, consists of appointed members and plays a nominal role in politics, with no power to approve or veto legislation. At the subnational level, a First Minister, the leader of the majority party in the provincial unicameral legislature, governs each of Canada's ten provinces and serves as the primary spokesperson for the interests of the territory and the party. A bifurcated party system, similar to that in Spain, permeates the federal relationship in Canada. Canadian politics are dominated by two centralized national parties—the Liberal Party and the Conservative Party—surrounded by increasing numbers of and support for regional parties, including the Bloc Quebecois, the Reform Party, and the Progressive Conservatives. Federal politics thus involve a complex process of inter- and intraparty negotiations. Few federal debates occur independent of electoral concerns, with regional and opposition parties using federal reform as a means to secure provincial support.

Despite the predominant role of political parties in policy making,[12] Canada has been labeled a system of "executive federalism," highlighting the dominance of the Prime Minister and First Ministers in intergovernmental negotiations and federal reform.[13] Since the 1960s, an annual First Ministers' Conference has become the principal institutional mechanism for intergovernmental negotiation and reform, supplemented by more informal ministerial meetings (Savoie 1999, 362). These meetings served as the forum for debates over the 1982 Canada Bill, the 1987 Meech Lake Accords, and the 1992 Charlottetown Agreement—the principal documents for recent federal reform. According to one observer, the annual conference "is the most significant unwritten development in the constitutional life of the country."[14] The closed-door conferences, free from public and interest group involvement, have provided opportunities to negotiate unpopular measures, such as the "distinct society" clause in the Meech Lake Accords (see below). Moreover, as the majority leaders of political parties that stress strict party discipline (Simeon 1972), first ministers often can easily pass such measures through the provincial legislatures, thus giving greater weight to the accusation of the conferences as essentially a mechanism for "backroom deals." According to one critic:

With their majority governments, the premiers could command the loyalties of their cabinet, their caucus, and their legislatures. Hence, the deals they made and the agreements they signed with the prime minister could, and did, become the law of the land. Administrative agreements between levels of government were proliferating [in the 1980s]. In the absence of a body representing the provinces at the centre, the premiers could claim to speak for their regions. It was an authority their predecessors could not have imagined, and it was growing all the time. Cooperative federalism was now co-optive federalism. (Cohen 1992, 50–1)

The unique bilateral relationship between the province of Quebec and the federal government highlights the asymmetries in Canada's federal system and serves as the focal point for federal reform. The federal government recognized the special status of Quebec as the country's only French-speaking province and granted it substantial political autonomy including, for example, the right to carry out relations with francophone countries without Ottawa's interference (Burgess 1993; Elazar 1994, 54). Yet it was not until the 1960s and the rise of Quebec nationalism that provincial demands became a threat to the unity of Canada. The goals of the Quebec government have fluctuated over the last thirty years, but they have focused principally on the constitutional recognition of Quebec as a "distinct society," self-determination as part of the Canadian Federation or as a sovereign state, and the decentralization of fiscal decision-making power to the province.[15] In the 1960s, the Canadian government began to negotiate constitutional reform with the provinces to incorporate the demands of Quebec. Although they made little progress in rewriting the constitution, the central government found more success in negotiating bilaterally with the leaders of Quebec. The center agreed to decentralize powers to the province, including areas of taxation and social policy, as a short-term measure to respond to the demands of the Québécois in lieu of a new constitution. As Richard Simeon points out, "The contracting-out legislation for Quebec in 1965 was a response to immediate Quebec demands; few federal decision makers at the time perceived the consequences this *de facto* special status would have for the future" (Simeon

1972, 293). Ottawa chose to address Quebec demands bilaterally at a time when territorial interests were subordinate to party allegiances. As opposed to the outcry after Russia's treaty with Tatarstan, the Canadian provinces did not see the agreement with Quebec as an opportunity to negotiate their own special arrangements. Nevertheless, it reinforced Quebec's self-identification as a "distinct society" within Canada and created a "Quebec model" of decentralized power as a subnational goal for federal reform, particularly among the Western provinces.

The problem of Quebec's special status arose during the next round of constitutional reform in the late 1970s and brought renewed demands from Quebec for political autonomy within the federation. Prime Minister Trudeau, however, used the opportunity of a failed referendum for sovereignty within the province to carry out a "federal *coup de force*" and negotiate a document that emphasized provincial equality rather than political and cultural asymmetries (Rocher 1992, 33–4). With provisions for provincial authority over natural resources to please the western provinces and federal commitment to fiscal equalization to gain the support of the Atlantic provinces, the provincial legislatures, with the exception of Quebec, approved the 1982 Constitution Act (Burgess 1993, 366). Although the document was legally binding for Quebec, Canada had not yet resolved the problem of federal unity—an issue it would address with the Meech Lake Accords in 1987.

The asymmetrical model of federalism, symbolized by the special status and authority of Quebec within the federation, structured the agenda for the negotiations at Meech Lake. The Quebec government proposed a package of five constitutional reforms, including recognition of Quebec as a "distinct society," the right to veto all constitutional matters, and the limitation of federal spending power in areas of provincial jurisdiction (Stein 1997, 316). As opposed to Russia and Spain, where the center relied on bilateral deals to address the federation's asymmetries, the Canadian federal government rejected the bilateral approach of the 1960s in favor of a multilateral solution to Quebec's reform agenda. In part, collective action appeared more attainable among Canada's ten provinces than Russia's 89 regions. In addition, the initiation of the First Ministers' conferences in the 1960s as part of the system of executive federalism emphasized cooperation[16] and interdependence in reaction to a previously more confederal system. Although both Russia and Canada relied on bargaining among executive leaders rather than legislative debate to resolve federal issues, the Canadian federal government hoped to address the needs and demands of the provinces and the unity question simultaneously through multilateral negotiations. Despite its use of bilateralism in the 1960s, Canada had never envisioned the process to extend beyond the special case of Quebec to the rest of the federation. Once the approach failed to eliminate threats of sovereignty from the province, the federal government looked for support from other provinces within multilateral forums to dilute the bargaining power of Quebec. But the center also had to face the potential costs of collective action by the provinces *against* the center[17]—a limited possibility due to the factionalizing Quebec issue—and the problem of balancing past concessions to Quebec autonomy with constitutional declarations of provincial equality.

At the First Ministers' Conference at Meech Lake, Ottawa's solution to these problems was the "provincialization" of Quebec's demands—similar to Madrid's "coffee for all" solution in Spain—with the exception of the "distinct society" clause. The Québecois felt strongly about its symbolic importance and the center did not wish to renew this heated debate and increase the hostility of the Quebec government to the Meech Lake negotiations. Instead, the government chose to focus on the less symbolic and more practical concerns for equality among the other nine provinces. All of the provinces received wider authority over areas such as financial allocations and immigration and a veto over constitutional reform matters. According to one observer, "The mutual gains accruing to the negotiating provinces ... were substantial, and they came without major losses or costs to any single negotiator, apart from perhaps the federal government. . . . However, the federal government may not have been viewed as an overall political loser in the negotiations if the benefits it derived from constitutionally integrating Quebec had been seen as offsetting its losses in political power" (Stein 1997, 318 and n. 21). Despite the support of the First Ministers and the successful marriage of provisions for federal unity and decentralization in the Meech Lake Accord, the agreement failed the ratification stage in the provincial legislatures. Provincial elections following the negotiation of the agreement brought opposition parties into power in three provinces: New Brunswick, Manitoba, and Newfoundland. Each of the provincial leaders had the power to nullify the agreement with the consent of his or her party in as much as the constitution demanded the approval of all ten provincial legislatures. Moreover, significant opposition to the accord had emerged, particularly over the "distinct society" clause, much to the surprise and ire of the federal government. Native populations, both in the territories and in Manitoba, protested that the statement recognized the status of French-speaking Québecois but not other ethnic groups within Canada. Other interest groups, such as women's coalitions, resented any bequest of special status to one group versus another (Stein 1997, 320). With public and elite opinion coalescing, the Meech Lake Accord died in the provincial legislatures in 1990.[18]

Since 1990, the Canadian government has attempted to resolve the federal unity issue with the 1992 Charlottetown Accord and subsequent First Ministers' conferences. Yet the more recent negotiations have faced even stronger opposition, failing to go beyond the stage of executive bargaining. Given the center's commitment to cooperative federalism, individual provinces hold enormous power by threatening a veto and resisting compromise. As the economic differences between the Atlantic provinces and the Western provinces have grown, their agendas and their positions on Quebec's autonomy have become increasingly disparate. Even negotiations over more circumscribed issues, such as Ottawa's fiscal powers, have been unable to navigate this divide. The poorer Atlantic provinces do not wish to limit the spending powers of the center, particularly during conditions of fiscal crisis, whereas the Western provinces resent federal programs that impose the brunt of the cost on the resource-rich West. Moreover, the Western provinces, led by Alberta's popular premier, Ralph Klein, argue that federal law must establish a clear division of federal and provincial responsibilities (*Maclean's*, 15 December 1997). In part to ensure the implementation of a comprehensive federal rulebook, the Western provinces have also argued for a "Triple-E Senate" (elected, effective, and equal) to replace the current appointed and ceremonial upper house of parliament. Despite the support of the Atlantic provinces for a more institutionalized forum to negotiate regional agendas, Quebec has opposed equal representation in the senate without a corresponding increase in its representation in the House of Commons.[19] Senate reform has continued to stumble as more populous provinces resist equal representation and provincial leaders focus on more popular issues such as economic and social reforms.

Canada's shift from bilateral to multilateral intergovernmental forums[20] has limited both the possibilities for federal reform and the opportunities for subnational bargaining. As in any federal system, Canadian provinces can sign individual intergovernmental agreements with the central government in areas of housing, employment, and other concrete social issues.[21] Yet issues that alter the long-term rules of the game—resource control, control over spending allocations, environmental policy, and other broad issues that constituted the bilateral agreements in Russia— now fall within the realm of multilateral negotiations. Moreover, the federal government retains the right to unilaterally alter or abandon bilateral agreements, a power it had agreed to relinquish in the rejected Charlottetown Accord (Burgess 1993, 375). Bilateral agreements thus lack the credible commitment of the federal government; only the thorny process of multilateral negotiations and reform can guarantee long-term changes to the rules of intergovernmental interaction. Yet as the failed Meech Lake and Charlottetown Accords reveal, even a hard-fought compromise can unravel as a result of the extraconstitutional, nontransparent nature of executive federalism. Without the accountability and legitimacy of a parliamentary institution, the federal reforms that are so desired by Canada's provinces to define the nature of the federal bargain seem unattainable.

Even politically unified regions where First Ministers can easily pass intergovernmental reforms and agreements through the cabinet and legislature have limited power to alter the rules of federalism. For example, Alberta's First Minister, Ralph Klein, aggressively pursued federal reform with the Meech Lake and Charlottetown Accords. Klein, buoyed by a healthy and expanding local economy and substantial electoral and elite support despite austere fiscal measures, attempted to find a compromise between provincial equality and existing asymmetries by proposing an "all-against-one" strategy of decentralizing authority and resources. The autonomy that Quebec achieved in its bilateral negotiations and subsequently used as the basis for its special relationship with Ottawa became the objective for the government of Alberta and other provinces. As in Russia, the benefits of national unity for the central government offset the price of regional autonomy set forth in the agreements. Regardless of their power to set the agenda, however, provincial leaders such as Klein could not control the ratification process in other provinces, a situation only exacerbated by recent legislation in Alberta and Manitoba requiring territorial referendums for federal reform accords. In spite of recent votes on Quebec sovereignty that have raised the fear of federal dissolution, provincial and central leaders have moved away from broader issues of federal reform and have instead turned to more realizable reform in such areas as social policies, health care, and environmental regulation, largely as a result of the constraints of Canada's multilateral arrangements.

The 1999 Social Union demonstrates the tensions between symmetry and asymmetry and bilateralism and multilateralism that prevail in Canada as a result of its frequent attempts to negotiate the rules of the game. The First Ministers—with the exception of the leader of Quebec—and Prime Minister Chrétien signed *A Framework to Improve the Social Union for Canadians* (SUFA), a wide-reaching program that covers health, education, and welfare. According to Alain Noël, "For the first time broad agreement codified the new rules that would govern intergovernmental relations in all areas of social policy, but also, by extension in a number of sectors not considered in the document."[22] Despite the harmonizing impulse of the agreement, provinces may opt out of federal social programs if they have a similar program in place and can finance it at the provincial level. This gives a double advantage to wealthier provinces such as British Columbia: they may come up with their own programs without federal intervention and use the federal financing for other areas of their choosing (Smith 2002). Moreover, Quebec still remains in its own category, left to negotiate independently with the federal government over social policy and to extend the opportunities for bilateral negotiations into the future.

RUSSIA IN COMPARATIVE PERSPECTIVE

The above comparisons with Spain and Canada suggest that intergovernmental bargaining over the rules of federal interaction provides a dynamic source of interdependence and change in federal systems, even in systems more established than the Russian Federation. In particular, asymmetrical federations require constant negotiation to balance regional diversity with national unity (Tarlton 1965). Central and regional elites bargain frequently over distributional outcomes and specific federal policies, but they also focus on the rules of the game during periods of change or uncertainty. In both Russia and Spain, the political upheaval of a democratic transition provided opportunities for regional elites to structure the definition of federalism. In Canada, the uncertainty over Quebec's position in the federation served as the impetus for the renegotiation of the balance of federal and provincial power. Each of these countries used bilateral negotiations to address threats to national unity, thereby placing the federal rulebook on the intergovernmental bargaining table. Moreover, the initial decision of the central government to create or extend the asymmetrical relationships with its constituent units instituted a discordant system of federalism. Regions constantly employed strategies of "comparative grievance" to renegotiate their arrangements with the center, creating a costly and volatile environment for intergovernmental relations. In Russia, regional elites protested the privileges of the republics and a handful of provinces. Similarly, subnational leaders in Spain resented the power held by the historical territories. Even the four territories—Basque, Catalonia, Galacia, and Navarre—with enhanced autonomy competed among themselves for equal or greater administrative and fiscal control. In Canada, as the Western provinces grew in population and wealth, they began to seek decentralized control similar to that of Quebec and reject the notion of a "distinct society."

In each of these countries, institutional arrangements structured the way in which the central government negotiated with subnational elites and the opportunities for individual regions to alter the rules of federalism. The level of interdependence in a modern federation assures that central and regional elites will need some mechanisms to negotiate jurisdictional boundaries on a regular basis. This was particularly true in the new Russian Federation, due to the profound nature of the political transition from communism and to the design of the 1993 Constitution. The sheer number of joint competencies that the constitution explicitly lays out, perhaps unequaled in any other federal constitution, forced intergovernmental dialogue and cooperation to enact its provisions.

The absence of strong, territorial representation at the national level similar to the United States Senate or the German Bundesrat increased the need for and the scope of bilateral bargaining in Russia, as well as in

Canada and Spain. Subnational elites channeled their demands for changes to the federal rulebook directly to the central government rather than through a representative institution with an established set of rules. The failure of federal reform in Canada illustrates this point. Without a "Triple-E" (elected, effective, and equal) Senate, the Canadian government relied on executive federalism—meetings among the provincial First Ministers—to negotiate federal reform, leaving the government open to accusations of undemocratic practices. Despite the opportunities for consensus that a small, sequestered conference might present, Canada also instituted substantial hurdles, including unanimous regional approval, which increased the power of individual provinces to block federal reform but limited their power and the power of the federal government to achieve comprehensive reform. The structure of political parties only exacerbated the problem. Regional parties, such as the Reform Party or the Bloc Quebecois, that were seeking to gain a foothold in local politics and contest the dominance of the two major national parties had ample reason to use provincial legislatures and federal reform as their battleground. As in Spain, decentralization and regional autonomy became the mantra for many regional and ethnic parties and thereby further politicized the process of federal reform. As a result, the changes to the balance of power in Canada have been achieved either within a narrow scope and limited time frame or through bilateral bargaining—an outcome that has only increased the competition among provinces and the desire of the central government to depend on multilateral negotiations for further changes.

In comparison to Spain and Canada, with their inconsequential Senates, the Russian Federation has the foundations for more effective territorial representation in the Federation Council. Members of the Council, under the rules of 1993–2000 or the new legislation under President Putin[23] primarily serve in the interests of their regions rather than the federal government, unlike in Canada. In theory, the Council, in cooperation with the Duma and the government, has the power to design and enact agendas for federal reform. Yet under Yeltsin the center relied on the flexibility of bilateralism to hammer out the balance of power in the federation. Rather than face the potential of collective action by the regions and the opposition of a hostile Duma during a period of political and fiscal weakness, the center negotiated with individual regions and validated an asymmetrical federal system. The Russian government assumed that bilateralism would give it more bargaining power in relation to the regions than any multilateral forum. Instead, bilateralism gave a group of wealthier and politically unified regions the opportunities—including issue-linkage within the Federation Council—to construct and negotiate advantageous agendas to decentralize extensive decision-making powers.

Yet the failure to develop the role of the Federation Council to balance "super-presidentialism" in Russia has left the regions vulnerable to attempts to recentralize power. As Colomer remarks in the case of Spain, if the regions "rely only upon strategic action and not on institutions fostering more stable relationships between the centre and the [territories], they may be vulnerable to changes in the centre" (1998, 51). President Putin used his honeymoon period to increase federal oversight of the regions and reduce the powers of regional governors, including their participation in the Federation Council. Yet the results of bilateralism leave some regions more vulnerable than others and Putin will have to devote sizable resources to eliminating the autonomy already achieved by some regions under bilateralism. Indicative of this conclusion is the fact that in 2001 and 2002 more than twenty regions had agreed to invalidate their bilateral treaties with the federal government. As of this time, however, Putin is still negotiating with Tatarstan and Bashkortostan over their treaties and republic constitutions with little sign of appeasement. In the future, he likely will be faced with a choice similar to that of Yeltsin after the passage of the 1993 Constitution. Either President Putin will have to operate within the Federation Council to pass further centralizing and equalizing federal reforms and face the potential of regional collective action, or he will have to continue to rely on bilateralism to renegotiate intergovernmental relationships. In the first two years of Putin's presidency, the Federation Council has shown few signs of regional cooperation against the aims of the federal government. But attempts to significantly alter the balance of power through eradicating regional asymmetry, reducing the number of federation subjects, or implementing and expanding the federal power to dismiss subnational leaders, may breathe new life into the upper parliamentary chamber. Like Yeltsin, Putin may eventually conclude that the center will have more power within a bilateral rather than a multilateral bargaining situation.

Retaining some degree of asymmetry might be the price of maintaining the Rikerian bargain in a multiethnic, diverse federation,[24] but it nevertheless brings the tenets of that bargain into question more often. It might also be the case that bilateralism will become less of a threat to federal stability when bargaining focuses solely on distributional outcomes rather than the federal rulebook. Stephen Krasner (1984) and Reinhard Bendix (1977) argue that conflicts over allocation decisions replace struggles over the rulebook during the process of state consolidation.[25] Yet federalism may offer an exception to the notion of the rulebook versus the pocketbook distinction as a developmental issue. Since federalism produces a broad range of de facto or de jure areas of joint jurisdiction and overlapping competencies, elites can continue to contest the rules of the game, even in more consolidated democracies such as Canada. Political changes, such as the incorporation of the eastern states into the German Federation, may reopen even the most stable federal systems to negotiation over the federal structure. In states without effectual territorial representation, conflict converges on the direct relationship between the central and individual regional governments. Without the constraints of institutional rules and collective decision making, disputes over allocation decisions may easily develop into struggles over the rules of the game.

Nevertheless, bilateral bargaining over the intergovernmental rules does not necessarily threaten the sustainability of federalism. Instead, center-regional bargaining provides an essential foundation of federalism, allowing both federal and subnational elites to bargain their agendas and revise the federal rulebook as resources and power shift. Moreover, overlapping jurisdictions and interdependence—as important a part of federalism as autonomous spheres of activity—must be renegotiated in response to changing circumstances. Regime changes, the creation of the European Union, the growth of international trade and regulations, and technological advancements all affect subnational governments and their relationship with the federal center. Rather than requiring a particular set of institutional structures or norms, the survival of federalism—whether in Russia, India, Brazil, or Canada—depends on the capacity for regional and federal leaders to renegotiate and redefine the rules of interaction under changing circumstances and new demands.

NOTES

1. I take the language of "co-opting" versus "expropriating" from Shleifer and Treisman's work on the political economy of economic reforms in Russia. In *Without a Map* (2000), the authors artfully outline the political strategies available to political leaders in dealing with "stakeholders," such as enterprise managers and bankers, in the economic transition. Here, regional leaders represent stakeholders in the democratization process; the federal government must decide whether to co-opt their participation in the reforms by offering them rents or expropriate their political power and exclude them from policy making.

2. In April 2002, the Constitutional Court upheld the these laws after a challenge by the President of Chuvashia and the legislatures in the republics of Adygeya and Sakha. But the Court also raised the hurtles for the implementation of the laws by requiring more judicial oversight in determining whether the violation of the law is serious enough to warrant expulsion (*EWI Russian Regional Report* 7, 14 (April 2002)).

3. Smiryangin (2001) notes that the Federation Council is likely to be the arena for center-regional conflicts in the future.

4. The decree, upheld by the Constitutional Court, essentially "grandfathered" leaders who had been elected before 1999 when the two-term limit law was passed. This particularly benefited the most powerful regional leaders, such as Shaimiyev in Tatarstan, Luzhkov in Moscow, and Titov in Samara, who have held their posts since Russia's independence.

5. In fact, the inherent premise of symmetrical intergovernmental relationships based on the U.S. federal model steered Spain away from federalism (Linz 1989).

6. The *ley paccionada* (negotiated law) of 1841, which determined the status of

Navarre following the civil war, served as one of the foundations for the autonomous communities (Linz 1989).

7. There is a growing literature on the relationship between federalism and political parties. Riker (1987) argues that strong national parties with decentralized party organizations most successfully integrate a federal state and protect subnational autonomy, whereas strong regional parties tend to segment elites and interests. Others suggest that simultaneous regional and federal elections further state integration (Linz and Stepan 1992). The case of Spain is somewhat ambiguous. Certainly, regional parties have advanced the drive for subnational autonomy. In fact, there is some evidence that decentralization has increased the support for regional parties, particularly in the nonhistoric ACs (Hamann 1999). Nevertheless, with a few exceptions such as Catalonia's CiU, regional parties still play a much stronger role in elections within the ACs and the two major national parties, the PP and PSOE, dominate national politics (Van Houten 2002).

8. This is similar to the case of India under the Congress Party, where state representatives retained significant bargaining power within the party. See, for example, Lijphart (1996).

9. The formula for selecting the members of the Constitutional Court involves a broad spectrum of political bodies and, as a result, all of the major political parties: 4 members are elected by Congress, 4 by the Senate, 2 appointments on the proposal of the Government Council and 2 appointments on the proposal of the General Council of Judicial Power (Watts 1999, 101). According to Moreno (2001), this accords the Court a high degree of respect.

10. I focus here on the ten provinces, rather than the self-governing Yukon Territory and Northwest Territories, which do not participate directly in the constitutional and federal debates.

11. Canada also has a governor general in Ottawa and lieutenant governors in the provinces, who serve mostly ceremonial roles (Elazar 1994).

12. Tanguay argues that it is precisely because of the party system—in particular, the strict party discipline and the nature of the Westminster parliamentary system—that gives the prime minster and first ministers so much power. He states that, "[P]arty politics in Canada is leader-dominated to an extent unrivalled in almost any other industrialized democracy" (Tanguay 2002, 305).

13. Smiley (1970, 3). Cited in Simeon (1972, 5).

14. Cheffins (1969, 15). Cited in Simeon (1972, 283).

15. There exists a large literature on Quebec nationalism and Quebec politics. See, for example, Weaver (1992), McRoberts (1997), Cook (1986), and Mathews (1990).

16. Cooperation and cooperative federalism imply joint decision making and unanimity rather than lack of conflict; the Quebec issue has certainly generated intense strife and heated debates.

17. Putnam refers to this as an "all-on-one" versus a "one-on-one" bargaining strategy (1993, 22).

18. The Accord formally died when the single Aboriginal member of the Manitoba legislature, Elijah Harper, succeeded in blocking its passage using procedural tactics (Burgess 1993, 370).

19. This became one of the major stumbling blocks in the 1992 Charlottetown

Accords. Quebec demanded a permanent increase of 25 percent in its parliamentary representation in exchange for a Triple-E senate (Stein 1997).

20. I differentiate here between an intergovernmental forum, which focuses purely on matters of center-provincial relations, and a national forum such as the Senate, which addresses questions that are broader in scope.

21. Despite opportunities to negotiate bilateral arrangements—Alberta, for example, signed a three-year deal to control job-training programs on its territory (*Canada and the World Backgrounder*, March 1998)—the Canadian government has continually stressed federal health and social programs and national income and economic policies (*Maclean's*, 22 December 1997).

22. Noël 2000. Cited in Simeon and Cameron (2002).

23. From 1993–2000 the governor (or Republic President) and head of the regional legislature also served as members of the Federation Council. Recent legislation creates a new system that bears some resemblance to the makeup of the German Bundesrat. The regional government and legislature each appoint a representative to the Federation Council but may no longer serve in the upper chamber themselves.

24. I am referring here in particular to federations where regional and ethnic boundaries coincide. Switzerland might be an exception due to its use of more confederal arrangements. See, for example, Watts 1999a.

25. David Woodruff (1999) applies this distinction to Russia, arguing that the fragmentation of monetary control and the fight over how the state should govern its money supply suggest that Russia has still not entered the state consolidation phase of development. I thank Steven Solnick for suggesting the state-building aspect of the rulebook and mentioning the above sources to me.

Bibliography

Agranoff, Robert. 1996. "Federal Evolution in Spain." *International Political Science Review* 17 (4):385–401.

Agranoff, Robert and J. Gallarin. 1997. "Toward Federal Democracy in Spain: An Examination of Intergovernmental Relations." *Publius: The Journal of Federalism* 27 (4):1–38.

Ames, Barry. 1987. *Political Survival: Politicians and Public Policy in Latin America.* Berkeley: University of California Press.

Andrews, Josephine and Kathryn Stoner-Weiss. 1995. "Regionalism and Reform in Provincial Russia." *Post-Soviet Affairs.* 11 (4):384–406.

Axelrod, Robert. 1984. *The Evolution of Cooperation.* New York: Basic Books.

Bacharach, Samuel. 1981. *Bargaining: Power, Tactics, and Outcomes.* San Francisco, CA: Jossey Bass.

Bahl, Roy and Christine Wallich. 1996. "Intergovernmental Fiscal Relations in the Russian Federation." In *Decentralization of the Socialist State,* Ed. R. Bird, R. Ebel and C. Wallich. Aldershot, England: Avebury.

Bahry, Donna. 1987. *Outside Moscow: Power, Politics, and Budgetary Policy in the Soviet Republics.* New York: Columbia University.

Bakvis, Herman and William Chandler, Eds. 1987. *Federalism and the Role of the State.* Toronto: University of Toronto Press.

Balzer, Marjorie and Irina Vinokurova. 1996. "Nationalism, interethnic relations and federalism: The Case of Sakha Republic (Yakutia)." *Europe-Asia Studies.* 48:101–20.

Bates, Robert. 1981. *Markets and States in Tropical Africa.* Berkeley: University of California Press.

Bednar, Jenna, William Eskridge, Jr. and John Ferejohn. 1997. *A Political Theory of Federalism.* Mimeo.

Beissinger, Mark. 2002. *Nationalist Mobilization and the Collapse of the Soviet State.* Cambridge: Cambridge University Press.

Belin, Laura. 1997. "Russia's 1996 Gubernatorial Elections and the Implications for Yeltsin." *Demokratizatsiia* 5 (2).

Belin, Laura and Robert Orttung. 1997. *The Russian Parliamentary Elections of 1995: The Battle for the Duma.* Armonk, NY: M.E. Sharpe.

Bellows, Heather. 1993. "The Challenge of Informationalization in Post-Communist Societies." *Communist and Post-Communist Studies.* 26 (2):144–64.

Belyakov, Vladimir and Walter Raymond, Eds. 1994. *Constitution of the Russian Federation.* Lawrenceville, VA.

Bendix, Reinhard. 1977. *Nation Building and Citizenship: Studies of Our Changing Social Order.* Berkeley: University of California Press.

Bikalova, Nadezhda. 2001. "Intergovernmental Fiscal Relations in Russia." *Finance and Development.* 38 (3):36–9.

Birkenes, Robert. 1996. *The Development of Fiscal Federalism in Economics in Transition: Problems in the Russian Federation.* Indiana University.

Borodulina, Nadezhda. 1997. *Geographicheskie aspekti otnoshenii mezhdu tsentrom i regionami Rossii v budzhetno-nalogovoi sphere.* Instityt Geographii RAN.

Bowman, J. 1989. "Transaction Costs and Politics." *European Journal of Sociology.* 30:150–68.

Bradfield, Michael. 1992. "Failing to Meet Regional Needs." In *Constitutional Politics,* Ed. Duncan Cameron and Miriam Smith. Toronto: James Lorimer & Company.

Bradshaw, Michael and Phillip Hanson. 1994. "Regions, Local Power, and Reform in Russia." In *The Postcommunist Economic Transformation,* Ed. Robert Campbell. Boulder: Westview.

Bradshaw, M., A. Stenning, et al. 1998. "Economic Restructuring and Regional Change in Russia." In *Theorising Transition,* Ed. John Pickles and Adrian Smith. London: Routledge.

Brams, Steven. 1990. *Negotiation Games.* New York: Routledge.

Brennan, Geoffrey and James Buchanan. 1985. *The Reason of Rules.* Cambridge: Cambridge University Press.

Breslauer, George. 1982. *Khrushchev and Brezhnev as Leaders: Building Authority in Soviet Politics.* London: George Allen & Unwin.

Breton, Raymond. 1992. *Why Meech Failed: Lessons for Canadian Constitutionmaking.* Toronto: C. D. Howe Institute.

Brudny, Yitzhak. 1998. *Reinventing Russia: Russian Nationalism and the Soviet State, 1953–1991.* Cambridge, MA: Harvard University Press.

Buchanan, James and Gordon Tullock. 1965. *The Calculus of Consent.* Ann Arbor, MI: The University of Michigan Press.

Burgess, Michael. 1993. "Constitutional Reform in Canada and the 1992 Referendum." *Parliamentary Affairs.* 46 (3):363–379.

Burgess, Michael and Alain-G. Gagnon, Eds. 1993. *Comparative Federalism and Federation: Competing Traditions and Future Directions.* New York: Harvester Wheatsheaf.

Caillaud, Benoit, B. Jullien, et al. 1996. "National vs. European Incentive Policies: Bargaining, Information and Coordination." *European Economic Review.* 40: 91–111.

Cappelli, O. 1988. "Changing Leadership Perspectives on Centre-Periphery Relations." In *Elites and Political Power in the USSR*, Ed. David Lane. Aldershot, England: Edward Elgar.

Cheffins, R.I. 1969. *The Constitutional Process in Canada*. Toronto: McGraw-Hill.

Chorney, H. 1992. "A Regional Approach to Monetary and Fiscal Policy." In *The Constitutional Future of the Prairie and Atlantic Regions of Canada*, Ed. James McCrorie and Martha MacDonald. Regina, Saskatchewan: University of Regina, Canadian Plains Research Center.

Chubb, John. 1985. "Federalism and the Bias for Centralization." In *The New Directions in American Politics*, Eds. J. Chubb and P. Peterson. Washington, D.C.: Brookings.

Chung, Jae Ho. 1995. "Studies of Central-Provincial Relations in the People's Republic of China: A Mid-Term Appraisal." *The China Quarterly.* (142): 487–508.

Clark, Susan and David Graham. 1995. "The Russian Federation's Fight for Survival." *Orbis.* 39:329–42.

Clark, William. 1989. *Soviet Regional Elite Mobility after Khruschev.* New York: Praeger.

Clark, W. R. 1998. "Agents and Structures: Two Views of Preferences, Two Views of Institutions." *International Studies Quarterly.* 42:245–270.

Cohen, Andrew. 1992. "Executive Federalism and the Lessons of Meech Lake." In *Federalism in Peril*, Ed. A. R. Riggs and Tom Velk. Vacouver: The Fraser Institute.

Collier, David. 1991. "The Comparative Method: Two Decades of Change." In *Comparative Political Dynamics: Global Research Perspectives*, Ed. Dankwart Rustow and Kenneth Paul Erickson. New York: Harper Collins.

Collier, David and Deborah Norden. 1992. "Strategic Choice Models of Political Change in Latin America." *Comparative Politics.* 24:229–43.

Collier, David and J. Mahoney. 1996. "Insights and Pitfalls: Selection Bias in Qualitative Research." *World Politics.* 49 (October):56–91.

Colomer, Josep. 1998. "The Spanish 'State of Autonomies': Non-Institutional Federalism." *West European Politics* 21 (4):40–52.

Colomer, Josep. 1995. *Game Theory and the Transition to Democracy.* Aldershot, England: Edward Elgar.

Cook, Karen and Margaret Levi, Eds. 1990. *The Limits of Rationality.* Chicago: The University of Chicago Press.

Cook, Ramsey. 1986. *Canada, Quebec, and the Uses of Nationalism.* Toronto: McClelland and Stewart.

Cortell, Andrew and Susan Peterson. 1999. "Altered States: Explaining Domestic Institutional Change." *British Journal of Political Science.* 29:177–203.

Cottrell, Robert. 1996. "Russia's Parliamentary and Presidential Elections." *Government and Opposition.* 31 (Spring):160–74.

Cox, Robert and Erich Frankland. 1995. "The Federal State and the Breakup of Czechoslovakia: An Institutional Analysis." *Publius: The Journal of Federalism,* 25 (1):71–88.

Cremer, H., Marianne Marchand, et al. 1997. "Interregional Redistribution through Tax Surcharge." In *Fiscal Aspects of Evolving Federations*, Ed. David Wildasin. Cambridge: Cambridge University Press.

Davenport, Paul. 1983. "The Constitution and the Sharing of Wealth in Canada." *Law and Contemporary Problems.* 45 (4):109–47.

Desai, Padma and Todd Idson. 2002. *Work Without Wages: Russia's Nonpayment Crisis.* Cambridge, MA: MIT Press.

Diaz, C. 1981. "The State of the Autonomic Process in Spain." *Publius: The Journal of Federalism,* 11 (3–4):193–219.

DiMaggio, Paul and Walter Powell, Eds. 1991. *The New Institutionalism in Organizational Analysis.* Chicago: University of Chicago Press.

Dion, Douglas. 1998. "Evidence and Inference in the Comparative Case Study." *Comparative Politics.* 30 (2):127–45.

Dmitriev, Mikhail. 1996. *Budzhetnaya politika Rossii v usloviyakh finansovoi stabilizatsii.* Moscow: Carnegie Center.

Donnithorne, Audrey. 1981. *Centre-Provincial Economic Relations in China.* Canberra: Contemporary China Centre, Australian National University.

Dowley, Kathleen. 1998. "Striking the Federal Bargain in Russia: Comparative Regional Government Strategies." *Communist and Post-Communist Studies.* 31 (4):359–380.

Duchacek, Ivo. 1970. *Comparative Federalism: the Territorial Dimension of Politics.* New York: Holt, Rinehart, and Winston.

———. 1973. *Power Maps: Comparative Politics of Constitutions.* Santa Barbara, CA: ABC-Clio.

Dunlavy, Coleen. 1992. "Political Structure, State Policy, and Industrial Change: Early Railroad Policy in the United States and Prussia." In *Structuring Politics,* Ed. S. Steinmo, K. Thelen and F. Longstreth. Cambridge: Cambridge University Press.

Dupré, Joseph. 1987. "The Workability of Executive Federalism in Canada." In *Federalism and the Role of the State,* Eds. Herman Bakvis and William Chandler. Toronto: University of Toronto Press.

Easter, Gerald. 1996. "Personal Networks and Postrevolutionary State Building: Soviet Russia Reexamined." *World Politics.* 48 (July):551–78.

———. 1997. "Redefining Centre-Regional Relations in the Russian Federation: Sverdlovsk *Oblast'.*" *Europe-Asia Studies.* 49 (4):617–635.

Echols, John. 1975. "Politics, Budgets, and Regional Equality in Communist and Capitalist Systems." *Comparative Political Studies.* 8 (3):259–93.

Eggertsson, Thrainn. 1990. *Economic Behavior and Institutions.* Cambridge: Cambridge University.

Elazar, Daniel. 1966. *American Federalism: A View from the States.* New York: Thomas Y. Crowell Company.

———. 1985. "Federalism and Consociational Regimes." *Publius: The Journal of Federalism.* 15 (2):17–34.

———. 1987. *Exploring Federalism.* Tuscaloosa, AL: University of Alabama Press.

Elazar, Daniel, Ed. 1994. *Federal Systems of the World: A Handbook of Federal, Confederal, and Autonomy Arrangements.* Harlow, Essex: Longman Group.

Elazer, Daniel. 1995. "Comparative Federalism." *Polis.* 5.

Ellis, Richard. 1987. *The Union at Risk.* Oxford: Oxford University Press.

Elster, Jon, Ed. 1986. *Rational Choice.* Readings in Social and Political Theory. New York: New York University Press.

Enloe, Cynthia. 1977. "Internal Colonialism, Federalism, and Alternative State Development Strategies." *Publius: The Journal of Federalism*, 7 (Fall):145–60.

Fainsod, Merle. 1958. *Smolensk Under Soviet Rule*. Cambridge, MA: Harvard University Press.

Farmer, Kenneth. 1992. *The Soviet Adminitrative Elite*. New York: Praeger.

Filippov, Mikhail. and Olga Shvetsova. 1999. "Asymmetric Bilateral Bargaining in
the New Russian Federation: A Path-Dependence Explanation." *Communist
and Post-Communist Studies*. 32:61–76.

Fisher, R. C. 1997. "Intergovernmental Fiscal Relations: Policy Developments and
Research Prospects." In *Intergovernmental Fiscal Relations*, Ed. R. C. Fisher.
Boston: Kluwer Academic Publishers.

Freinkman, Lev and S. Titov. 1994. "The Transformation of the Regional Fiscal
System in Russia: the Case of Yaroslavl'." *World Bank Discussion Paper*, report IDP-143 (August).

Friedgut, Theodore and Jeffrey Hahn, Eds. 1994. *Local Power and Post-Soviet Politics*.
Armonk, NY: M.E. Sharpe.

Friedrich, Carl. 1968. *Trends of Federalism in Theory and Practice*. New York: Fred-
erick A. Praeger.

Furubotn, Eirik and Rudolph Richter, Eds. 1991. *The New Institutional Economics*.
College Station, TX: Texam A&M.

Gaddy, Clifford. 1996. *The Price of the Past: Russia's Struggle with the Legacy of a
Militarized Economy*. Washington, D.C.: Brookings Institution.

Gaddy, Clifford and Barry Ickes. 1997. "Russia's Virtual Economy." *Foreign Affairs*.
77 (5):53–67.

Gallik, Daniel, Cestmir Josina, and Stephen Rapawy. 1968. *The Soviet Financial
System*. Washington, D.C.: U.S. Bureau of the Census, Foreign Demographic
Analysis Division.

Geddes, Barbara. 1990. "How the Cases You Choose Affect the Answers You Get:
Selection Bias in Comparative Politics." *Political Analysis*. 2:131–52.

———. 1994. *Politicians' Dilemma: Building State Capacity in Latin America*. Berkeley:
University of California Press.

Gel'man, Vladimir. 1996. *Transformatsiia zakonodatel'noi politiki i federativniie otnosh-
eniia v Rossii*. Evropeiskogo Universiteta, St. Petersburg.

George, K. K. 1988. *Centre-State Financial Flows and Inter-state Disparities*. Delhi:
Criterion Books.

Gibson, James and Philip Hanson, Eds. 1996. *Transformation from Below: Local Power
and the Political Economy of Post-Communist Transitions*. Studies of Communism in Transition. Cheltenham, UK: Edward Elgar.

Goble, Paul. 1994. "Regions, Republics, and Russian Reform: Center-Periphery
Relations in the Russian Federation." In *The Successor States to the USSR*,
Ed. John Blaney. Washington, D.C.: Congressional Quarterly, Inc.

Goodman, David and Gerald Segal, Eds. 1994. *China Deconstructs*. London:
Routledge.

Gorbatova, L. 1995. "Formation of Connections Between Finance and Industry in
Russia." *Communist Economies and Economic Transformation*. 7 (1):121–34.

Gorenburg, Dmitri. 1999. "Regional Separatism in Russia: Ethnic Mobilisation or
Power Grab?" *Europe-Asia Studies*. 51 (2):245–74.

Goskomstat. 1996. *Sotsial'no-ekonomicheskoe polozhenie Rossii, yanvar'-noyabr' 1996 g.* Goskomstat RF.

Goskomstat. 1997. *Sotsial'no-ekonomicheskoe polozhenie Rossii, yanvar'-noyabr' 1996 g.* Moscow: Goskomstat RF.

Guboglo, Mikhail. 1997. *Federalizm vlasti i vlast' federalizma.* Moscow: State Duma of the Russian Federation, Commitee on Federal and Regional Policy and the Russian Academy of Sciences, Institute of Ethnology and Anthropology.

Gunlicks, Arthur. 1994. "German Federalism after Unification: The Legal/Constitutional Response." *Publius: The Journal of Federalism.* 24 (Spring): 81–98.

Gustafson, Thane. 1981. *Reform in Soviet Politics: The Lessons of Recent Policies on Land and Water.* New York: Cambridge University Press.

Gustafson, Thane and D. Mann. 1988. "Gorbachev and the 'Circular Flow of Power'." In *Elites and Political Power in the USSR,* Ed. D. Lane. Aldershot, England: Edward Elgar.

Hahn, Gordon. 2001. "Putin's Federal Reforms: Reinterpreting Russia's Legal Space or Upsetting the Metastability of Russia's Asymmetrical Federalism." *Demokratizatsiya.* 9 (4):498–531.

Hahn, Jeffrey. 1988. *Soviet Grassroots: Citizen Participation in Local Soviet Government.* Princeton: Princeton University Press.

———. 1991. "Developments in Local Soviet Politics." In *Perestroika at the Crossroads,* Ed. A. Rieber and A. Rubinstein. Armonk, NY: M.E. Sharpe.

———. 1993. "Attitudes Toward Reform Among Provincial Russian Politicians." *Post-Soviet Affairs.* 9 (1):66–85.

———. 1994. "Reforming Post-Soviet Russia: The Attitudes of Local Politicians." In *Local Power and Post-Soviet Politics,* Ed. T. Friedgut and J. Hahn. Armonk, NY: M.E. Sharpe.

Hall, Peter. 1986. *Governing the Economy: the Politics of State Intervention in Britain and France.* New York: Oxford University Press.

Hamann, Kerstin. 1999. "Federalist Institutions, Voting Behavior, and Party Systems in Spain." *Publius* 29 (1):111–21.

Hanson, Philip. 1991. "Property Rights in the New Phase of Reforms." In *Milestones in Glasnost and Perestroyka,* Ed. E. Hewett and V. Winston. Washington, D.C.: The Brookings Institution.

———. 1993. "Local Power and Market Reform in Russia." *Communist Economies and Economic Transformation.* 5 (1):45–60.

———. 1996. "Economic Change and the Russian Provinces," In *Transformation from Below: Local Power and the Political Economy of Post-Communist Transitions.* Eds. John Gibson and Philip Hanson. Cheltenham, UK: Edward Elgar.

Hanson, Philip. 1997. "Samara: A Preliminary Profile of a Russian Region and its Adaptation to the Market." *Europe-Asia Studies.* 49 (3):407–429.

Hay, C. and D. Wincott. 1998. "Structure, Agency and Historical Institutionalism: Comment on P. A. Hall and R. C. R. Taylor." *Political Studies.* 46 (5):951–7.

Helf, G. and J. Hahn. 1992. "Old Dogs and New Tricks: Party Elites in the Russian Regional Elections of 1990." *Slavic Review.* 51 (Fall):511–30.

Henderson, J. 1991. "Legal Aspects of the Soviet Federal Structures." In *Soviet Federalism, Nationalism, and Economic Decentralization,* Ed. A. McAuley. Leicester: Leicester University.

Hesse, Joachim and Vincent Wright. 1996. *Federalizing Europe?* Oxford: Oxford University Press.

Hewitt, Ed and V. Winston. 1991. "Entering the 1990s: Editors' Introduction." In *Milestones of Glasnost and Perestroyka*, Ed. E. Hewitt and V. Winston. Washington, D.C.: Brookings Institution.

Higley, John, Judith Kollberg, et al. 1996. "The Persistence of Post-Communist Elites." *Journal of Democracy*. 7 (2):133–47.

Hill, Ronald. 1980. *Soviet Politics, Political Science, and Reform*. White Plains, NY: M.E. Sharpe.

———. 1977. *Soviet Political Elites: The Case of Tiraspol*. New York: St. Martin's.

———. 1983. "The Development of Soviet Local Government Since Stalin's Death." In *Soviet Local Politics and Government*, Ed. Everett Jacobs. London: George Allen & Unwin.

Hopmann, Terrence. 1996. *The Negotiation Process and the Resolution of International Conflicts*. Columbia, SC: University of South Carolina Press.

Hough, Jerry. 1969. *The Soviet Prefects: the Local Party Organs in Industrial Decision-making*. Cambridge, MA: Harvard University Press.

———. 1997. *Democratization and Revolution in the USSR 1985–1991*. Washington, D.C.: The Brookings Institution.

Huang, Yasheng. 1991. *The Politics of Inflation Control in China: Provincial Responses to Central Investment Policies, 1977–1989*. Harvard University.

———. 1996. *Inflation and Investment Controls in China: The Political Economy of Central-Local Relations During the Reform Era*. Cambridge: Cambridge University Press.

Hueglin, Thomas. 2000. "From Constitutional to Treaty Federalism." *Publius* 30 (4):137–53.

Hughes, James. 1996. "Moscow's Bilateral Treaties Add to Confusion." *Transition*. 20 (September):39–43.

Hughes, James. 1997. "Sub-national Elites and Post-communist Transformation in Russia: A Reply to Kryshtanovskaya and White." *Europe-Asia Studies*. 49 (6):1017–36.

Hutchings, Raymond. 1983. *The Soviet Budget*. Albany: State University of New York Press.

Hyde, Matthew. 2001. "Putin's Federal Reforms and their Implications for Presidential Power in Russia." *Europe-Asia Studies* 53 (5):719–43.

Ickes, Barry, Peter Murrell, and Randi Ryterman. 1997. "End of the Tunnel? The Effects of Financial Stabilization in Russia." *Post-Soviet Affairs*. 13 (2):105–33.

Ickes, Barry and Randi Ryterman. 1993. "Roadblock to Economic Reform: Inter-Enterprise Debt and the Transition to Markets." *Post-Soviet Affairs*. 9 (3): 231–52.

Igudin, A. G. 1998. "Pochemu ne snizhayetsya ostrota protivorechii v mezhbud-zhenikh otnosheniyakh." *Finansi* 2:9–12.

Ikenberry, G. John. 1989. "Conclusion: An Institutional Approach to American Foreign Economic Policy." In *The State and American Foreign Economic Policy*, Ed. G. J. Ikenberry, D. A. Lake and M. Mastanduno. Ithaca, NY: Cornell University.

Immergut, Ellen. 1992. *Health Politics: Interests and Institutions in Western Europe.* Cambridge: Cambridge University Press.

———. 1998. "The Theoretical Core of the New Institutionalism." *Politics & Society.* 26 (1):5–34.

Instityt zakonodatel'stva I sravnitel'nogo pravovedeniya. 1996. "Dogovornii protsess: vchera, sogodnya, zavtra." *Federatsiia* 19:17–19.

Ivanov, Vasili 1998. "Vnutrifederal'nie dogovori 1997 goda uvelichili kolichestvo privelegirovannikh subyektov Rossiiskoi Federatsii." *Federalizm.* 3:137–164.

Jacobs, Everett., Ed. 1983. *Soviet Local Politics and Government.* London: Allen and Unwin.

Jeffery, Charlie. 1999. "From Cooperative Federalism to a 'Sinatra Doctrine' of the Länder?" In *Recasting German Federalism,* Ed. Charlie Jeffery. London: Pinter.

Jeffrey, Charlie. 1999. "Party Politics and Territorial Representation in the Federal Republic of Germany." *West European Politics.* 22 (2):130–66.

Jeffery, Charlie and S. Collins. 1998. "The German Länder and EU Enlargement: Between Apple Pie and Issue Linkage." *German Politics.* 7 (2):86–101.

Johnson, Juliet. 1997. "Russia's Emerging Financial-Industrial Groups." *Post-Soviet Affairs.* 13 (4):333–65.

Jowitt, Kenneth. 1992. *New World Disorder: The Leninist Extinction.* Berkeley: University of California Press.

Kahn, Jeffrey. 2002. *Federalism, Democratization, and the Rule of Law in Russia.* New York: Oxford University Press.

Kato, Junko. 1996. "Review Article: Institutions and Rationality in Politics—Three Varieties of Neo-Institutionalists." *British Journal of Political Science.* 26: 553–82.

Kempton, Daniel. 1996. "The Republic of Sakha (Yakutia): the Evolution of Centre-Periphery Relations in the Russian Federation." *Europe-Asia Studies.* 48:587–613.

King, Desmond. 1992. "The Establishment of Work-Welfare Programs in the United States and Britain: Politics, Ideas, and Institutions." In *Structuring Politics,* Ed. Sven Steinmo, K. Thelen and F. Longstreth. Cambridge: Cambridge University Press.

King, D. S. 1989. "Political Centralization and State Interests in Britain: The 1986 Abolition of the GLC and MCCs." *Comparative Political Studies.* 21 (4): 467–94.

King, Gary, Robert Keohane, and Sidney Verba. 1994. *Designing Social Inquiry.* Princeton: Princeton University Press.

King, Preston. 1982. *Federalism and Federation.* London: Croom Helm.

Kirkow, Peter. 1995. "Regional Warlordism in Russia: The Case of Primorskii *Krai.*" *Europe-Asia Studies.* 47 (6):923–47.

Kirkow, Peter. 1996. "Distributional Coalitions, Budgetary Problems and Fiscal Federalism in Russia." *Communist Economics and Economic Transformation.* 8 (3):277–98.

———. 1998. *Russia's Provinces: Authoritarian Transformation Versus Local Autonomy.* New York: St. Martin's Press.

Kivelson, Valerie. 1996. *Autocracy in the Provinces.* Stanford: Stanford University Press.

Knight, Jack. 1992. *Institutions and Social Conflict*. Cambridge: Cambridge University.

Kokov, V. and Iu. Liubimtsev. 1997. "Fiscal Federalism." *Problems of Economic Transition*. 39 (11):22–41.

Kolsto, Pål. 2000. *Political Construction Sites*. Boulder, CO: Westview.

Krasner, Stephen. 1984. "Approaches to the State: Alternative Conceptions and Historical Dynamics." *Comparative Politics*. 16 (2):223–46.

Kryshtanavskaya, Olga. and Stephan White. 1996. "From Soviet Nomenklatura to Russian Elite." *Europe-Asia Studies*. 48 (5):711–34.

Kux, Stephan. 1990. *Soviet Federalism: A Comparative Perspective*. New York: Institute for East-West Studies.

Laikam, K. E. and V. V. Sharamova. 1998. "Mesto i rol' nalogovoi politiki v sovershenstvovanii mezhbudzhetnikh otnoshenii." *Finansi*. (6):12–14.

Lane, David, Ed. 1988. *Elites and Political Power in the USSR*. Aldershot, England: Edward Elgar.

Lapidus, Gail and Edward Walker. 1995. "Nationalism, Regionalism, and Federalism: Center-Periphery Relations in Post-Communist Russia." In *The New Russia: Troubled Transformation*, Ed. G. Lapidus. Boulder: Westview.

Lapshova, Y. 1996. *Vibori gubernatora Samarskoi oblasti*. International Institute of Humanitarian-Political Studies.

Lavrov, Aleksei. 1995. "Budzhetnii federalizm v Rossii: itogi I yroki 1994 g." *Federalizm I regionalnaia politika: Problemi Rossii I zarubezhnii opit*. Ed. V. E. Seliverstov. Novosibirsk: Rossiskaya akademiya nauk.

———. 1998. "Budgetary Federalism." In *Conflict and Consensus in Ethno-Political and Center-Periphery Relations in Russia*, Ed. J. Azrael and E. Payin. Santa Monica, CA: RAND.

Lavrov, Alexei, Jenny Litwack, and D. Sutherland. 2001. "Fiscal Federalist Relations in Russia: A Case for Subnational Autonomy." *OECD Center for Cooperation with Nonmembers*. Paris: Organization for Economic Cooperation and Development.

Lebow, Richard Ned. 1997. *The Art of Bargaining*. New York: Columbia University Press.

Le Houerou, Philippe. 1996. *Fiscal Management in Russia*. Washington, D.C.: The World Bank.

Le Houerou, Philippe and Michael Rutkowski. 1996. "Federal Transfers in Russia: Their Impact on Regional Revenues and Incomes." *Comparative Economic Studies*. 38 (2/3):21–44.

Lemco, Jonathan. 1991. *Political Stability in Federal Governments*. New York: Praeger.

Leonardy, Uwe. 1999. "The Institutional Structures of German Federalism." In *Recasting German Federalism*, Ed. Charlie Jeffery. London: Pinter.

Levi, Margaret. 1988. *Of Rule and Revenue*. Berkeley: University of California.

———. 1997. "A Model, a Method, and a Map: Rational Choice in Comparative and Historical Analysis." In *Comparative Politics: Rationality, Culture, and Structure*, Ed. M. I. Lichbach and A. S. Zuckerman. Cambridge: Cambridge University Press.

Lewis, C. W. 1977. "Comparing City Budgets, the Soviet Case." *Comparative Urban Research*: 46–57.

Li, Linda. 1998. *Centre and Provinces: China 1978–1993*. Oxford: Clarendon Press.

Liebschutz, Sarah. 1991. *Bargaining Under Federalism: Contemporary New York*. Albany: SUNY.

Lijphart, Arend. 1996. "The Puzzle of Indian Democracy: A Consociational Approach." *American Political Science Review*. 90 (2):258–68.

Linz, Juan. 1989. "Spanish Democracy and the Estado de las Autonomias." In *Forging Unity Out of Diversity*, Eds. R. Goldwin, A. Kaufman, and W. Schambra. Washington, D.C.: American Enterprise Institute for Public Policy Research.

Linz, Juan and Alfred Stepan. 1992. "Political Identities and Electoral Sequences: Spain, the Soviet Union, and Yugoslavia." *Daedalus* 221 (2):123–39.

Lipton, David and Jeffrey Sachs. 1992. "Prospects for Russia's Economic Reforms." *Brookings Papers on Economic Activity*. 2:213–66.

Litvack, Jennie. 1994. "Regional Demands and Fiscal Federalism." In *Russia and the Challenge of Fiscal Federalism*, Ed. C. Wallich. Washington, D.C.: World Bank.

Lopez, C. D. 1985. "Centre-Periphery Structures in Spain: From Historical Conflict to Territorial-Consociational Accommodation?" In *Centre-Periphery Relations in Western Europe*. Eds., Yves Meny and Vincent Wright. London: George Allen & Unwin.

Lowndes, V. 1996. "Varieties of New Institutionalism: A Critical Appraisal." *Public Administration*. 74 (Summer):181–97.

Lusztig, Michael. 1995. "Federalism and Institutional Design: The Perils and Politics of a Triple-E Senate in Canada." *Publius: The Journal of Federalism*. 25 (1):35–50.

Lynn, Nicholas and Aleksei Novikov. 1997. "Refederalizing Russia: Debates on the Idea of Federalism in Russia." *Publius*. 27 (2):187–203.

Lysenko, Vladimir. 1995. *Razvitie federativnikh otnoshenii v sovremennoi Rossii*. Moskva: Institute sovremennoi politiki.

Ma, Jun. 1997. *Intergovernmental Relations and Economic Management in China*. New York: St. Martin's Press.

Mackenstein, H. and C. Jeffery. 1999. "Financial Equalization in the 1990s: On the Road Back to Karlsruche?" In *Recasting German Federalism*, Ed. C. Jeffery. London: Pinter.

Mahler, Gregory. 1987. *New Dimensions of Canadian Federalism*. Rutherford, NJ: Farleigh Dickinson University Press.

March, James and Johan Olsen. 1984. "The New Institutionalism: Organizational Factors in Political Life." *American Political Science Review*. 78:738–49.

Martinez-Vazquez, Jorge. 1994. "Expenditures and Expenditure Assignment." In *Russia and the Challenge of Fiscal Federalism*, Ed. Christine Wallich. Washington, D.C.: The World Bank.

Martinez-Vazquez, Jorge and Jameson Boex. 2001. *Russia's Transition to a New Federalism*. Washington, D.C.: The World Bank.

Mathews, Georges. 1990. *Quiet Resolution: Quebec's Challenge to Canada*. Toronto: Summerhill Press.

Matsuzato, Kimitaka. 1997. "The Split and Reconfiguration of Ex-Communist Party Factions in the Russian Oblasts: Chelyabinsk, Samara, Ulyanovsk, Tambov, and Tver (1991–5)." *Demokratizatsiya*. 5 (1):53–88.

Matveev, Vladimir. 1997. *Zakonodatel'nie prioriteti regional'noi ekonomicheskoi politiki v Rossii.* Russian Federation State Duma.

Mau, Vladimir and Vadim Stupin. 1997. "The Political Economy of Russian Regionalism." *Communist Economies and Economic Transition.* 9 (1):5–25.

May, Ronald. 1970. "Decision-making and Stability in Federal Systems." *Canadian Journal of Political Science.* 3 (1):73–87.

McAuley, Alastair. 1997. "The Determinants of Russian Federal-Regional Fiscal Relations: Equity or Political Influence." *Europe-Asia Studies.* 49 (3):431–444.

McAuley, Mary. 1992. "Politics, Economics, and Elite Realignment in Russia: A Regional Perspective." *Soviet Economy.* 8 (1):46–88.

McGrath, Troy. 2002. *Nations in Transit: Report on Russia.* Washington, D.C.: Freedom House.

McLure, Charles. 1995. "Revenue Assignment and Intergovernmental Fiscal Relations in Russia." In *Economic Transition in Eastern Europe: Realities of Reform,* Ed. Edward Lazear. Stanford: Hoover Institution.

McRoberts, Kenneth. 1997. *Misconceiving Canada: The Struggle for National Unity.* Toronto: Oxford University Press.

McRoberts, Kenneth and Patrick Monahan, Eds. 1993. *The Charlottetown Accord, the Referendum, and the Future of Canada.* Toronto: University of Toronto Press.

Mitchneck, Beth. 1993. "An Assessment of the Growing Local Economic Development Function of Local Authorities in Russia." *Economic Geography.* 150–69.

Moe, Terry. 1985. "The New Economics of Organization." *American Journal of Political Science.* 28 (4):739–77.

Montinola, G., Y. Qian, et al. 1995. "Federalism, Chinese Style: The Political Basis for Economic Success in China." *World Politics.* 48:50–81.

Moore, Barrington. 1966. *Social Origins of Dictatorship and Democracy.* Boston: Beacon Press.

Moravcsik, Andrew and K. Nicolaidis. 1999. "Explaining the Treaty of Amsterdam: interests, influence, institutions." *Journal of Common Market Studies.* 37 (1):59–85.

Moreno, Luis. 2001. *The Federalization of Spain.* London: Frank Cass.

Morgan, T. Clifton. 1994. *Untying the Knot of War.* Ann Arbor: University of Michigan Press.

Moses, Joel. 1985. "Regionalism in Soviet Politics: Continuity as a Source of Change, 1953–1982." *Soviet Studies.* 37 (2):184–211.

Musgrave, Richard. 1959. *The Theory of Public Finance.* McGraw-Hill.

Noël, Alain. 2002. "Is Decentralization Conservative?" In *Stretching the Federation,* ed. R. Young. Kingston: Institute of Intergovernmental Relations, Queen's University.

North, Douglass. 1987. "Institutions, Transaction Costs and Economic Growth." *Economic Inquiry.* 25 (July):419–28.

———. 1990. *Institutions, Institutional Change and Economic Performance.* Cambridge: Cambridge University.

———. 1991. "A Transaction Cost Approach to the Historical Development of Politics and Economies." In Ed. Furbotn and Richter.

———. 1991. "A Transaction Cost Approach to the Historical Development of Poltics and Economies." In *The New Institutional Economics,* Ed. Eirik Furbotn and Rudolf Richter. College Station, TX: Texas A & M.

Nove, Alec. 1986. *The Soviet Economic System.* Boston: Unwin Hyman.

Oates, Wallace, Ed. 1977. *The Political Economy of Fiscal Federalism.* Lexington, Mass.: Lexington Books.

OECD. 1995. *OECD Economic Surveys. The Russian Federation.* Paris: OECD.

———. 1998. *OECD Economic Surveys 1997–1998: Russian Federation.* Paris: Organization for Economic Cooperation and Development.

———. 2002. *OECD Economic Surveys. The Russian Federation.* Paris: OECD.

Oksenberg, Michael and J. Tong. 1991. "The Evolution of Central-Provincial Fiscal Relations in China, 1971–1984: the Formal System." *The China Quarterly.* 125 (March):1–32.

Ordeshook, Peter. 1995. "Institutions and Incentives." *Journal of Democracy.* 6: 46–60.

Ordeshook, Peter and Olga Shvetsova. 1997. "Federalism and Constitutional Design." *Journal of Democracy.* 8 (1):27–41.

Orlov, Aleksandr. 1997. "Budzhet pod nozhom sekvestra." *Rossisskaya federatsiya.* (10):41–2.

Orttung, Robert. 1995. "Battling Over Electoral Laws." *Transition* 32–6.

———. 1995. *From Leningrad to St. Petersburg: Democratization in a Russian City.* New York: St. Martin's Press.

Ostrom, Elinor. 1990. *Governing the Commons: The Evolution of Institutions for Collective Action.* Cambridge: Cambridge University Press.

———. 1995. "New Horizons in Institutional Analysis: Review Article." *American Political Science Review.* 89:174–8.

Panorama. 1996. *Rossiyskiy sbornik.* Moscow: Panorama.

Pantsirev, Vladimir. 1996. *Podgornovskie miliardi.* Vologda: Russkii Sever—Partner.

Pearson, Raymond. 1991. "The Historical Background to Soviet Federalism." In *Soviet Federalism, Nationalism, and Economic Decentralisation,* Ed. Alastair McAuley. Leicester: Leicester University.

Peters, B. Guy. 1999. *Institutional Theory in Political Science: The "New Institutionalism".* London: Pinter.

Peterson, Paul. 1981. *City Limits.* Chicago: The University of Chicago Press.

Peterson, Paul. 1995. *The Price of Federalism.* Washington, D.C.: The Brookings Institution.

Pichardo, Nelson. 1988. "Resource Mobilization: An Analysis of Conflicting Theoretical Variations." *The Sociological Quarterly.* 29 (1):97–110.

Pinter, Walter and Don Rowney, Eds. 1980. *Russian Officialdom.* Chapel Hill: University of North Carolina Press.

Podporina, I. 1997. "Budzhetnii kodeks i nekotorie aspekti ekonomicheskikh otnoshenii." *Ekonomist.* (9):69–77.

Pohl, J. Otto. 1997. *The Stalinist Penal System.* Jefferson, NC: McFarland and Co., Inc.

Powell, Walter and P. DiMaggio, Eds. 1991. *The New Institutionalism in Organizational Analysis.* Chicago: The University of Chicago.

Pozgalev, Vyacheslav. 1997. "Sud'ba u kazhdogo svoya, otvetstvennost' za Rossiyu—obshaya (The fate of each of us is our own, the responsibility for Russia is everyone's)." *Federalizm.* Special issue:17–40.

Przeworski, Adam. 1991. *Democracy and the Market.* Cambridge: Cambridge University Press.

Putnam, Robert. 1993. *Making Democracy Work.* Princeton, NJ: Princeton University.

———. 1976. *The Comparative Study of Political Elites.* Englewood Cliffs, NJ: Princeton University.

Remington, Thomas. 1989. "Renegotiating Soviet Federalism: Glasnost' and Regional Autonomy." *Publius.* 19 (3):145–65.

———. 1999. *Politics in Russia.* New York: Longman.

Rich, Michael. 1993. *Federal Policy-making and the Poor: National Goals, Local Choices, and Distributional Outcomes.* Princeton, NJ: Princeton University.

Rigby, Thomas. 1990. *Political Elites in the USSR.* Aldershot: Edward Elgar.

Riker, William. 1964. *Federalism: Origin, Operation, Significance.* Boston: Little, Brown & Co.

———. 1982. *Liberalism Against Populism.* San Francisco: W. H. Freeman.

———. 1987. *The Development of American Federalism.* Boston: Kluwer Academic Publishers.

Rocher, F. 1992. "Quebec's Historical Agenda." In *Constitutional Politics,* Ed. Duncan Cameron and Miriam Smith. Toronto: James Lorimer & Co.

Rodionova, V. M. 1998. "Sovremennya trebovaniya k budzhenomu zakonodatel'stvu." *Finansi* 7:8–11.

Roeder, Phillip. 1994. "Varieties of Post-Soviet Authoritarian Regimes." *Post-Soviet Affairs.* 10 (1):61–101.

———. 1993. *Red Sunset: The Failure of Soviet Politics.* Princeton, NJ: Princeton University.

Rogowski, Roanld. 1989. *Commerce and Coalitions: How Trade Affects Domestic Political Alignments.* Princeton: Princeton University Press.

Romanov, P. and I. Tartakovskaya. 1998. "Samara *Oblast*': A Governor and his Guberniya." *Communist Economies and Economic Transformation.* 10 (3): 341–361.

Ross, Cameron. 1987. *Local Government in the Soviet Union.* London: Croom Helm.

Rossiter, Clinton, Ed. 1999. *The Federalist Papers.* New York: Penguin.

Roth, Alvin, Eds. 1985. *Game-theoretic Models of Bargaining.* Cambridge: Cambridge University Press.

Rowney, Don. 1989. *Transition to Technocracy: The Structural Origins of the Soviet Administrative State.* Ithaca, NY: Cornell University Press.

Russian Federation. 1993. *Novoe nologovoe zaakonodatel'stvo Rossii.* Moskva: Profizdat.

Rutland, Peter. 1994. "The Economy: The Rocky Road from Plan to Market." In *Developments in Russian and Post-Soviet Politics,* Ed. S. White, A. Pravda and Z. Gitelman. Durham, NC: Duke University Press.

Sally, R. and D. Webber. 1994. "The German Solidarity Pact: A Case Study in the Politics of the Unified Germany." *German Politics.* 3 (1):18–46.

Sartori, Giovanni. 1970. "Concept Misinformation in Comparative Politics." *APSR* 64 (4):1033–53.

Savoie, Donald. 1999. *Governing from the Centre: The Concentration of Power in Canadian Politics.* Toronto: University of Toronto Press.

Scharpf, Fritz. 1997. *Games Real Actors Play: Actor-centered Institutionalism in Policy Research.* Boulder, CO: Westview Press.

Schelling, Thomas. 1960. *The Strategy of Conflict.* Cambridge, MA: Harvard University Press.

Schroeder, Gertrude. 1991a. "Anatomy of Gorbachev's Economic Reform." In *Milestones in Glasnost and Perestroyka,* Ed. E. Hewitt and V. Winston. Washington, D.C.: Brookings Institution.

Schroeder, Gertrude. 1991b. "Perestroyka in the Aftermath of 1990." In *Milestones of Glasnost and Perestroyka,* Ed. Ed Hewitt and V. Winston. Washington, D.C.: Brookings Institution.

Senatova, Olga and Andrei Yakurin. 1997. "Vybori gubernatorov v kontekste sotsial'no-politicheskogo razvitiya regionov Rossii." *Mezhdunarodnii institut gumanitarno-politicheskikh issledovannii. Politicheskii monitoring.* 1 (60):1–22.

Sharlet, Robert. 1993. "Russian Constitutional Crisis: Law and Politics Under Yeltsin." *Post-Soviet Affairs.* 9:316–320.

Sharlet, Robert. 1994. "The Prospects for Federalism in Russian Constitutional Politics." *Publius: The Journal of Federalism.* 24:115–27.

Shevtsova, Liliia. 1996. "The Constituency Nexus in the Russian and Other Post-Soviet Parliaments." In *Democratization in Russia: The Development of Legislative Institutions,* Ed. Jeffrey Hahn. Armonk, NY: Sharpe.

Shirk, Susan. 1993. *The Political Logic of Economic Reform in China.* Berkeley: University of California Press.

Shleifer, Andrei and Daniel Treisman. 2000. *Without a Map.* Cambridge, MA: MIT Press.

Sikkink, Kathrine. 1991. *Ideas and Institutions: Developmentalism in Brazil and Argentina.* Ithaca: Cornell University Press.

Simeon, Richard. 1972. *Federal-Provincial Diplomacy: The Making of Recent Policy in Canada.* Toronto: University of Toronto Press.

Simeon, Richard and David Cameron. 2002. "Intergovernmental Relations and Democracy: An Oxymoron If There Ever Was One?" In *Canadian Federalism: Performance, Effectiveness, and Legitimacy.* Eds. Herman Bakvis and Grace Skogstad. Oxford: Oxford University Press.

Skocpol, Theda. 1992. *Protecting Soldiers and Mothers: The Political Origins of Social Policy in the United States.* Cambridge, MA: Belknap Press of Harvard University Press.

Slider, Daniel. 1996. "Elections to Russia's Regional Assemblies." *Post-Soviet Affairs.* 12 (3):243–264.

Smiley, D.V. 1970. *Constitutional Adaptation and Canadian Federalism Since 1945,* Ottawa: Documents of the Royal Commission on Bilingualism and Bilculturalism.

Smirnyagin, Leonid. 2001. "Federalizm po Putinu ili Putin po federalizmu (zheleznoi pyatoi)?" *Briefing Paper.* Moscow: Moscow Carnegie Center.

Smith, Gordon. 1980. *Public Policy and Administration in the Soviet Union.* New York: Praeger.

Smith, Graham. Ed. 1995. *Federalism: The Multiethnic Challenge.* London: Longman.

———. 1996. "Russia, Ethnoregionalism and the Politics of Federation." *Ethnic and Racial Studies.* 19 (2):391–410.

Smith, Jennifer. 2002. "Informal Constitutional Development: Change by Other Means." In *Canadian Federalism: Performance, Effectiveness, and Legitimacy.* Eds. Herman Bakvis and Grace Skogstad. Oxford: Oxford University Press.

Snyder, Glenn and Paul Diesing. 1977. *Conflict Among Nations*. Princeton: Princeton University Press.

Sobyanin, A., E. Gel'man, et al. 1993. "The Political Climate in Russia in 1991–1993." *Mirovaya ekonomika i mezhdunarodnye otnosheniya*. 9:20–32.

Solnick, Steven. 1995. "Federal Bargaining in Russia." *East European Constitutional Review*. 43 (6):13–25.

———. 1996. "The Political Economy of Russian Federalism: A Framework for Analysis." *Problems of Post-Communism*. 43 (6):13–25.

———. 1998a. *Stealing the State*. Cambridge, MA: Harvard University Press.

———. 1998b. "Will Russia Survive?" In *Post-Soviet Political Order*, Ed. B. Rubin and J. Snyder. London: Routledge.

Starodubrovskaia, I. 1995. "Financial-Industrial Groups: Illusions and Realities." *Communist Economies and Economic Transformation*. 7 (1):5–19.

Stavrakis, Peter. 1993. *State Building in Post-Soviet Russia: The Chicago Boys and the Decline of Administrative Capacity*. Kennan Institute.

Stein, Michael. 1997. "Improving the Process of Constitutional Reform in Canada: Lessons from the Meech Lake and Charlottetown Constitutional Rounds." *Canadian Journal of Political Science*. 30 (2):307–338.

Steinmo, Sven, K. Thelen, et al., Eds. 1992. *Structuring Politics: Historical Institutionalism in Comparative Analysis*. Cambridge: Cambridge University Press.

Stepan, Alfred. 1999. "Federalism and Democracy: Beyond the U.S. Model." *Journal of Democracy*. 10 (4):19–34.

Stevenson, Garth. 1982. *Unfulfilled Union: Canadian Federalism and National Unity*. Toronto: Gage Publishing Limited.

Stoner-Weiss, Kathryn. 1997. *Local Heroes: The Political Economy of Russian Regional Governance*. Princeton, NJ: Princeton University Press.

———. 1999. "Central Weakness and Provincial Autonomy: Observations on the Devolution Process in Russia." *Post-Soviet Affairs*. 15 (1):87–106.

Sury, M. M. 1998. *Fiscal Federalism in India*. Delhi: Indian Tax Institute.

Szporluk, Roman. 1994. *National Identity and Ethnicity in Russia and the New States of Eurasia*. Armonk, NY: M.E. Sharpe.

Tabata, S. 1998. "Transfers from Federal to Regional Budgets in Russia: A Statistical Analysis." *Post-Soviet Geography and Economics*. 39 (8):447–460.

Tanguay, A. Brian. 2002. "Political Parties and Canadian Democracy: Making Federalism Do the Heavy Lifting." In *Canadian Federalism: Performance, Effectiveness, and Legitimacy*. Eds. Herman Bakvis and Grace Skogstad. Oxford: Oxford University Press.

Tarlton, Charles. 1965. "Symmetry and Asymmetry as Elements of Federalism: A Theoretical Speculation." *Journal of Politics*. 27:861–74.

Tarr, Alan. 1999. "Creating Federalism in Russia." *South Texas Law Review*. 40 (689).

Teague, Elizabeth. 1993. "North-South Divide: Yeltsin and Russia's Provincial Leaders." *RFE/RL Research Report*. 2 (47):7–23.

Theen, Rolf. 1993. "Russia at the Grassroots: Reform at the Local and Regional Levels." *In Depth*. 3 (1):53–90.

Thimmaiah, G. 1985. *Burning Issues in Centre-State Financial Relations*. New Delhi: Ashish Publishing House.

Tompson, William. 1997. "Old Habits Die Hard: Fiscal Imperatives, State Regulation and the Role of Russia's Banks." *Europe-Asia Studies*. 49 (7):1159–1185.

Treisman, Daniel. 1996. "The Politics of Intergovernmental Transfers in Post-Soviet Russia." *British Journal of Political Science*. 26 (July):299–335.

———. 1997. "Russia's Ethnic Revival: The Separatist Activism of Regional Leaders in a Postcommunist Order." *World Politics*. 49 (2):212–249.

———. 1998a. "Deciphering Russia's Federal Finance: Fiscal Appeasement in 1995 and 1996." *Europe-Asia Studies*. 50 (5):893–906.

———. 1998b. "Fiscal Redistribution in a Fragile Federalism: Moscow and the Regions in 1994." *British Journal of Political Science*. 28:185–222.

———. 1999. *After the Deluge: Regional Crises and Political Consolidation in Russia*. Ann Arbor, MI: The University of Michigan Press.

———. 2000. *Fiscal Pathologies and Federal Policies: Understanding Tax Arrears in Russia's Regions*. Published on-line (May).

Tsebelis, George. 1990. *Nested Games: Rational Choice in Comparative Politics*. Berkeley: University of California Press.

Urban, Michael. 1990. *More Power to the Soviets: The Democratic Revolution in the USSR*. Aldershot, England: Edward Elgar.

Van Houten, Pieter. 2002. *National Parties in Regional Party Systems*. Paper presented at 98th meeting of the American Political Science Association.

Vsya Moskva. 1994. *Novaia Rossiia. Informatsionno statisticheskii aalmanakh*. Moscow: SP "Vsya Moskva"

Walker, David. 1981. *Toward a Functioning Federalism*. Cambridge, MA: Winthrop Publishers, Inc.

Wallich, Christine. 1992. *Fiscal Decentralization: Intergovernmental Relations in Russia*. Washington, D.C.: World Bank.

———. 1996. *Russia and the Challenge of Fiscal Federalism*. Washington, D.C.: World Bank.

Wallich, Christine. and R. Nayyat. 1993. "Russia's Intergovernmental Fiscal Relations: A Key to National Cohesion." *Challenge*. 36:46–52.

Watts, Ronald. 1999a. *Comparing Federal Systems*. 2d ed. Kingston, Ontario: Queen's University.

———. 1999b. "German Federalism in Comparative Perspective." In *Recasting German Federalism*, Ed. C. Jeffery. London: Pinter.

Webb, J. C. 1993. *The Regional Russian Leadership Formation Process, 1987–1993: Four Case Studies*. Georgetown University.

Wegren, Stephen. 1997. "Land Reform and the Land Market in Russia: Operation, Constraints and Prospects." *Europe-Asia Studies*. 49 (6):959–987.

Wheare, K. C. 1953. *Federal Government*. London: Oxford University Press.

Whittington, Keith. 1996. "The Political Constitution of Federalism in Antebellum America: The Nullification Debate as an Illustration of Informal Mechanisms of Constitutional Change." *Publius: The Journal of Federalism*, 26 (2): 1–24.

Wildasin, David. 1997. "Fiscal Aspects of Evolving Federations: Issues for Policy and Research." In *Fiscal Aspects of Evolving Federations*, Ed. David Wildasin. Cambridge: Cambridge University Press.

Wildavsky, Aaron. 1998. *Federalism and Political Culture*. Eds, D. Schliecher and B. Swedlow. New Brunswick, NJ: Transaction Publishers.

Willerton, John. 1992. *Patronage and Politics in the USSR*. Cambridge: Cambridge University.

Williamson, Oliver. 1975. *Markets and Hierarchies.* New York: Free Press.

Wilson, Woodrow. 1885. *Congressional Government.* Reprint 1956. New York: Meridian Books.

Winiecki, Jan. 1991. *Resistance to Change in the Soviet Economic System: A Property Rights Approach.* London: Routledge.

Wollman, H. 1993. "Change and Continuity of Political and Administrative Elites in Post-Communist Russia." *Governance.* 6 (3):325–40.

Woodruff, David. 1999. *Money Unmade: Barter and the Fate of Russian Capitalism.* Ithaca, NY: Cornell University Press.

Young, Oran. 1975. "Strategic Interaction and Bargaining." In *Bargaining: Formal Theories of Negotiation,* Ed. O. Young. Chicago: University of Illinois.

Zielonka, Jan. 1994. "New Institutions in the Old East Bloc." *Journal of Democracy.* 5 (2):87–104.

Index

About the Author

ELIZABETH PASCAL is Visiting Assistant Professor, Department of Government at Connecticut College.